ENTERTAINING
WITH *Wholefood*

ENTERTAINING
WITH

JANETTE MARSHALL

TREASURE PRESS

First published in Great Britain in 1984 by
Thorsons Publishers Limited under the title
The Wholefood Party Book

This edition published in 1986 by
Treasure Press
59 Grosvenor Street
London W1

© Janette Marshall 1984

ISBN 1 85051 122 5

Printed in Hungary

Contents

For Mary, Hugh and Mothy

Acknowledgements

Thanks to Harrods for kind co-operation in the loan of crockery, glassware and other props for the colour pictures.

Thanks to Jacky Gibson for taking such care from her side of the camera, and to everyone at John Welburn Associates.

Thanks to Michael and Elizabeth Wilson for the opportunity to have such fun cooking for Ruth's wedding to Graham de Baerdemaerker on May 14, 1983. Many of the recipes from the wedding appear in the book.

Thanks to The Barbecue Shop, Weybridge, Surrey for advice on/loan of barbecue and equipment.

Thanks to the authors of two enlightening books, *The World Atlas of Wine*, by Hugh Johnson (Mitchell Beazley, 1977), and *The Great British Cheese Book*, by Patrick Rance (Macmillan, 1982), who have fed my interest in these subjects.

Introduction

Welcome to Entertaining With Wholefood. Perhaps we could begin our acquaintance with an explanation about why I wrote this book.

Since changing to a healthier way of eating a few years ago I have noticed that there is no comprehensive source of menus or recipes for parties based on wholefood ingredients. When having friends to stay for the weekend, guests for dinners and more formal occasions to cater for I have looked through my old Cordon Bleu style recipe books to find only dishes laden with cream, fats and sugar. So, I have made healthier versions of classic dishes or invented dishes of my own.

I have also noticed a misconception among others that because I now eat wholemeal bread, brown rice, wholemeal spaghetti etc., it means I no longer enjoy myself! I was at first regarded as 'converted', and greeted with slightly offended looks as though delicious dinner parties would now be a thing of the past.

Those who already eat a wholefood diet will know this is not the case. Very often the reason for watching what we eat is to make us feel a lot healthier and therefore more full of energy with more time for enjoying ourselves and having fun. So, the parties are just as good, the food is even better and the guests no longer run the risk of feeling slightly off colour after the party because of over-rich food or indigestible mixtures.

I therefore decided it was time to write a book that showed how wholefood ingredients can be used when entertaining, together with all the hints and tips I have amassed on planning (and having) some excellent parties.

I have also included menus and recipes which cater for larger numbers, because I have always found it infuriating (and boring) to have to work out from the basic 'Serves 4' how to convert it into a quantity suitable for a party.

I do hope you enjoy the book. It is designed to help you have fun and enjoy good food with your family and friends. For how to make best use of the book have a look at the first chapter, 'How to Use this Book'.

1.

How to Use This Book

There are two ways in which to make the best use of Entertaining With Wholefood. The first is as a source of recipes put together in menus to suit certain types of parties.

The second is as a source of information and advice on how to plan successful parties, as well as using the menus and recipes for each occasion. Chapter 3, 'Planning a Party', tells you how to get things organized by outlining all the major points involved in giving a party. These notes are expanded, where necessary, at the beginning of each party chapter.

But remember, the notes in Chapter 3 refer to all the parties, so if you are not confident about your party read this chapter before or after you have looked at the recipes for the occasion.

The notes at the beginning of the section on catering for a wedding reception are more extensive than those heading other chapters because this is a more complicated event to co-ordinate, but it is not a specific time-table of what to do when, or a countdown to the wedding, because each wedding is different and will need its own tailored plan of action.

The aim of the book is to stimulate the reader into preparing his or her own timetable by showing all the points that have to be taken into consideration. So, once you have decided on your menu, it is a good idea to make a shopping list for food and other requirements, and to write down an order of work covering the day, or days, before the party.

How to read this book
If you are confident about the success of your parties, but just want some new ideas for recipes and menus then go straight to the chapter for the type of party you are planning. However, you might find it useful to look at Chapter 3, 'Planning a Party'.

The other approach is to read 'Planning a Party' and then turn to the chapter containing the menus and recipes relevant to your party.

There is, of course, no reason why you can not swap a dish from one menu to another if you prefer a particular dessert, for instance. However, do bear in mind when swapping dishes that the menus have been designed so that the meal is balanced. For instance, if there is cream in one course of the meal it will not be used in another course, so check that you are not adding a course very similar to the one preceding it.

Texture and colour are also important. It is not a good idea to have a mousse as a starter, followed by soft-textured main course and a soufflé for dessert. Look out for this if you are swapping the recipes around.

About the recipes and menus

Continuing from the point above, all the menus have been designed so that the ingredients involved are all in season at the same time.

This means that they should be cheaper because they are more readily available. It also means you will not be disappointed when trying to shop for a menu.

Nature also seems to have a way of arranging that things which are good together are around together. Hence combinations like mackerel and gooseberries in the spring — the tartness of the gooseberries complements the oily fish very well.

All the recipes are calorie counted so you can see at a glance how your combinations of dishes are adding up. This is also helpful if you have some slimmers coming for a meal, and it will give you an idea of which foods (if you do not already know), are higher in calories than others.

The number of servings is also indicated. This is essential information when catering for a greater number than you are used to. Quantities for parties often pose problems for people, but this book aims to take the hard work out of guessing how much pasta to cook for 20 people, etc. As a rough guide you will find that:

2 oz (50g) brown rice cooks to 6 oz (175g)
2 oz (50g) pulses cooks to 4 oz (100g)
3 oz (75g) wholemeal pasta cooks to 8 oz (225g)

The recipes are also designed to suit the occasion, by making the job as easy as possible for the cook. So, for instance, the recipes in the section Impromptu Parties are all easy and very quick to prepare. In circumstances where the cook has more time available there are more complicated recipes for those who would like to try them.

If you haven't made something before don't be put off. Have a go. When you have done it once it will be so much easier the second time.

Do remember always to read the recipe through before you start work. That includes not only the list of ingredients for the shopping list, but also the method. You will find it a lot easier if you assemble all the ingredients and all the tools you need before you start work. That way you won't have floury fingerprints to clean off the cupboards and drawers when you have finished!

You will also discover if you have run out of something before you start cooking, so you won't be disappointed or waste the rest of your ingredients if the vital one is missing and the shops are closed.

To those new to wholefoods

Chapter 2 explains what wholefoods are and gives the basic outline of a wholefood diet.

Wholefoods are being used increasingly by all sorts of people as more evidence comes to light of the links between the typical Western/British diet and ill health. Modern health problems like constipation, varicose veins, hernias, diverticulitis and diabetes as well as heart disease and cancer are being linked with the kind of diet that is high in fat, sugar and salt and low in the main ingredients of the wholefood diet: fibre, fresh fruit and vegetables, and low-fat, low-sugar and low-salt foods.

See the next chapter for more information.

To those who 'knock' wholefoods

As Assistant Editor of *Here's Health* I come in contact with a lot of people who tell me that wholefoods are a big 'con' set up by the people who market certain foods, and that all foods are equally good for us.

There is much documented evidence to prove that many people have been helped with certain health problems by changing their diet, and that most people who give wholefoods a go feel a lot better for it and don't want to go back to their old way of eating.

There are also those who do not understand the term wholefoods and who rightly get annoyed by so-called wholefood restaurants that serve sugary foods on the basis that the sugar in them is not harmful to health because it is brown rather than white.

These complaints are, of course, justified. All sugar is equally bad, as is an excess of fat whether it is saturated or unsaturated. So there is no point in eating chips five days a week and thinking they are healthy because they are fried in sunflower oil.

If you have been put off wholefoods by these kind of instances, but have nonetheless read this far, I hope you will go on to read, and try, the recipes and menus that will show you how delicious these foods can be and that they really do try to cut down on the amount of sugar, fats and salt without just paying lip service to a desire for healthier food.

The book also aims to dispel the myth held by many wholefood critics that people who eat healthily are a bunch of killjoys who want to control what others eat.

This certainly isn't the aim of this book. It hopes to provide the information to enable an informed choice about the type of foods that will keep you healthy and full of energy, so that you can get even more fun out of life.

Hopefully it will also show those who 'don't like' wholefoods that there is such a wealth of good food to choose from, in so many combinations, that there must be something they like, even if it does happen to be good for them!

If you are used to eating meat every day, or even more than once a day, you are bound to be put off if someone suggests going vegetarian or switching to beans and other pulses rather than meat.

Any changes in eating habits should be gradual, and a slow introduction to a different way of eating is best to give both mind and body time to adjust and to get to like new foods. Of course you won't like everything in a wholefood diet just as you don't like everything in a non-wholefood diet. We all have our likes and dislikes.

But, just because you have not enjoyed a meal at a wholefood restaurant or one cooked by friends try not to be put off everything labelled wholefood. Taste some of the dishes in this book that you think you might like.

To those who already enjoy wholefoods
If you already enjoy the type of foods and ingredients used in this book I hope you will find lots of new and interesting combinations to share with your family and friends.

You might have experienced some disappointment with so-called wholefood restaurants and come to the conclusion that the only way to ensure good quality food of a high standard is to prepare it yourself at home. The many menus for different occasions in this book should help you to do that.

The book will also, I trust, convey the idea that cooking for special occasions is not a chore but a rewarding and enjoyable way to spend your time. When planning and preparing food for parties I always look forward to eating the food as much as I hope my guests do. That way I think you make sure that the food will be really good.

I have received many letters at *Here's Health* from people who want to cater for their own larger functions such as weddings, but do not know what to put on the menu or how to approach the event. I have tried in this book to solve these problems by pointing out all the major points to be considered about the catering and to provide detailed menus and recipes for large numbers of people.

I have catered for two wedding receptions,

my own and my dear friend Ruth's, and I have found them extremely challenging. They are hard work, but they are a lot of fun and very rewarding; especially when everyone likes the food so much and obviously enjoys something so very different from the usual caterer's parade of white sandwiches, sausage rolls and vol-au-vents and dried-up chicken drumsticks.

But I'm not vegetarian . . .

A wholefood diet is not a vegetarian diet but it does use less meat than the average diet. This is because meat is a source of saturated fats which have been linked with the risk of heart disease.

It is also because there are other sources of protein available which have more to offer than meat. Meat contains no fibre, unlike vegetable proteins such as bean pulses, cereals, seeds and nuts, which also contain unsaturated fats. These fats are essential to health (unlike saturated fats) and also are thought to be protective against heart disease.

Modern methods of rearing animals for meat may also result in drug residues in the meat. There are also other considerations of animal husbandry and individual conscience.

Most entertaining evolves around a meat-based meal whether it's a dinner party or an informal barbecue and although a wholefood diet uses meat only occasionally it is likely to use it when entertaining. This book, therefore, does contain some meat recipes, but it is also a source of many non-meat orientated meals for entertaining.

But you don't drink . . .

Many people ask you, if you eat a wholefood diet, are you 'allowed' to drink.

It is true that many people prefer not to drink spirits and stronger alcoholic drinks but wine, beer (real ale) and cider are not thought to be harmful in moderation; in fact they may be valuable aids to relaxation.

Chapter 6 deals in detail with the type of wine that is chosen for healthy drinking and it also gives a brief guide to buying wine, getting to know wine and how to choose a wine to suit the party you are catering for.

You can do it!

Armed with the information and recipes and menus in this book you can now go out and cancel the hired caterers and make an excellent job of catering for your own parties!

You will be amazed at what you can do and your family and friends will be too.

If you enjoy cooking then the rewards are tremendous, especially when you see people enjoying food and a party atmosphere that has been prepared with thought and care.

So make your parties ones that your friends really look forward to rather than those they invent 'prior engagements' to avoid, or their hearts (and stomachs) sink with the thud of your invitation on the doormat.

2.

For Those New to Wholefoods

This chapter explains what wholefoods are and what the term means. It also gives an outline of the basic principles of wholefood eating.

It is a reflection of modern thinking about the link between our standard of health and the food we eat. Many processed foods have been linked with the risks of, or development of, several 'modern' health problems. For this reason the wholefood diet has evolved in an attempt to combat the ill effects of a modern diet by a return to less processed, more natural foods.

What are wholefood ingredients?
The term 'wholefood' is used to describe foods that are as near to their natural, and therefore 'whole', state as possible. It is applied to wholemeal flour which has not had the fibre or the valuable vitamins, minerals and wheatgerm removed during milling. It is applied to wholemeal pasta which is made from the whole flour, complete with all its goodness. It is applied to brown rice which has not been polished to remove its natural bran and vitamins.

There are many other foods to which it is applied, but the idea is the same for all. Wholefoods are foods that have not been processed or had anything taken away from them.

Wholefoods are also those foods that have not had anything added to them. This usually goes hand-in-hand with processing out ingredients. In removing natural parts of foods it is often necessary to put back other artificial ingredients to restore the lost flavour, or the lost vitamins, or the lost fibre. And in processing foods it is also necessary to add chemicals to lengthen the shelflife and keep food fresh long after it would naturally have gone stale.

Colourings and flavourings are added because the customer wants them, we are told. In reality it is because we have become accustomed to the unnatural colours and highly spiced flavours needed to make many processed, or second rate foods, palatable.

In the same way we have become used to food that is highly salted or has a lot of sugar added. A wholefood diet trys to avoid these ingredients because they have been linked with the rise in incidence of certain health problems.

In party terms this means producing appetizing and unusual foods that do not have artificial colourings, flavourings or any other additives. It also means not using lots of salt and sugar and it means making party foods with wholemeal flour, brown rice and all the other whole ingredients.

There is also less emphasis on fatty foods and not as much meat as is used generally when entertaining. The types of meat used are also different and there is a greater emphasis on fish.

Fresh fruit and vegetables play an important role too, and spices sweeten, where necessary, rather than lots of sugar or sugary confections like meringues.

The type of wine you choose might also be different. Yes, wine *can* play a part in a wholefood diet, for entertaining it is far preferable to heavy and strong cocktails, spirits and liqueurs.

The way food is prepared makes all the difference too. There is much more flavour in freshly prepared fruits and vegetables. There is no deep fat frying, it's not French fries with everything and fats and oils are lighter and used sparingly.

Guests will also thank you for sparing them the cream and sugar and the need to 'diet' the next day as part of their usual erratic entertainment and post-entertainment eating patterns. Because meals are less fattening and fatty this goes hand-in-hand with them being more easily digestible.

After a wholefood party the guests will go home feeling well; not with that over-fed, 'rather nice, but rather too rich' or sickly feeling. They will like *you* better for not having to get up in the night to find the *Alka Seltzer* or the aspirin.

Going out should not be paid for by a penance of indigestion or a hangover the next day. They will suddenly discover that is not what entertaining is all about. There's no need to feel ill to have a good time!

Wholefood eating guidelines
Outlined here is the type of eating pattern that makes up a wholefood diet. It reflects current medical opinion (long-held by many 'alternative' medical practitioners) that diet has a great bearing on how well or ill we are.

Nutrition is now a subject being treated with greater respect by doctors, but for a long time many people have been discovering for themselves that they feel a lot better for eating a sensible, balanced 'wholefood' diet.

Giving the body the right 'fuel' results in better performance. If you feel good and have more energy you are likely to have more fun, and be more fun to be with, which all augurs well for good parties!

Protein. Most of us eat too much of this. We only need about 2-3 oz (50-75g) a day and this does not have to be from meat. Aim to eat less meat, about one or two meat meals a week. Use meats like lamb (less likely to contain antibiotics or residues of growth hormones and other drugs because it is younger) or game, free-range poultry or liver. Fresh fish is an excellent source of protein, easily digested and containing unsaturated fats, unlike animal proteins.

Vegetarians gain their protein from pulses, grains, nuts and seeds; eat more meals based on these ingredients, choosing two out of the three groups at each meal to ensure that all the essential amino acids for protein building in the body are available. Do not use too much dairy produce (cheese and eggs) for protein, use them sparingly and buy unprocessed cheeses and free-range eggs.

Fresh fruit and vegetables. Eat more, aiming for some raw food such as a salad every day. Try to buy organically grown produce because it is free from chemical residues such as chemical fertilizers, pesticides, fungicides etc. It also tastes better.

If cooking vegetables and fruit use stainless steel pans and use the minimum of water to lessen vitamin and mineral loss. Use a good, stainless steel, sharp knife to minimize bruising and do not prepare them until ready to cook — never leave vegetables soaking in water because the vitamins and minerals will leach out. Similarly, use vegetable cooking water in stocks, soups and gravies (remember cabbage water does not keep, so throw it away if not used that day).

Fat. Reduce the amount of fat you eat. There is still much controversy over the butter vs. margarine, saturated vs. unsaturated fats debates. If you use butter, make it unsalted and if you use margarine choose a soft vegetable brand high in polyunsaturates. Either way be mean with it, aim for under 3 oz (75g) a day — including that lurking in pastry, cakes, sauces, chocolate, nuts, biscuits. Cooking oil is a fat too, cut down on its use (sauté in stock or stir-fry instead of frying) except in salad dressings where a good quality cold-pressed oil can be used. Choose olive oil, sunflower and safflower for dressings (or more exotic walnut, sesame etc.) and stable-at-high-temperature oils like corn and soy for cooking. Make these unsaturated oils at least half of your daily allowance. When you do have to fry foods, use an 'oil well' and brush to regulate the amount of oil needed to just coat the pan.

Sugar. Reduce the amount you eat. It is possible to do without it in the kitchen, and that does not mean substituting raw cane sugars for white or using honey, molasses, fructose instead. It really means cutting down on all added sugar. You do not need it in drinks, on cereal, in sandwiches(!) in salad dressings or sauces, and remember it's in many processed foods, canned and bottled. Read the labels and avoid it. For breakfast spreads, or in cakes, use no-added-sugar preserves. If you do want to use sugar in baking, most recipes are just as good with far less sugar, or even no sugar. Spices and some

herbs give a sweet effect as do dried fruits and fresh fruits.

Salt. While reading those labels looking for sugar, avoid salt and the sodium-based additives too. There is much evidence to link salt and hypertension so get out of the salt habit *before* you get high blood pressure. Do not salt vegetables when cooking or at table and stop using it in baking as far as possible. This means using a potassium-based baking powder too, instead of the sodium-based baking powders.

Additives. Shun all the other chemical additives to processed food — which really means avoiding all processed foods. You do not need them, there is a wealth of food to choose from without resorting to tins and ready-made products. Additives like colouring, preservatives, flavourings, emsulsifiers, antioxidants, nitrites and so on are there to make food palatable and stop it going bad after it would normally have gone off. Who wants to eat second-rate food that needs this treatment or stale food held together with chemicals?

Drinks. Drink less tea, coffee and cocoa because they contain stimulants that interfere with the body's metabolism. They are addictive. That may not sound serious, but who wants to be addicted to anything? Cola and soft drinks are high in sugar and may contain some stimulants. The slimmers' varieties are usually sweetened with saccharin, another additive that is banned in some countries. They are also high in flavourings and colouring.

Choose fresh and carton, bottled or frozen fruit and vegetable juices, decaffeinated coffee, herb teas and tisanes, and mineral water.

3.

Planning a Party

The following notes are designed to cover the major points in the planning of any kind of party. They can be applied to any party in the book so they have been put together at the beginning to save repeating them in each chapter.

However, there are further notes on specific types of parties, where necessary, in the relevant chapters, or in the menus and recipes where they naturally arise.

You can read this chapter and then refer to the chapter dealing with the type of party you are planning, or you can look at the party menu and then return to this chapter to check that you have not forgotten anything in your plans.

Each party has its own natural order of work. There is no one timetable or countdown of order of work that would be suitable for all parties, but using these notes you can sort out your own order of work, write it down and then tick things off as they are done. This will help you make sure that everything is 'all right on the night' and that you and your guests have a good time.

Planning a party
Thought is probably the most important ingredient for a successful party. Think about the following points before you send out your invitations:

- What is the party for?
  You do not have to have a reason to give a party, but make sure you *want* to have it before you settle on the final date. If you do have a reason, let your guests know what you are celebrating, or make sure they know when they are invited if it is going to be a fancy dress or an outdoor party etc., so they can dress for it and feel confortable. They will also want to give it some thought and make an effort with costumes, if necessary, to make it a success for you.
- Think about the people you are inviting. This is only applicable to small groups, but do consider if they will all get on with each other. They do not have to become bosom friends, but try to mix and match your guests well.
- Issue your invitations in plenty of time. Some people plan events a long time ahead and would like to make sure they can come. Others need babysitters or to make travel arrangements, or perhaps arrange somewhere to stay.
- Find out beforehand if your guests dislike a particular food or have any food allergies. It's up to you whether you go ahead and have what you planned, making them something different, or whether you plan the meal around them. Either way do not embarrass

them about it, or even let them know.

● Plan your menu some time ahead of the event and check that the ingredients for the dishes you want to make are available. You might fancy a strawberry gateau in midwinter but strawberries are either going to be very expensive if fresh or not very nice if frozen or tinned.

● Similarly, plan within your budget. Do not go over the top with expensive items you cannot afford and then resent having spent the money on your guests. Fresh seasonal food is much nicer, prepared properly, than out of season extravagances.

● Bear in mind the type of food your guests normally eat. Do not give them a bean-based vegetarian meal if they are three-meat-meals a day people. Choose something more suited to their taste; you will be able to judge if they would like fresh fish for a change, or choose a wholefood meat and cook it without added fat.

● If you have friends who regularly eat with you, or eat with you periodically, keep a record of the meals you enjoy together. It might sound an affected thing to do, but when those weekend guests come again it will be a help in remembering what you gave them last time so you do not repeat the weekend meal for meal. Also make a note of whether they *really* liked something or did not appear to like it. (See page 187.)

● Never give people large portions. Always be slightly 'mean' with the option that they can come back for more. There is nothing worse than sitting in front of a mountain of food — it does not look appetizing, and it's worse if you do not like it much.

● Do not press alcoholic drinks on people and *never* disguise strong spirits and liqueurs in drinks without the guests knowing — especially if they are driving home afterwards.

● Make them welcome by organizing yourself so you are not in the kitchen from the moment they arrive until they leave. They have come to see you, not to stare at your wallpaper.

● Think about the music for your party. If it's a bring-a-bottle party it is a good idea to make a series of tapes beforehand with a mixture of items to suit the people, mood and whether there is dancing or not. For a dinner party, instrumental records are probably more suitable. If you do not know your guests' tastes choose some light classical music as a background to start with.

● If there is to be dancing at the party it's an idea to move the carpets (if necessary) or furniture out of the dancing area. In the summer it's possible to put some of the furniture in the garden, or use garden furniture, and pretty lights make all the difference in the garden.

● Tell the immediate neighbours if you are having a party, either to warn them about possible noise, or, if they are not being invited, to give them the chance of going out for the evening should they want to. Similarly, old people may be worried by a lot of activity if they do not know what's going on.

● No matter how proud of some ornaments you may be, if it is a large and very informal party it is best to move breakables out of the way.

● Make sure you have enough glasses. Most Off Licences will hire out both wine and beer glasses for functions such as weddings (see Chapter 4) and other large parties. Get them from the Off Licence where you are buying the drink and there may be no charge.

● If you are having beer of the real ale type order it well in advance so that the wine merchant can deliver it with plenty of time to settle. Beer drinkers are very fussy about their pints!

• Make it clear on the invitation whether it is necessary to bring a bottle to a large party. Most guests will bring a bottle of wine, but do not bank on it! Always plan the wine for the evening to go with the food and if a 'clashing' bottle is brought, just pop it in your 'cellar'.

• For the sake of having fresh fruit and vegetables do not be afraid to have a short lapse between courses. For instance, the vegetables can be put on to boil just before the starter is served, or use a microwave to cook them between courses. For fruit desserts make the fruit salad just before the guests arrive but do not do any fruit garnishes until just before the course is served.

• If having ice-cream or sorbets remember to get them out of the freezer before serving the preceding course because they will need 30 minutes or so in the fridge to become soft enough to serve. If they are too cold they will be unpleasant to eat. Their flavour developes more as they thaw a little; but do not overdo it and have runny ices.

Although fresh is best, for large parties a freezer is invaluable, especially for events like weddings where it is often necessary to be free from the kitchen to perform other tasks nearer the day (see Chapter 4). Batch baking for these events is very useful and the freezer is an invaluable aid.

Good preparation is the key to all successful catering events. Planning the menus well in advance and doing all the necessary shopping in plenty of time saves last minute dashes to the shops in the middle of cooking something — only to be disappointed because they are shut or have run out of what you want. Non-perishable goods can be bought and stored away a few at a time, if this is easier, to free time for perishable shopping just before the ingredients are wanted.

It makes sense to plan your party well ahead and give yourself plenty of time because then you will not be too exhausted from rushing around to enjoy it yourself. Baking is particularly tiring and if this can be done in advance and frozen then all you need to do on the day of the party is remember to remove it from the freezer in time and make the salads and fruit salads, prepare any home-made soft cheeses etc.

Giving yourself time to think beforehand without having to rush around too much will make all the difference in your approach to the party and will give you time to do little extras like decorating tables prettily with flowers or other seasonal arrangements, and perhaps leave you enough puff to blow up a few balloons and strew a few streamers!

See the introductions to party chapters for specific tips on each type of party.

4.
The Wedding Reception or the Wedding Breakfast

The Reception

A wedding is probably one of the most exciting events to cater for. It is entertaining on a large scale and it's a real challenge to break away from the usual wedding food of sausage rolls, sandwiches, meat pies, limp salads, soggy vol-au-vents that have lost their 'puff' and all the other dishes rolled out at every wedding.

With some forward planning and the help of a chest freezer and some friends, it is possible to make a wedding a gastronomic event to surpass most outside caterers, incorporating the type of wholefood ingredients _you_ want to use. I know from personal experience that it works and how much people enjoy it.

Planning ahead

If you cater for your own wedding, or that of a friend (I have done both) it is important to think well ahead. Most weddings offer long advance notice. Start off with a chat with the bride (or a good talking to yourself!) about the number of guests. Be ruthless if necessary and do not take on more than you can handle. Up to 50 is possible for most people, 100 for the more experienced cook and 150 for the well-organized enthusiast. Talk about the type of food you would like and draw up a list of proposed dishes then think it over for a week or two.

Try to come to a decision about the menu about three months ahead of the date (though of course it can still be changed). It is at this stage that you might like to start some of the cooking and begin freezing it. For the bride who is doing her own catering it is best to make an early start so she can be free for other things nearer the date.

Using a freezer

From the suggested menus in this chapter there are lots of things that can be made and frozen, such as all the flans, Spinach Choux Puffs (either filled or unfilled), Smoky Pancakes (filled or unfilled) Tahini and Sesame Patties, Apricot Gateaux (ready decorated), Apple Bateaux and Lemon Cups (filled or unfilled) and Mini Pizzas.

It is easier to cook the flans in batches and each recipe gives the ingredients for three flans. It is necessary to have three flan rings of the same size and three baking trays. The pastry is made and the flans baked blind while the filling is prepared. The quiches are left until completely cold before being wrapped in cling film and then foil. They are frozen on a flat surface (lid of a box or board) in the freezer before being stacked.

The Spinach Puffs can be packed into containers such as ice-cream boxes, in layers of not more than three deep with sheets of freezer layering tissue between each layer. Frozen filled they keep their shape better. The Pancakes can also be frozen filled. They are easier to fill if both the pancakes and filling are left to get cold before filling. They can then be packed in layers in polythene boxes with layering tissue between each level. The Patties can be packed in the same way, not more than two deep in case the weight crushes those beneath. The pizzas are lighter and may be packed in deeper layers, again it is useful to have tissue between the layers to prevent any sticking. They can also be unpacked more easily if they have tissue between them, because it prevents them freezing together. The gateaux are best frozen when completely decorated and ready for use. Place them on the lid of a large *Tupperware*-type box and place the box over the top of them as a lid. They can easily be slid off the lid onto a serving plate when wanted. The Bateaux Lemon Cups may be packed in layers like the patties.

As most of the wedding dishes are free from heavy cream, fats and sugars a soufflé might be enjoyed. Raspberries and strawberries make delicious summer soufflés and lemons can be used in the winter, or decaffeinated coffee and stem ginger, or carob. These can also be frozen.

Choosing a colour scheme
It is best to aim for all the advance dishes to be prepared a month in advance of the wedding. During the months leading up to the wedding, when the venue has been decided on the table decorations can be thought about. It is nice to have a colour theme and Ruth chose pink for her wedding (see the picture opposite page 32). The marquee on the lawn was filled with boughs of pink and white apple blossom and the cake was decorated with frosted buds of real blossom. The tables were covered with pastel pink paper cloths with tiny white blobs, on top

of white linen cloths. The serviettes were in the same pink and white and the bride wore the palest pink dress with five 'pink' bridesmaids with blonde hair, carrying baskets of pink and white apple blossom. They looked beautiful in the May sunshine.

Choosing crockery
To match the crockery to the colour theme is a good idea. Telephone several hire firms in the area to see what lines each carries. There will also be widely differing prices. Book early, especially for summer weddings, because it's surprising how many people want to hire the crockery on the same date as you! Have the crockery delivered a day or two before you want it and check it in as it is delivered. Make sure you have the right number of plates etc., before it's too late to do anything about it and check that things are clean at least the day before, so they can be washed without any last minute rushes. Find somewhere to stack them out of the kitchen so you have room to work. If the marquee is up, place them inside, or if you are hiring a hall have them delivered directly there.

Shop around for wine
The wine can be left until nearer the date, but it is a good idea to have visited the wine merchant of your choice and ordered the wine, the glasses and the ice about a month or three weeks before the event.

Before committing yourself, visit a few wine merchants or wine warehouses in the area and ask for lists of the wines they carry and their prices, plus charges for glass hire (usually free if buying wine), delivery and whether they offer a sale or return service so you can return any unopened bottles.

A wedding buffet will need three types of drink. The drink offered to guests on arrival (traditionally sherry but now being replaced by either a cocktail or a wine-based drink) wine to drink with the buffet and champagne for the toast. In summer we have found a sparkling wine drink like Bucks Fizz (fresh orange juice and sparkling wine) very successful instead of sherry. The sparkling wine for this drink need not be expensive or of a very high quality, a dry sparkling Spanish or French wine will be sufficient but make sure it is made by the *Méthode Champenoise*. Do not make it up in advance because a *vin moussec* will not be fizzy enough but get a couple of helpers to pour the juice into the glasses and add the sparkling wine just before it is served. Put the wine and the orange juice on ice before use, your wine merchant should be able to provide plastic dustbins (or other containers) and ice in which to place this wine and the wine for the toast. A Bucks Fizz needs about 1 part orange juice to 3 parts sparkling wine. Serve it in a fluted wine glass. Fluted wine glasses are the best type to hire because they can be used for all three drinks, the sparkling wine as people arrive, the wine during the meal and the toast.

During the meal offer either red or white drinking wine. As you are going to buy a large amount the wine merchant should let you taste the wines before you order them. Any good wine merchant will keep bottles of his main stock available for customers to taste, unfortunately we are behind the French in this matter. They would never dream of buying 'blind', and we should expect the same, especially when buying a large quantity of wine. However, for smaller buys it is often a good idea to keep your own tasting notes in a little booklet simply so you know whether you have enjoyed a wine or not, or what you thought it went well with so you can buy the same again — or avoid it!

Red, white or rosé?

Usually ⅓ red to ⅔ white wine is drunk at most functions. You may get away with a cheaper white wine, but the red must be a good quality for general drinking. At a wedding you are catering for many tastes so the choice is rather limited by the common denominator. Whether you like it or not many people favour the sweet wines of the Rhine, especially Liebfraumilch. (Personally I think they are *too* sweet.)

I would choose something a little different for the bulk of the white wine, such as the slightly crisper wines of the Mosel which are a little drier than the hocks (see Chapter 6 for further information) or, if possible, a Riesling wine from the Alsace, or if you have a larger budget, a Chablis from Burgundy. You could have two types of white wine, a general German wine and a drier French wine, this, however, is probably complicating things for home-catering.

The prices of Bordeaux and Burgundy reds will probably make them rather prohibitive for the red wine so it will be necessary with many weddings to look further afield and consider some of the excellent wines from the Rhône, such as as A. C. Côtes-du-Rhône-Villages or another wine from the south such as a red from the Rouissillon or Languedoc areas.

Should you have champagne?

Most people decide against champagne for the toast because of the prohibitive price, and because it is wasted with fruit cake!

Because of the way champagne is made, and the grapes it is made from, there is a definite difference in taste and appearance of the wine. For instance the 'sparkle' in champagne will last a lot longer than that of sparkling wine, the bubbles are finer and the wine is much crisper. Second best to champagne is the sparkling wine made from the *méthode champenoise*, which means the wine has had a double fermentation in the bottle rather than having carbon dioxide pumped into it to make it sparkle. There are many excellent sparkling wines made by the *méthode champenoise* from France, Germany, Italy, Spain and California. The main French regions are Vouvray on the Loire where the wine varies from *petillant* (naturally very slightly sparkling) to fully sparkling; Die on the river Drôme (part of Rhône region of wines) with sparkling Clairette de Die; Limoux in Roussillon with Blanquette de Limoux; and then there is blanc de blancs.

Among the German sparkling wines are perlwein which is slightly sparkling, and schaumwein, which is slightly better than perlwein, but for a wedding toast wine consider only the sekt wines, made to a strict quality control or the Deutscher Sekt, the top quality German sparkling wines made by the *méthode champenoise*. From the Piedmont area of Italy comes Asti Spumante available either sweet or dry, or try the superior Ferrari Brut a *méthode champenoise* wine from the Trento area of Italy.

The best Spanish sparkling wine comes from the Penedès region, the main production being at San Sadurní de Noya. From California come some excellent 'champagnes' especially from the Korbel on the Russian River and areas of the Napa valley. Sweet 'champagne' is the speciality of the New York producers on the Finger Lakes.

Although many wines are produced by the *méthode champenoise* only those from the Champagne country in northern France that have been made by that method are true champagnes.

Having the sparkling wine for the toast on ice in large dustbins or buckets will be sufficient because it does not have to be icy, just pleasantly chilled. It can then be opened and poured into glasses on trays during the speeches (if there are any) or distributed before so that people have a glass for the toast, or it can be circulated with the cake.

How much to order

Allow one glass of Bucks Fizz per guest which will mean about seven bottles per 50 guests and two cartons of orange juice (1 litre size). If you are offering sparkling wine on its own allow nine bottles of sparkling wine. The same amount of champagne/sparkling wine is required for the toast. You may like to order a little more, especially if it is on sale or return.

For drinking wine during the buffet allow half a bottle of wine per person, which is the equivalent of three glasses of wine.

Tea or coffee?

After the toasts and the champagne many guests like a coffee before their journey home. The easiest way to do this for large numbers is to use *Rombouts*-style decaffeinated coffee filters. They can be put on top of cups which are laid out ready in the kitchen (or other area) after the food preparation is finished. An urn, borrowed from local church or caterer, will boil the water which can be poured into jugs and then into the filters. This way you do not make up enormous amounts of coffee that are not drunk and the unused filters can be used afterwards.

For those who prefer tea, large teapots from churches, village halls etc., can usually be borrowed or hired. The same water from the urns will also make tea when required. Ceylon tea is lower in tannin. China is best for black tea drinkers and herb teabags cater for individual taste.

When to make the salads

Fruit salads can be made up the evening before the wedding and stored in plastic containers in the fridge overnight. If well covered with orange juice (rather than sticky made-up syrup) the fruit will not discolour.

If the wedding is not too early in the morning then the green salads should be prepared at this

24

late stage. The lettuce, watercress, onions, cress, cucumber etc., can be washed and stored in a large wine-making bin or clean new dustbin standing in a cool place. As they are required the ingredients can be shredded into salad bowls and the dressing, ready made up and stored in screwtop jars in the fridge, poured over.

Other salads, such as tomato salad, improve with marination in the dressing, and potato salad and courgette salad can be made the day before and stored in containers in the fridge or a cool cupboard if the weather is not hot. Preparing the potato or tomato salad can be a bit punishing if faced with about 20 lb of vegetables so share these sort of jobs between several helpers.

Borrow a fridge

If you are catering at home it is a good idea to borrow an extra fridge in which to put all the salad things and the soufflés and gateaux while they defrost. It will also be useful for cheese, should you buy the cheeseboard ingredients a few days before the wedding, but remember to allow it to come to room temperature during the night or day before the reception.

Avocado dip is very simple to make and with the help of a processor could easily be made in 20 minutes on the morning of the reception. Keep covered in the fridge until required for use with crudités and the welcome drink as guests arrive.

A 5 a.m. trip to the market

To make sure the vegetables and fruit are fresh it is a good idea to buy them from your local wholesale fruit and vegetable market. This will mean an early start on the wedding morning or, more easily, the day before. Most markets open at 4 a.m. and you will find greengrocers, buyers for larger shops and restaurateurs there choosing the best produce. Check beforehand, but usually anyone can buy from the suppliers at the market.

Walk around the stalls and see which looks the best quality produce and which has most of the things you want. It will mean buying in large quantities (which is just what you want for a wedding) at cost prices — an ideal arrangement. Some suppliers will give you half boxes of goods and if you let them know in advance they might prepare smaller quantities of fruits and vegetables from split boxes that they have.

It is a good idea to enquire a week or so before you want to buy because a lot of the goods are under-ripe as shopkeepers buy them and keep them for a few days. A nice friendly supplier will keep you a couple of trays of tomatoes or whatever so that they are ready for use when you collect them, or buy them and ripen them at home.

Warn the baker!

Similarly visit your local baker a week or so beforehand to order the number of bread rolls or loaves that you want. Ask for a special discount on a large order, this is often forthcoming, but not if you don't ask! The bread should be collected on the morning of the wedding.

If friends have access to cash and carry markets this could be an ideal place to buy the ingredients for your cooking — if they carry wholemeal flour and pasta and the type of ingredients you require. If not, perhaps your local wholefood or health food shop could provide discount on a small sack of flour or large quantities of other goods. Butter wrapped in individual portions is very handy to have for a wedding and this is usually available from cash and carry places, but butter curls are prettier and can be made in advance and frozen.

What friends are for

With a little help from your friends, catering

Wedding Menus — Quantities Required

	Batches of recipes for number of guests		
	50	100	150
Main Course			
Mackerel Pâté (page 27)	1	2	
Avocado Dip (page 27)	1	2	
Spinach Choux Puffs (page 31)	1	2	3
Asparagus Quiche (page 28)	1	1½	2
Mushroom Quiche (page 29)	1	1½	2
Finnan Haddock and Avocado Quiche (page 30)	1	1⅓	2
Tomato Quiche (page 29)	1	1⅓	2
Smoky Pancakes (page 32)	1	2	3
Stuffed Courgettes (page 34)	1	2	2
Stuffed Tomatoes (page 34)	1	2	2
Pizzas (page 33)	1	2	3
Tahini and Sesame Patties (page 30)		1	2
Green Salad (page 36)	1	2	3
Tomato Salad (page 35)	1	2	3
Courgette Salad (page 35)	1	2	3
Potato Salad (page 35)	1	2	3
Home-cured Ham (optional)	3 lb (1.3 kilos)	6 lb (2.5 kilos)	8 lb (3.5 kilos)
Cold Roast Beef (optional)	3 lb (1.3 kilos)	6 lb (2.5 kilos)	8 lb (3.5 kilos)
Dessert			
Fresh Fruit Salad (page 36)	1	2	3
Apple Bateaux (page 38)			1
Lemon Cups (page 38)			1
Raspberry Soufflé (page 40)	3		
Orange Cheesecake (page 39)		1	3
Apricot Gateau (page 37)		1	2
Cheeseboard Select cheese from Chapter 6.	6 lb (2.5 kilos)	10 lb (4.5 kilos)	15 lb (7 kilos)
Wholemeal Bread Rolls (page 73)	50	100	500
Cheese Biscuits	1 tin (or equivalent)	2 tins (or equivalent)	3 tins (or equivalent)

for a wedding can be a lot of fun and a great success. So, for the two days beforehand arrange a rota of friends whereby you can have them spending a couple of hours each helping you in the kitchen (or two pairs of extra hands if it is a large affair). People love to help and they will get a kick out of seeing the courgettes they stuffed or the tomatoes they cut up on the wedding buffet on the big day.

What can I do?

For some reason you never have to ask for help with the clearing up. It seems people just love to get to grips with a teatowel and there are always steadfast relations and friends who will stick to kitchen sinks like limpets. All you need to do is hire plenty of crockery and glasses so that no washing up is needed during the reception and then keep an eye on them afterwards to see that they don't overdo it and everyone has their fair share with the teatowels. Incidentally, if friends ask what they can do to help let them send round some teatowels or trays because you can't have enough of either, or perhaps some bin liners for clearing up.

Avocado Dip

Serves 50 with crudités, used as a dip when guests arrive; 65 calories per person (approx)

6 large ripe avocados, about 10 oz (275g) each
2 lemons
4 × 10½ oz (287g) boxes *tofu*
1 tablespoonful Worcestershire sauce (optional)
8 oz (225g) prawns
Freshly ground black pepper

1. Cut the avocados in half and remove the stones. Scoop out the flesh and mash with the juice from the lemons.

2. Add the drained tofu and mix well.

3. Stir in the Worcestershire sauce and the prawns.

4. Season to taste with freshly ground black pepper.

5. Serve with selection of *crudités*: Cut a selection of seasonal vegetables into julienne strips and arrange on plates around bowls of dip placed on individual tables or trays with the drinks or near the place where guests collect their welcoming drink.

Mackerel Pâté

Serves 50; 135 calories per portion

12 smoked mackerel
4 blades of mace, pounded
12 oz (325g) unsalted butter, softened
2 lb (900g) cottage cheese
2 lemons
Freshly ground black pepper

1. Flake the fish from the skin and bones and mix with the mace in a bowl.

2. Beat the butter to soften it and add to the mackerel. Either mix thoroughly by hand or place in a liquidizer to blend.

3. Press the cottage cheese through a sieve and add to the fish mixture together with the lemons. Season to taste and either blend again or mix well.

4. Serve with tiny pieces of toast and a selection of *crudités*, or place in cold, wetted fish-shaped (or other) moulds and press down lightly. Chill for a couple of hours before unmoulding.

Asparagus Quiche

*Makes 3×9-inch (23cm) quiches. Each
quiche serves 12; 175 calories per portion
(Illustrated opposite page 161)*

Pastry:

1½ lb (675g) wholemeal flour
12 oz (325g) unsalted butter or soft vegetable margarine
3 free-range egg yolks
Water to mix

1.   Sieve the flour into a mixing bowl and add the fat. Rub the fat into the flour until the mixture resembles breadcrumbs in texture.

2.   Stir in the egg yolks mixed with a little water to make a soft dough.

3.   Divide the dough into three and roll out each third on a lightly-floured surface.

4.   Lightly oil a 9-inch (23cm) flan ring and baking tray and line the ring with the pastry. Cover with greaseproof paper and weigh down with baking beans.

5.   Bake in a pre-heated oven at 400°F/200°C (Gas Mark 6) for 10 minutes. Remove from heat and remove beans and paper. The flan case is now ready for filling. Repeat with the other portions of pastry.

Filling:

4×15oz (425g) tins asparagus
4 oz (100g) wholemeal flour
4 oz (100g) unsalted butter or soft vegetable margarine
1 pint (600ml) skimmed milk
½ pint (300ml) chicken stock
1 pint (600ml) single cream
6 free-range eggs, beaten
Freshly ground black pepper

1.   Drain the tins of asparagus and purée the contents of two tins. Retain the other two.

2.   Place the flour and fat in a saucepan and stir together over a moderate heat to make a roux. Cook for 2 minutes, stirring continuously.

3.   Gradually add the milk to the roux, stirring continuously to prevent lumps forming. Then add the chicken stock. Allow to cool.

4.   Stir the cream into the cooled sauce. Add the asparagus purée.

5.   Stir in the beaten eggs and add the seasoning.

6.   Arrange the asparagus spears in the flan cases in a cartwheel arrangement with tips pointing inwards. Pour the filling over the top and bake in a pre-heated oven at 375°F/190°C (Gas Mark 5) for 30-40 minutes until set and golden-brown.

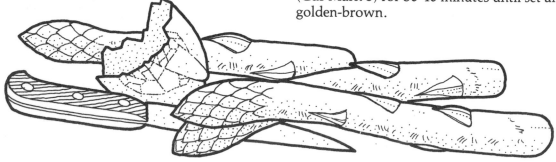

Mushroom Quiche

Makes 3 × 9-inch (23cm) quiches. Each quiche serves 12; 160 calories per portion (Illustrated opposite page 161)

1½ lb (675g) mushrooms
3 free-range eggs
3 free-range egg yolks
1 pint (600ml) thick set natural yogurt
8 oz (225g) Quark or similar low-fat soft white cheese
¾ pint (150ml) single cream
1 tablespoonful freshly chopped basil
Freshly ground black pepper
3 × 9-inch (23cm) flan cases, baked blind (page 28)

1.   Clean the mushrooms and place in a heavy-based saucepan lightly brushed with oil. Add three tablespoonsful of water and cook with the lid on for about 5 minutes or until mushrooms are starting to soften slightly. Remove from heat and drain.

2.   Beat the eggs, egg yolks, yogurt, cheese and cream together in a bowl and stir in the basil and pepper.

3.   Place the drained mushrooms in the baked flan cases and pour over the filling.

4.   Bake in a pre-heated oven at 375°F/190°C (Gas Mark 5) for 35-40 minutes until set and golden-brown in colour.

Tomato Quiche

Makes 3 × 9-inch (23cm) quiches. Each quiche serves 12; 160 calories per portion

2 bunches spring onions
3 × 9-inch (23cm) flan cases, baked blind (page 28)
2 lb (900g) small ripe tomatoes
¾ pint (450ml) thick set natural yogurt
8 oz (225g) Quark or similar low-fat soft white cheese
4 free-range eggs, lightly beaten
4 tablespoonsful finely chopped chives
Freshly ground black pepper

1.   Clean the spring onions and cut into small pieces. Lightly sauté in a smear of vegetable oil for about 5 minutes. Remove from heat and place in the bottom of the prepared pastry cases.

2.   Wash the tomatoes and cut in half. Arrange, cut side uppermost, in the pastry cases.

3.   In a bowl mix together the yogurt, cheese and eggs. Stir in three tablespoonsful of chives and season with pepper.

4.   Pour the filling into the pastry cases and sprinkle the remaining chives into the centre of each quiche. Bake in a pre-heated oven at 375°F/190°C (Gas Mark 5) for 25 minutes or until the filling is set and golden-brown.

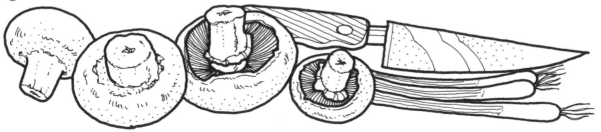

Finnan Haddock and Avocado Quiche

Makes 3 × 9-inch (23cm) quiches. Each quiche serves 12; 180 calories per portion (Illustrated opposite page 161)

1½ lb (675g) Finnan haddock*

3 large ripe avocados

2 lemons

1 pint (600ml) natural yogurt

¼ pint (150ml) double cream

4 free-range eggs

Freshly ground black pepper

3 × 9-inch (23cm) pastry cases, baked blind (page 28)

1.   Place the haddock in a large saucepan with about ½ pint (300ml) water and cover. Bring to the boil. Lower the heat and simmer for about 15 minutes until the fish is cooked.

2.   Remove the fish from the heat and when cool enough to handle flake from the skin and bones into a large mixing bowl.

3.   Halve the avocados, remove the stones and the peel and slice carefully into another bowl. Cover with the juice from the lemons to prevent browning.

4.   Lightly beat the yogurt, cream and the eggs together and mix thoroughly with the fish. Season to taste and pour into the prepared pastry cases.

5.   Arrange the avocado slices on top of the quiche and push down slightly into the filling.

6.   Bake in a pre-heated oven at 375°F/190°C (Gas Mark 5) for 30-40 minutes until filling is set and golden-brown.

Tahini and Sesame Patties

Makes 50; 70 calories per patty

1½ lb (675g) brown continental lentils

2 bay leaves

6 onions, diced

1 dessertspoonful vegetable oil

10 oz (275g) wholemeal breadcrumbs

6 oz (175g) tahini

2 teaspoonsful ground cumin

1 teaspoonful ground coriander

2 free-range eggs, beaten

Large plateful sesame seeds

Vegetable oil for frying

1.   Wash the lentils and pick them over removing any grit or stones. Place in a large saucepan with 2½ times their volume of water. Add the bay leaves and boil for about 20 minutes until well cooked. Drain, remove bay leaves.

2.   Place the onions and the oil in a saucepan and cover. Cook for 10 minutes until soft and transparent. Do not brown.

3.   Place the breadcrumbs in a large mixing bowl and add the cooked lentils. Pound well to make a soft paste.

4.   Add the onions, tahini and spices to the lentil mixture and form into small patty shapes.

5.   Dip the patties into the beaten egg and then roll in sesame seeds before lightly frying in a small amount of vegetable oil until golden on both sides. Allow to cool.

Spinach Choux Puffs

Makes 50; 130 calories per puff

Choux Pastry:

1½ pints (900ml) water
10 oz (275g) unsalted butter or soft vegetable margarine
1¼ lb (550g) 85 per cent wholemeal flour
2 teaspoonsful paprika
10-12 free-range eggs

1.   Place water and fat in a saucepan and heat until the fat has melted and the water is boiling.

2.   Add the sieved flour and paprika to the pan and remove from the heat. Beat the flour into the water until it is smooth and shiny and leaves the sides of the pan.

3.   Allow to cool slowly then beat in one egg at a time ensuring each is completely integrated before adding the next. Do not make the paste too wet because it has to be piped into shape. Depending on the size of the eggs 10 may be enough. Stop adding the eggs at any stage after 8 if the mixture is becoming too wet.

4.   Lightly oil a baking sheet and place the paste in a piping bag with a ½-inch (1cm) plain nozzle. Place a knife in a jug of hot water and use this to cut off the paste after piping each ball onto the tray. Glaze with remaining egg or some milk.

5.   Bake in a pre-heated oven at 425°F/220°C (Gas Mark 7) for 20 minutes then lower the heat to 375°F/190°C (Gas Mark 5) for a further five minutes to dry out the puffs.

6.   Remove from oven and leave to cool on a wire cooling tray.

Note: The puffs will fill three or four baking trays. If your oven is not large enough to take them all in one session the choux paste will keep, covered, in the fridge until the first batch is baked.

Filling:
For 50 choux puffs:

8 oz (225g) unsalted butter or soft vegetable margarine
8 oz (225g) wholemeal flour
2 pints (900ml) stock
1½ lb (675g) frozen spinach

For 100 choux puffs:

10 oz (275g) unsalted butter or soft vegetable margarine
10 oz (275g) wholemeal flour
2½ pints (1.5 litres) stock
2 lb (900g) frozen spinach

1.   Stir together the fat and flour in a saucepan to make a roux. Cook the roux for 2 minutes, stirring all the time.

2.   Gradually stir in the stock, cooking between additions and stirring continuously to prevent lumps forming.

3.   The spinach can be added from frozen by stirring into the hot sauce.

4.   Once all the spinach has been stirred in assess the consistency of the mixture and thin, if necessary by adding a little skimmed milk.

5.   Leave the mixture to cool. When cold enough to handle place some in a piping bag fitted with a ⅛-inch (.25cm) plain nozzle.

6.   Pierce the choux puffs with the nozzle and pipe the mixture into the centre.

Smoky Pancakes

Makes 50; 85 calories per portion

Batter:

1 lb (450g) wholemeal flour

Pinch sea salt (optional)

4 free-range eggs

2 pints (900ml) skimmed milk

1.   Sieve the flour into a mixing bowl with the salt, if using.

2.   Lightly beat the eggs and make a well in the centre of the flour.

3.   Add the eggs to the flour and gradually work in the flour using a fork. Work from the centre towards the sides of the bowl.

4.   When the eggs have absorbed as much flour as they can, gradually start adding the milk until a smooth paste is achieved, then add the remainder of the milk. Leave to stand for 10 minutes.

5.   Lightly oil an omelette pan or frying pan and heat it until very hot.

6.   Using a jug pour in a small amount of batter and tip the pan so it thinly coats the base. Allow to set and slip a palette knife under. When the pancake comes away easily flip it over and cook the other side for a few seconds.

7.   Remove from pan and pile onto a plate until the stuffing is ready.

Note: The first pancake often sticks to the pan. In Brittany this one is always thrown out for the birds for luck! The pancakes can be frozen either by lying them flat and layering with sheets of freezer tissue, or rolling them up and packing in polythene boxes to prevent them being damaged in the freezer.

Filling:

3 lb (1.3 kilos) smoked cod, poached and cooled

6 onions, diced

1 lb (450g) mushrooms

3 × 14 oz (375g) tins of tomatoes

4 oz (100g) Gruyère cheese, grated

1.   Flake the cooled, smoked cod from the bones and skin and place in a large mixing bowl.

2.   Place the onions in a large saucepan with a smear of oil. Cover and cook for 5 minutes.

3.   Clean the mushrooms and slice. Add to the onions and cook for another 5 minutes.

4.   Add the tomatoes and break them up with the back of a wooden spoon. Continue cooking over a fast heat with the lid off the pan to reduce the juice a little.

5.   When the mixture has reduced add it to the bowl containing the fish and mix thoroughly.

6.   Stir in the cheese. As soon as the mixture is cool enough to handle pour off excess liquid and stuff the pancakes.

7.   Serve cold or place in an ovenproof dish and reheat at 350°F/180°C (Gas Mark 4) for 15-20 minutes.

Note: For a cocktail or drinks party these pancakes can be cut in half, when stuffed, to make finger-size nibbles. Choose a naturally smoked cod rather than a dyed bright yellow one which will have colouring and possibly other additives. Real smoked fish is pale in colour without a shiny artificial appearance.

Opposite: The perfect Wedding Reception. (Photograph by Janette Marshall.)

Anchovy Mini Pizzas

Serves 50; 120 calories per pizza

1 quantity of pizza dough (page 50, Tomato and Olive Pizza)
1 quantity of topping (page 50, same recipe), plus an extra 2 oz (50g) black olives
2 × 1½ oz (38g) tins anchovy fillets

1. Make the dough as instructed in recipe for Tomato and Olive Pizza (page 50). Make the topping from the same recipe.

2. Roll out the dough and cut into individual pizzas using a plain circular biscuit cutter of 3-3½ inches (8-9cm) in diameter. Place the pizzas on a lightly-oiled baking tray and brush with a smear of olive oil.

3. Place a spoonful of topping on each pizza and then add part of an anchovy fillet and a black olive.

4. Top with thinly sliced Mozzarella cheese and bake for 20-25 minutes in pre-heated oven at 400°F/200°C (Gas Mark 6).

Mushroom Mini Pizzas

Serves 50; 115 calories per pizza

1 quantity of pizza dough (page 50, Tomato and Olive Pizza)
1 quantity of topping (page 50, same recipe) plus an extra 2 oz (50g) black olives
12 oz (325g) thinly sliced mushrooms

1. Make the dough as instructed in recipe for Tomato and Olive Pizza (page 50). Make the topping from the same recipe.

2. Roll out the dough and cut into individual pizzas using a plain circular biscuit cutter of 3-3½ inches (8-9cm) in diameter. Place the pizzas on a lightly-oiled baking tray and brush with a smear of olive oil.

3. Place a spoonful of topping on each pizza and then add slices of mushroom and a black olive.

4. Top with thinly sliced Mozzarella cheese and bake for 20-25 minutes in a pre-heated oven at 400°F/200°C (Gas Mark 6).

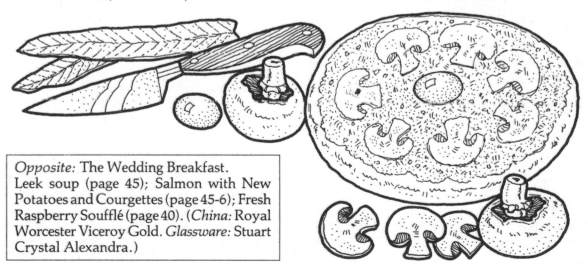

Opposite: The Wedding Breakfast. Leek soup (page 45); Salmon with New Potatoes and Courgettes (page 45-6); Fresh Raspberry Soufflé (page 40). (*China:* Royal Worcester Viceroy Gold. *Glassware:* Stuart Crystal Alexandra.)

Stuffed Courgettes

Serves 50; 50 calories per courgette half

25 courgettes
2 lb (900g) onions, diced
4 cloves garlic (optional)
1 tablespoonful vegetable oil
3 lb (1.3 kilos) mushrooms, diced
8 oz (225g) wholemeal breadcrumbs
Freshly grated nutmeg
Blade mace, pounded
Freshly grounded black pepper

1. Wash the courgettes and top and tail them. Plunge into boiling water and cook for 8 minutes until just cooked, but still firm. Drain and plunge into cold water to stop them cooking further. Drain again.

2. Cut the courgettes in half lengthways, and use a teaspoon to scoop out the pulp from the centre leaving a hollow boat shape. Reserve the pulp.

3. Place the onions and garlic in a pan with a tablespoonful of vegetable oil and cook over a moderate heat for 5 minutes.

4. Add the mushrooms and continue cooking for another 10 minutes. Drain any excess liquid from the pan and allow the mushrooms to cool slightly before liquidizing.

5. Stir half the courgette pulp into the mushrooms and add the breadcrumbs and the seasoning.

6. Stuff the courgettes shells with the mixture.

Stuffed Tomatoes

Makes 50; 50 calories per tomato

50 ripe but firm tomatoes
2½ lb (1 kilo) cottage cheese
1 lb (450g) smoked cod's roe
Juice of 2 lemons
2½ fl oz (75ml) tin tomato purée
8 oz (225g) wholemeal breadcrumbs
Freshly ground black pepper

1. Wash the tomatoes and slice off the tops. Retain the tops and scoop out the pulp and pips from the tomatoes. Turn upside down on wire cooling racks to drain.

2. Drain any excess liquid from the cottage cheese and press it through a sieve into a mixing bowl.

3. Peel the skin from the cod's roe. If it does not come away easily place the roe in a liquidizer and blend to remove any hard pieces. Add the lemon juice to the cod's roe.

4. Mix the roe, cheese and other ingredients together and spoon the mixture into the tomato shells.

Note: Do not make these too far in advance because the liquid from the cheese and tomatoes will begin to leak out after about 12 hours. This does not impair the flavour or mean they are 'off' but it does look rather messy.

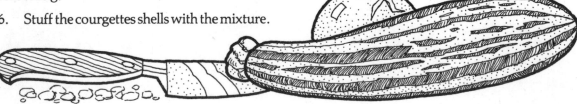

Courgette Salad

Serves 50; 60 calories per portion

6 lb (2.5 kilos) courgettes
¾ pint (450ml) olive oil
Juice of 6 lemons
2 tablespoonful white wine vinegar
Freshly ground black pepper
1 large bunch fresh chives

1. Wash the courgettes and slice very thinly into a bowl containing the juice from two of the lemons. Toss from time to time to ensure the courgettes are well coated and prevent them from browning.

2. In a clean screwtop jar place the olive oil, the rest of the lemon juice and the white wine vinegar, pepper and chives. Shake the jar well.

3. Toss the courgettes in the dressing and cover. Refrigerate until ready for use.

Tomato Salad

Serves 50; 95 calories per portion

8 lb (3.5 kilos) ripe tomatoes
1¼ pints (750ml) olive oil
8 fl oz (250ml) cider vinegar
2 bunches chives, finely chopped
2 teaspoonful ready-made stoneground or meaux mustard

1. Plunge the tomatoes into boiling water and leave them for about 4 minutes. Drain and cover with cold water.

2. Remove the skin from the tomatoes and discard.

3. Slice the tomatoes thinly and place them in a large plastic container with a lid.

4. Place the rest of the ingredients in a clean screwtop jar and shake vigorously. Pour over the tomatoes and leave to marinate in the fridge for several hours before use.

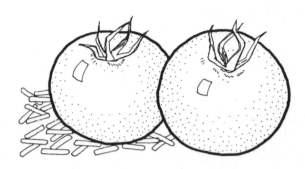

Potato Salad

Serves 50; 95 calories per portion

8 lb (3.5 kilos) new potatoes
Sprigs of fresh mint
2 × 12 oz (325ml) jars safflower mayonnaise
2 bunches parsley, finely chopped

1. Scrub the potatoes in plenty of cold water and plunge into large saucepans of boiling water. Cook for about 10 minutes with some fresh mint in the water. Check the potatoes regularly because if they are over-cooked they will crumble.

2. When the potatoes are cooked remove from the water and run under a cold tap in a colander for a few minutes to stop them cooking further.

3. As soon as they are cool enough to handle, chop the potatoes into a bowl and dress them with the mayonnaise and parsley.

Green Salad

Serves 50; 100 calories per portion with dressing

8 cos or Webb's lettuce

6 bunches watercress

4 punnets mustard and cress

4 bunches spring onions

2 large cucumbers

1¼ pints (750ml) sunflower oil

½ pint (300ml) cider vinegar

2 tablespoonsful ready-made stoneground or meaux mustard

Freshly ground black pepper

1.   Have ready a large plastic bucket such as a wine-making container.

2.   Wash the lettuce thoroughly.

3.   Wash the watercress and discard any yellowing leaves and excess stalks or roots.

4.   Wash the mustard and cress. Clean the spring onions and leave whole. Shake all the ingredients vigorously to drain excess water before putting in the large bucket.

5.   Wash the cucumber, but do not peel.

6.   Before serving, shred the lettuce into salad bowls and add the other washed ingredients. Snip the spring onions into small pieces using kitchen scissors and slice the cucumber. (A food processor will do this job in seconds.)

7.   Make the salad dressing by combining the oil, vinegar, mustard and pepper in a clean screwtop jar and shaking vigorously. Toss the salad in the dressing just before serving.

Note: Leave it as late as possible before preparing the green salad because it will wilt if prepared too far in advance. Once washed and stored in a cool airy place the ingredients will last overnight, but do not shred them until just before serving.

The salad dressing can be made in advance and stored in jars in the fridge. Do not dress green salad before it is required because it will go slimy and unpleasant.

Fresh Fruit Salad

Serves 50; 60 calories per portion

1 large pineapple

2 litre cartons orange juice

8 bananas

8 apples

8 pears

8 oranges

2 lb (900g) grapes

1.   Slice the pineapple in half and place the cut sides on a work surface. Cut away the outer skin and cut in half through the core. Make a V section to remove the core then slice the pineapple and chop the slices into small cubes. Place in a large container.

2.   Pour the orange juice into the container.

3.   Peel the bananas and slice into the mixture.

4.   Wash and core, but do not peel, the apples and dice into the salad.

5.   Prepare the pears in the same way as the apples.

6.   Peel the oranges and remove all the pith. Slice four of the oranges into rounds, removing the pips, and add to the salad. Cut the remainder into natural segments.

7.   Wash the grapes well then halve and remove the pips before stirring into the salad.

Apricot Gateau

Makes 3 × 8-inch (20cm) gateaux. Each gateau serves 12; 145 calories per slice

6 oz (175g) **unsalted butter or soft vegetable margarine**

9 oz (250g) **wholemeal flour**

3 **tablespoonsful cornflour**

9 **free-range eggs**

8 oz (225g) **clear honey**

Filling:

1½ lb (675g) **dried apricots**

2 lb (900g) **Quark or similar low-fat soft white cheese**

'No-added-sugar' apricot jam (optional)

4 oz (100g) **toasted flaked almonds**

1.   Line three 8-inch (20cm) loose-bottomed cake tins with silicone baking paper or grease-proof paper. Oil the insides of the paper. Heat the oven to 375°F/190°C (Gas Mark 5).

2.   Melt the butter in a saucepan over a low heat. Remove and allow to cool.

3.   Sieve together the flour and cornflour and place on one side.

4.   Place the eggs and honey in an electric mixer bowl and beat until pale in colour, thick and ropey in texture.

5.   Carefully pour the melted butter into the egg mixture and mix in well.

6.   Quickly add the flour and fold in with a metal spoon.

7.   Pour the mixture into the three cake tins and bake for 20-25 minutes until firm and springy to the touch and golden-brown. Remove from oven and allow to cool before carefully slicing into three, horizontally, using a palette knife.

Filling and topping:

1.   While the cake is baking and cooling, wash the apricots and cook in boiling water for about 30 minutes until soft enough to purée.

2.   When the purée has cooled mix with the cheese.

3.   Spread the bottom layer of the gateaux with a thin layer of jam and top with a layer of apricot purée. Repeat with the second layer.

4.   Cover the top and sides of the cakes with the purée and smooth the surface with a palette knife.

5.   When all three cakes are assembled place, in turn, on a rotary icing stand and press toasted flaked almonds around the edges.

6.   Use the remaining purée to pipe small stars on top of the cakes, around the edge, and in spokes going into the centre of the gateaux.

Apple Bateaux and Lemon Cups

*Makes 40 of each; 95 calories per Apple
Bateau, 130 calories per Lemon Cup*

Sweet pastry:

2 lb (900g) wholemeal flour

1½ lb (675g) unsalted butter or soft
vegetable margarine

4 free-range egg yolks

Zest of 1 lemon

1. Sieve the flour into a mixing bowl and add
the fat. Rub in until the mixture resembles
breadcrumbs in consistency.

2. Make a well in the centre.

3. Beat the egg yolks with a little water and
add to the flour with the lemon zest.

4. Stir to make a soft dough adding a little
more water if necessary.

5. Turn the dough onto a lightly floured
surface and knead gently until pliable enough
to roll out.

6. Lightly oil some bateaux moulds (unless
you have access to a large number these will
have to be baked in batches) and some small
patty tins.

7. Line the bateaux moulds with pastry and
trim the edges. Use a small pastry cutter with
a fancy edge for the patty tins and line those.

8. Place small pieces of silicone paper or
greaseproof paper in the moulds and weigh
them down with baking beans. Bake blind for
about 7 minutes at 375°F/190°C (Gas Mark 5).

9. Remove from oven. Fill the bateaux
according to method below and return to the
oven for another 7 minutes.

10. Leave the patty moulds to cool before
filling.

Apple Bateaux Filling:

1½ lb (675g) cooking apples

Juice of 1 lemon

2 dessert apples with red skins

1. Peel the cooking apples and slice into a
large saucepan with 6 tablespoonsful of water
and half the lemon juice. Cook, covered over
a moderate heat until the apples are soft enough
to form a purée. Remove from heat and drain
any excess liquid.

2. Slice the unpeeled, but washed and cored,
dessert apples into the remaining lemon juice.
Make sure the slices are thin and even.

3. Pile the purée into the bateaux and into
each place two of the slices of dessert apples
with the skin showing uppermost like two
wings.

Lemon Cup Filling:

8 oz (225g) light brown Muscovado sugar

4 oz (100g) unsalted butter

3 lemons

3 free-range eggs

1. Place the sugar, butter, the grated rind of
all three well-scrubbed lemons and the juice of
two lemons together with the well-beaten eggs
in the top half of a double boiler.

2. Stir over a low heat until the mixture melts
then slowly thickens. Do not let it boil or it will
curdle.

Note: The lemon curd can be stored in clean,
screwtop jars in the fridge for several weeks.

Orange Cheesecake

Makes 3 × 8-inch (20cm) cheesecakes. Each serves 12; 145 calories per portion

Base:

1¼ lb (550g) wholemeal flour

12 oz (325g) unsalted butter or soft vegetable margarine

3 free-range eggs

1 teaspoonful ground cinnamon

1. Sieve the flour into a mixing bowl and add the fat. Rub in until mixture resembles breadcrumbs in texture. Stir in the spice.

2. Make a well in the centre and add the lightly beaten eggs.

3. Add two tablespoonsful of water and mix to a soft dough.

4. Turn out onto a lightly-floured surface and knead gently until pliable enough to roll out.

5. Lightly oil three 8-inch (20cm) loose-bottomed flan tins and line with the pastry.

6. Cover with greaseproof paper and fill with baking beans. Bake in a pre-heated oven at 400°F/200°C (Gas Mark 6) for 10 minutes.

7. Remove from oven and empty out the beans and paper. The case is now ready for filling.

Filling:

1 lb (450g) low-fat curd cheese

¼ pint (150ml) single cream

½ pint (300ml) natural yogurt

6 free-range eggs, separated

4 tablespoonsful clear honey

2 oranges

2 teaspoonsful ground cinnamon

1. Pound the cheese with the cream and yogurt and stir in the egg yolks. Mix in the honey and the finely grated rind of both oranges.

2. Whisk the egg whites until stiff, but not dry, and fold into the mixture with a metal spoon. Pour immediately into the prepared pastry cases and bake at 350°F/180°C (Gas Mark 4) for 25 minutes until set and golden brown.

3. While the cheesecake is cooking peel the pith from the oranges and cut into rounds, removing the pips. When cold decorate the cheesecakes with the oranges sprinkled with cinnamon.

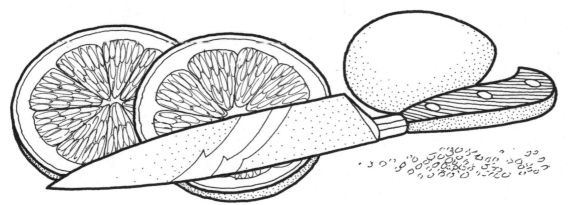

Raspberry Soufflé

Serves 20, 190 calories per portion
(Illustrated opposite page 33)

3 lb (1.3 kilos) fresh raspberries

10 free-range eggs, separated

6 oz (175g) fructose

1 pint (600ml) double cream

1½ oz (40g) gelatine

¼ pint (150ml) water

2 oz (50g) pistachio nuts

1.   Reserve some of the best raspberries for decoration and press the rest through a sieve or liquidize to a purée. This should make 1½ pints (900ml) juice.

2.   Make a greaseproof or silicone baking paper collar for two large soufflé dishes and tie in position so that the paper overlaps by about 2 inches where it joins, and stands a good 3 inches above the rim of the dish.

3.   Put the egg yolks and fructose in a bowl and whisk until thick and ropey. Pour in the purée. Stand on ice or in ice-cold water.

4.   Half whip the cream and fold into the mixture.

5.   Dissolve the gelatine in the water over gentle heat and allow to cool. When on the point of setting mix in thoroughly.

6.   Whisk the egg whites until stiff and fold in thoroughly using a metal spoon.

7.   Pour at once into the prepared soufflé dishes and place in fridge until set. Remove collar before serving and decorate the top with raspberries and pistachios.

The Wedding Breakfast

Wedding breakfasts can be enjoyed at any time of the day, as these menus show, but they are traditionally an early lunch, often after a register office wedding.

The menus offer a hot or a cold meal. The cold one is obviously easier for the host, who can prepare it in advance, but the hot meal is kept deliberately simple so that the minimum amount of time is spent in the kitchen. Part of it can be served cold. The soup could be turned into an iced vichyssoise and the salmon steaks could be served cold with a potato salad and a courgette salad; but this menu is better hot.

As these menus cater for a smaller number of guests you might prefer to serve champagne as a welcoming drink, or even throughout the meal because the food will compliment it well. Otherwise use a better quality white wine such as Chablis or a dry white from the Loire or Anjou (see Chapter 6 for further suggestions).

Both meals are essentially simple in their ingredients and they are light. They rely on the flavour of top-quality fresh foods, and colours that are subtle and attractive for the occasion.

If preferred, one of the desserts from the wedding reception, such as the Raspberry Soufflé, could be substituted for the suggested one. A cheese course is optional (see Chapter 6 on Cheese and Wine).

**Cold Wedding Breakfast
for 20 Guests**

Gazpacho

*Fresh Whole Salmon
Courgette Salad
Potato Salad*

*Pineapple, Orange and
Raspberry Sorbets*

Gazpacho

Serves 20, 65 calories per portion

3 lb (1.3 kilos) fresh, ripe tomatoes
2 cucumbers
2 bunches spring onions
2 red peppers
4 cloves garlic (optional)
4 oz (100g) fresh wholemeal breadcrumbs
6 tablespoonsful olive oil
2 tablespoonsful red wine vinegar
Freshly ground black pepper
4 tablespoonsful freshly chopped basil
½ pint (300ml) court bouillon
½ pint (300ml) cultured buttermilk or natural yogurt

1. Wash and chop the tomatoes, cucumber and spring onions and place in a large earthenware bowl.

2. Wash and de-seed the peppers. Dice and add to the other vegetables.

3. Peel and crush the garlic, if using. Add, with the breadcrumbs, to the vegetables.

4. Place the olive oil, vinegar, pepper and basil together in a clean screwtop jar and place on the lid. Shake vigorously and pour over the vegetables. Toss well and marinate for 30 minutes.

5. When marinated pour into a liquidizer and blend until smooth. Pour into a large container and stir in the court bouillon.

6. Just before serving stir in the buttermilk or yogurt, swirling round to make a marbled effect on the top of the soup.

Fresh Salmon

Serves 20; 135 calories per portion

Fresh salmon, served cold, looks far more attractive on the bone. It is also cheaper to buy three small whole salmon than it is to buy a salmon steak for each guest. The smaller salmon which are suitable for this type of cold buffet are often farmed salmon from Scotland, but they have a good coloured flesh and a good flavour. Ask the fishmonger to gut the fish. Take the trouble to make a court bouillon (page 140) in which to poach the salmon because it makes all the difference. Court bouillon is, in fact, very quick to make. Generally a fish kettle is used to poach salmon, but I find when cooking more than one that it is easier to poach them all together (in separate dishes) in the oven. Make sure you have a dish in which the fish can lie flat and so cook evenly in the liquid. If you do poach three at once in the oven, remember the one nearest the bottom of the oven will probably take longer than the others so check each separately.

3 × 3 lb (1.3 kilos) salmon
6 pints (3.5 litres) court bouillon
1 cucumber, for garnish
3 lemons, for garnish

1. Pre-heat the oven to 375°F/190°C (Gas Mark 5). Wash the fish under cold water, and place in the dish in which it is to be cooked. If it is a baking tin, line first with double layer of silicone paper. A glass ovenproof dish is often easier to use.

2. Pour 2 pints (1.2 litres) of court bouillon over each fish. Place in the oven. The fish nearest the top of the oven may need covering with a sheet of silicone or greaseproof paper to stop it from drying out.

3. After 15 minutes remove the fish from the oven and *very carefully* using a couple of fish slices, turn the fish to poach the other side.

4. After cooking for a further 15 minutes remove from the oven and place on a flat plate to cool. Lift the fish *very carefully* from the baking containers.

5. When the fish is cool enough to handle, very gently peel off the skin and scrape away any brown-coloured flesh with a sharp pointed knife. Leave the head and tail on the fish.

6. As the fish cools it will be sitting in a jelly of its own juices. Place the fish on the serving dish and use a pastry brush to glaze it with these jellied juices rather than using aspic for glazing.

7. Decorate with thin slices of cucumber and lemon and place small lemon wedges around the fish. If you are feeling extravagant spears of fresh boiled asparagus make a very impressive (and delicious) garnish. Serve with salads from the selection in the Reception section, Courgette Salad and Potato Salad (both page 35) go very well.

Note: Be careful at all times when handling a whole fish such as a salmon because it has delicate flesh, but is quite heavy and so is liable to fall to pieces if not handled with care.

Sorbets

Sorbets have become fashionable and popular dishes with the rise in fame of *Cuisine Minceur* and *Nouvelle Cuisine*. They are an excellent way of enjoying an ice-cream style dish without the heavy cream content. For most palates they require some sugar to be added, but the wholefood cook can use fructose which is a natural fruit sugar less disruptive to the metabolism than sucrose (ordinary white or brown sugars). Sorbets are best made fresh because the delicate aroma of the fruit is lost with storage.

Serve a selection of sorbets in a glass which shows off their wonderful colours in a delicious way. Or place *quenelles* of sorbet (parts of a scoop) on a white plate with slices of fresh fruit.

For a wedding and other large-scale catering it is better to stick with familiar flavours and serve raspberry, orange or pineapple sorbets. These are also cheaper than the more exotic mango, passion fruit or kiwi fruit sorbets which can be used for a smaller dinner party.

The following recipes will serve eight people, or they will provide each of the 20 guests with a *quenelle* of each flavour of the three sorbets. These would be served with segments of oranges on which all the skin has been cut away, sliced raspberries or strawberries and perhaps some tiny mint leaves.

These sorbets make the use of egg whites optional, because without them the taste of the fruit is much more pronounced. However, if a *sorbetier* is not available the egg whites will give a better texture when making sorbets by hand. They also do not strain the fruit pulp before freezing because this, too, loses some of the flavour and the fibre.

See also the Blackcurrant Sorbet recipe in Summer Dinner Parties (page 141).

This selection serves 20; average 100 calories per portion.

Pineapple Sorbet

2 ripe pineapples
4 oz (100g) fructose
Juice of 1 lemon
2 free-range egg whites (optional)

1.   Prepare the pineapple by dicing the flesh (not the central core) into small pieces. (See Hot Pineapple, page 47, if you have not used fresh pineapple before.)

2.   Place in a liquidizer with the fructose and lemon juice and blend.

3.   Pour into a *sorbetier*. If this is not available pour into a shallow tray and freeze until mushy. Remove from the freezer.

4.   Whisk egg whites until stiff and stir into frozen mixture.

5.   Return to freezer in container deep enough to remove sorbet in scoops.

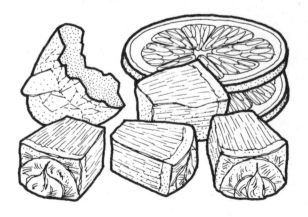

Orange Sorbet

2 lb (900g) oranges
Juice of 1 lemon
4 oz (100g) fructose
2 free-range egg whites (optional)

1. Scrub the oranges well and grate the rind from four into a bowl.

2. Cut the oranges in half and add the juice to the rind. Place with the fructose in a liquidizer and add the flesh left in the oranges — not the pith.

3. Pour the liquidized mixture into a *sorbetier*. If this is unavailable place in a shallow tray and freeze until mushy.

4. Remove from freezer and add the stiffly whisked egg white, if using. Return to the freezer in a container deep enough to remove scoops of sorbet from.

Raspberry Sorbet

1½ lb (675g) raspberries
4 oz (100g) fructose
Juice of 1 lemon
2 free-range egg whites (optional)

1. Pick over the raspberries and hull them. Wash and shake dry.

2. Liquidize with fructose and lemon juice.

3. Pour into a *sorbetier*. If this is not available pour into a shallow tray and freeze the mixture until mushy. Remove from freezer.

4. Whisk the egg whites until stiff and stir into the frozen mixture.

5. Return to the freezer in a container deep enough to remove scoops of sorbet from.

**Hot Wedding Breakfast
for 20 Guests**

Leek Soup

*Poached Salmon Steaks
New Potatoes
Courgettes*

*Hot Pineapple
Chantilly Cream*

3.   Place the butter in a large saucepan and melt over a gentle heat. Add the leeks and onions and cover. Leave to cook over a moderate heat for 20 minutes, stirring from time to time to ensure the vegetables are evenly cooked. They should become soft and transparent, but not browned.

4.   After about 5 minutes add the pepper and mace and stir well.

5.   In another large saucepan, warm the vegetable stock. When the leeks and onions are ready carefully spoon them into the stock and allow mixture to boil.

6.   Remove from heat and place in large tureen or individual serving bowls. Garnish with freshly chopped parsley.

Leek Soup

*Serves 20; 80 calories per portion
(Illustrated opposite page 33)*

4 lb (1.8 kilos) leeks

2 lb (900g) onions

4 oz (100g) unsalted butter

Freshly ground black pepper

Freshly ground blade mace

5 pints (2.8 litres) vegetable stock

2 tablespoonsful freshly chopped parsley

1.   Wash and trim the leeks. Run under cold water to completely remove grit and dirt. Dice very finely.

2.   Peel and finely dice the onions.

Poached Salmon

*Serves 20; 320 calories per portion
(Illustrated opposite page 33)*

When serving hot salmon for a wedding breakfast it is far easier to use individual salmon steaks, ready-cut by your fishmonger.

As you are bulk-buying he might agree to a discount. Ask for the steaks to weigh about 6 oz (175g) each. If there are children in the group you could have some 4 oz (100g) steaks. Turbot makes an excellent poached fish and can be used in place of salmon if preferred.

20 salmon steaks
6 pints (3.5 litres) court bouillon (page 140)
Freshly cut dill for garnish
3 lemons, each cut into 8 wedges

1.   Place the salmon steaks in very lightly buttered glass dishes or casseroles or other ovenproof containers.

2.   Pour over the court bouillon until steaks are just covered.

3.   Place in a pre-heated oven at 375°F/190°C (Gas Mark 5) and allow to poach for 15-20 minutes.

4.   Remove from oven and drain. Place on a serving dish and garnish with freshly-cut feathery dill and lemon wedges.

New Potatoes

Allow 6 lb (2.5 kilos) potatoes for 20 people

Both the hot and the cold salmon or turbot can be served with boiled new potatoes. Scrub the potatoes to remove the dirt and any loose skin, but do not scrape off more skin than is necessary. Place in boiling water with a generous sprig of fresh mint (it is not necessary to add salt) and boil until just cooked. Drain and toss in a small amount of unsalted butter.

If the cold salmon is used and there is neither time nor facilities at the reception for serving hot potatoes cook the potatoes as above, selecting only the tiniest ones. Drain them and leave them whole. Toss in a small amount of home-made or safflower mayonnaise to which freshly chopped chives have been added and serve as potato salad.

Courgettes

Allow 1 large courgette per person

Courgettes can be served hot or cold with the salmon or turbot. If serving hot, larger courgettes can be used and cut into slices. Place in a large, heavy-based saucepan which has been smeared with unsalted butter. Add the juice of a lemon and cover the pan with a well-fitting lid. Allow to cook over a low heat, in their own steam, for about 15 minutes. Stir from time to time to ensure even cooking. Do not allow the courgettes to be browned on the bottom of the pan.

If serving cold, choose baby courgettes and allow two or three per person depending on the size. Wash the courgettes and top and tail then drop whole into boiling water and allow to cook for a few minutes (again depending on size) until they are just cooked, firm but still offering resistance when bitten. Drain and plunge into cold water to stop them cooking. Drain again and toss, still whole, in a vinaigrette (see below).

Courgette Dressing

⅓ pint (200ml) olive oil
Juice of 1 lemon
Freshly ground black pepper

1.   Place all ingredients in a screwtop jar and shake vigorously.

Hot Pineapple

Serves 20; 290 calories with cream, 120 without

3 pineapples of moderate size or 2 of the very large varieties
½ pint (300ml) water
6 tablespoonsful kirsch
2-3 tablespoonsful Demerara sugar

1.   Slice the ends off the pineapple and then slice it in half through the circumference. Turn the largest cut surfaces face down on the work surface. This makes them easier to handle.

2.   Collect any juices that are lost from the pineapple. It is easier to do this by working on a chopping board and tipping the juices into a bowl as they escape.

3.   Slice away the rough outside pineapple skin and cut into the pineapple as far as is necessary to remove the inverted spikes that go into the flesh. Alternatively pinch them out.

4.   Slice into 20 rounds and remove the hard central core with either a sharp scone cutter or a small kitchen knife.

5.   Place the rounds in a large frying pan or gratin dish that can be used over a flame or electric ring.

6.   Pour over the water and kirsch and place over a low heat and gently heat through, turning the rings once.

7.   Heat the grill and sprinkle a small amount of sugar over the top of the rings. (The less the better. I prefer mine without but guests usually like some sugar.)

8.   When the sugar is on top flash the pineapple under the grill until it is melted and gives the rounds a golden-brown top. Serve at once.

Note: When choosing a pineapple make sure it is firm but that it is also soft enough to give *a little* when pressed. This will indicate that it is ripe and juicy. Often the outside flesh goes a more golden yellow than green when pineapples are ripe, but beware of very yellow-looking soft fruits because these will be over-ripe and the flesh will have started to discolour to a nasty brown around the edges.

Chantilly Cream

For 20 people use 2 pints of double cream and 4-6 egg whites

This can be offered with the pineapple. It is a way of making the cream go further and it also means you get less saturated fat per serving than ordinary double cream.

1.   Whisk the egg whites until stiff, but not dry.

2.   Whisk the cream until just firm. Mix the two ingredients together and whisk again for a few seconds.

3.   Place in a serving dish with an attractive spoon standing up in the mixture.

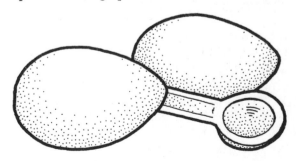

5.

Bring a Bottle

This is probably the most informal type of party, held for any or no particular reason! There are two party plans in this chapter, one for a small group of about 20 and one for a larger group of about 50.

The smaller party offers a selection of more expensive (but not too expensive!) and more complicated dishes which can also be prepared in smaller quantities. It makes use of delicious home-made wholemeal puff pastry in both sweet and savoury dishes. This can be made in advance and frozen uncooked in well wrapped parcels. The choux pastry can also be made in advance and frozen cooked, but both are better baked nearer the party. The Smoked Trout Mousse also freezes well.

Other dishes can be assembled on the day. The salads need to be left to the last minute, but the pasta for the salad can be boiled a while in advance.

The pastry for the Mille Feuille can be baked a day or two beforehand and kept, when cold, in airtight tins. The layers can be sandwiched together with the Bavarian cream and low-sugar jam in the morning and left in the fridge to chill. The pastry will stay crisp if it is kept dry and not put in a plastic box which will encourage condensation. The Gooseberry Fool can also be made in the morning. If gooseberries are not in season any dried fruit can be cooked and puréed to make a delicious fool.

Ingredients and dishes are much cheaper for the larger party which includes both hot and cold dishes for a winter party. Coleslaw-type salads are easy to make and a white cabbage goes a long way for a little money. The Brown Rice Rings make a nice splash of colour with their chopped vegetables, in a season otherwise devoid of colourful fruits and vegetable salads.

The pizzas can be made ahead and frozen, then served either hot or cold. The Chilli con Flageolli is obviously a hot dish (in several ways) and is good with rice, but could be served with pasta for a change, or crusty wholemeal French sticks.

Because the dishes for the winter party are hot it is an idea to use ceramic crockery. If using paper plates make sure they are quite deep and strong.

Opposite: Winter Bring a Bottle Party. Chilli con Flageolli (page 49) with Brown Rice; Tomato and Olive Pizza (page 50).

A Large Winter Party for 50

Chilli con Flageolli
Tomato and Olive Pizza
Baked Potatoes with Pineapple Cheese
or Ratatouille
Rice Rings
Coleslaw

Chilli con Flageolli

Serves 50; 240 calories per portion, or 215
calories per portion with meat
(Illustrated opposite page 18)

4 lb (1.8 kilos) red kidney beans,
soaked overnight

2 lb (900g) butter beans, soaked overnight

8 fresh green chillies

4 cloves garlic, crushed

2 lb (900g) onions, diced

¼ pint (150ml) vegetable oil

6 green peppers, de-seeded and diced

4 × 14 oz (400g) tins tomatoes

3 teaspoonsful cumin

3 teaspoonsful oregano

2 pints (900ml) water

3 lb (1.3 kilos) brown rice

Opposite: Summer Bring a Bottle Party.
Smoked Trout Mousse (page 54); Individual
Green Salad (page 55); Wholemeal Bread
Rolls (page 73).

1. Drain the beans and cook in boiling water for about 45 minutes or until soft. Drain.

2. Wash, de-seed and dice the chillies very finely. Be careful not to rub your eyes for some time after handling chillies because they make sensitive skin sting.

3. Place the chillies, with the garlic and onions and vegetable oil, in a large pan. Cover and cook for 10 minutes, stirring occasionally.

4. Add the peppers to the vegetables and pour in the tomatoes. Break up tomatoes with the back of the spoon.

5. Stir in the beans and add the spices and water. Continue cooking for 20 minutes with the lid off the pan. Stir occasionally to prevent burning.

6. Meanwhile boil the washed rice in 2½ times its volume of water for 25-30 minutes until cooked. Drain and place in warmed serving dish. Serve the chilli mixture in a separate dish.

Note: Beans are used in place of meat in this recipe, but 4 lb (1.3 kilos) red kidney beans and 4 lb (1.8 kilos) ground beef could be used. If using meat, add this to the saucepan with the onions at stage 3. Ensure the meat is thoroughly browned before proceeding to stage 4. The cooked kidney beans can be added at stage 5.

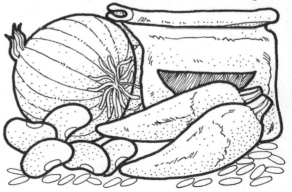

Tomato and Olive Pizza

Serves 50; 115 calories per portion
(Illustrated opposite page 48)

Base:

3 lbs (1.3 kilos) wholemeal flour
Pinch sea salt (optional)
1½ pints (900ml) lukewarm water
1½ oz (40g) fresh yeast
1 tablespoonful vegetable oil
25g vitamin C tablet, crushed

1. Sieve the flour and salt into a mixing bowl.

2. To achieve the correct temperature of water mix ⅓ boiling water with ⅔ cold water.

3. Crumble the yeast into the water and stir in the oil and vitamin C tablet. Leave to stand for 5 minutes.

4. Line three Swiss-roll tins with greaseproof paper and pre-heat the oven to 400°F/200°C (Gas Mark 6).

5. Make a well in the centre of the flour and pour in the yeast mixture. Stir to form a dough and turn onto a lightly floured surface and knead for 5 minutes.

6. Return dough to bowl, cover and leave to double in size while making the pizza topping.

Topping:

1 lb (450g) onions, diced
1 lb (450g) carrots, diced
2 red peppers, de-seeded and diced
2 cloves garlic, crushed
6 sticks celery
½ tablespoonful vegetable oil
2 × 14 oz (400g) tins tomatoes
2 teaspoonsful dried basil
1 tablespoonful tomato purée
Freshly ground black pepper
4 oz (100g) black olives
2 × 7 oz (200g) Mozzarella cheese packs

1. Place the onions, carrots, peppers, garlic and celery in a saucepan with the oil and cook, covered, over a low heat for 10 minutes, stirring occasionally to ensure all vegetables are cooked.

2. Add the tomatoes and break them up with the back of the spoon. Stir in the basil, tomato purée and pepper and continue to cook, uncovered over a moderate heat to reduce excess juice.

3. Roll out the pizza dough and line the three tins with the dough lapping up the sides of the tin by about one inch.

4. Pare thin slices of Mozzarella cheese using a cheese plane.

5. Spoon the tomato topping onto the pizzas and scatter olives over the top.

6. Top with cheese and bake for 25-30 minutes. Serve hot or cold.

7. Each pizza can be cut into 18 pieces by cutting in three along the length of the tin and in six across the width.

Baked Potatoes

Serves 50; 210 calories for pineapple cheese filling,
215 calorie for ratatouille filling

50 even-sized 7 oz (200g) potatoes

1.   Scrub the potatoes well and pierce all over using a fork.

2.   For a crispy skin rub the potatoes with butter or margarine wrappers or brush with a small amount of vegetable oil.

3.   Bake in a preheated oven at 375°F/190°C (Gas Mark 5) for about one hour, depending on the size of the potato.

4.   The potatoes may be cut across the top in a cross shape before baking to make it easier to open them when serving.

5.   Pile the baked potatos into a large dish or basket for serving and offer a choice of fillings in separate bowls.

Pineapple Cheese Filling. For 25 potatoes:
2 lb (900g) cottage cheese
1 fresh pineapple or 1½ lb (675g) pineapple, tinned in its own juice
Freshly ground black pepper

1.   Mash the cheese in a large bowl.

2.   Cut away the outer skin of the pineapple and cut it into rings. Slice out the hard central core and cut the rings into segments.

3.   Stir the pineapple into the cheese and season with pepper.

Ratatouille Filling. For 25 potatoes:
Make up a quantity of Ratatouille following the recipe on page 000, omitting the cheese.

Rice Rings

Serves 50; 95 calories per portion

2 lb (900g) brown rice
2 × 12 oz (325g) tins sweetcorn kernels
2 red peppers
2 green peppers
1 bunch spring onions
4 oz (100g) sunflower seeds
Freshly ground black pepper
12 oz (325g) jar safflower mayonnaise

1.   Wash the brown rice and cook in a large saucepan, in 2½ times its volume of water, for about 25-30 minutes.

2.   Drain the tins of sweetcorn and place in a large bowl.

3.   Wash and de-seed the peppers and dice finely. Add to the sweetcorn. Finely chop onions and add them to the bowl.

4.   Stir the sunflower seeds into the pepper mixture. Season.

5.   Allow the rice to cool before stirring it into the vegetable mixture and binding together with mayonnaise.

6.   Rinse out three savarin (or similar) moulds with cold water and do not dry. Press the rice mixture firmly into the moulds and leave in the fridge to chill.

7.   Unmould before serving by placing the moulds on a bed of lettuce on the serving dishes and giving them a sharp tap.

Coleslaw

Serves 50; 55 calories per portion

1 large white cabbage
2 lb (900g) carrots
1 head celery
8 crisp eating apples
8 oz (225g) sultanas
2 lemons
1 × 12 oz (325ml) jar cold-pressed safflower mayonnaise
Freshly ground black pepper
1 lb (450g) green grapes

1.   Finely shred the cabbages and grate the carrots.

2.   Slice the celery thinly and stir into the cabbage and carrots.

3.   Wash and core the apples but do not peel. Dice and toss at once in the lemon juice to prevent browning.

4.   Add the apples to the previous mixture and stir in the sultanas.

5.   Dress the salad with the mayonnaise. Add one jar only to begin with, and gradually add more as necessary, or to taste.

6.   Finally, halve the grapes and remove the pips before stirring in. Retain some for decoration on the top of the salad.

Note: When preparing a large amount of vegetables such as for this salad it is far less time-consuming to use a food processor and make use of the many different cutting edges they offer. Salads are far more interesting if the different ingredients retain their characteristics by being cut in different ways.

Because the vegetables are prepared quicker by a machine they will also suffer less vitamin and mineral loss and therefore be more nutritious. Food processors also have stainless steel blades which are good for vegetable preparation.

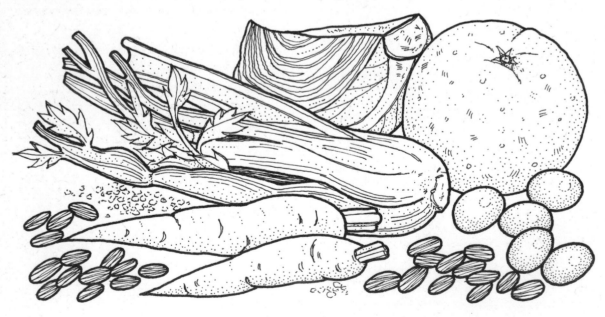

A Small Summer Party for 25

Tuna Bouchées
Gruyère Puffs

Smoked Trout Mousse
and Parsley Butter
Pasta Salad
Green Salad

Mille Feuille
Gooseberry Hazelnut Fool

Tuna Bouchées
Makes 24; 145 calories per portion

1 quantity wholemeal puff pastry (page 106)
2 × 7 oz (200g) tins tuna fish in brine
12 oz (325g) cottage cheese
1 free-range egg, beaten

1. Roll out the puff pastry to ¼-inch (.5cm) thickness and, using a pastry cutter with a plain or fancy edge, cut out 3½-inch (9cm) circles.

2. Place half the circles on a damp baking tray covered with damp greaseproof paper and carefully egg wash them.

3. Using a smaller cutter of about 1½ inches (4cm) cut out the centre of the remaining circles.

4. Place the two circles on top of the bases and carefully egg wash the tops only. Prick the centre bases with a fork.

5. Place the smaller circles on the baking tray and egg wash. These may be used as lids.

6. Bake in a pre-heated oven at 425°F/220°C, (Gas Mark 7) for 15-20 minutes until well risen and golden in colour.

7. Remove from oven leave until completely cold before filling.

8. Empty the tins of tuna and the cottage cheese into a liquidizer or blender and blend until smooth.

9. Spoon into the bouchée cases and place the lids on top. Sprinkle with freshly chopped parsley.

Gruyère Puffs

Makes 40; 80 calories per portion

8 oz (225g) unsalted butter or soft vegetable margarine
1 pint (600ml) water
12 oz (325g) 85 per cent wholemeal flour
6 free-range eggs
4 oz (100g) Gruyère cheese, grated
Pinch dry mustard
Freshly ground black pepper

1.   Place fat and water in a saucepan and heat until the fat has melted and the water is boiling.

2.   Quickly shoot the flour into the pan and remove from the heat. Beat the flour into the mixture until it is smooth and shiny and leaves the sides of the pan.

3.   Beat in one egg at a time ensuring each is completely integrated into the mixture before adding the next. Do not make the paste too wet because it has to be piped.

4.   Finally, beat in the grated cheese and seasoning.

5.   Lightly oil a baking sheet and place the paste in a piping bag with a ½-inch (1cm) plain nozzle. Place a knife in a jug of hot water and use this to cut off the paste after piping each ball onto the tray.

6.   Bake in a pre-heated oven at 425°F/220°C (Gas Mark 7) for 20 minutes then lower the heat to 375°F/190°C (Gas Mark 5) for a further 5 minutes.

7.   Serve hot or cold.

Smoked Trout Mousse and Parsley Butter

Serves 20; 180 calories per portion
(without toast or butter)
(Illustrated opposite page 49)

3 lb (1.3 kilos) smoked trout
1 lb (450g) Quark or similar low-fat soft white cheese
½ pint (300ml) soured cream
1 lemon
Freshly ground black pepper
2 oz (50g) freshly chopped parsley
8 oz (225g) unsalted butter
Basket of hot wholemeal toast

1.   Flake the trout from the bones and skin into a mixing bowl.

2.   Pound together with the Quark and stir in the soured cream.

3.   Add the juice and grate rind of half the lemon.

4.   Season to taste with pepper and place in serving bowl. Sprinkle with a small amount of the parsley.

5.   Soften the butter by pounding in a bowl and stir in the parsley. Place in the fridge and chill.

6.   When butter is chilled scoop out small butter balls using a Parisienne cutter.

7.   Serve the mousse and butter with hot wholemeal toast.

Pasta Salad

Serves 20; 130 calories per portion

2 lb (900g) wholemeal pasta rings

12 oz (325g) red kidney beans soaked overnight and then boiled for 40 minutes or 2 ready-cooked 15½ oz (440g) tins

3 lb (1.3 kilos) broad beans or 2 ready cooked 15½ oz (440g) tins borlotti beans

2 oranges

4 tablespoonsful olive oil

Freshly ground black pepper

1. Boil the pasta in plenty of water (about 8 pints/4.5 litres per 1 lb/900g is needed) to which 1 dessertspoonful of vegetable oil has been added.

2. Drain the tins of kidney beans, if using, and wash in cold water.

3. Shell the broad beans then boil for 10-12 minutes, if using. Drain.

4. Squeeze the juice from the oranges and place in a clean screwtop jar with the olive oil and pepper. Secure the lid and shake well.

5. Place the just-cooked pasta in a mixing bowl with the hot beans and the kidney beans and pour over the salad dressing. Toss well and serve warm or cold.

Green Salad

*Serves 20; 40 calories per portion or
85 with dressing
(Illustrated opposite page 49)*

4 cos lettuce

2 bunches watercress

2 bunches spring onions

2 ripe avocados

Juice of ½ lemon

2 large cooked beetroot

Dressing:

¼ pint (150ml) olive oil

4 tablespoonsful raspberry vinegar

Freshly ground black pepper

1. Wash the lettuce well and shred into a large container.

2. Wash the watercress discarding any yellowing leaves and some of the stalks. Break into small sprigs and add to the lettuce.

3. Clean the spring onions and chop into small pieces using kitchen scissors.

4. Halve the avocados and remove the stones. Peel the skin off and slice the avocado thinly. Toss in lemon juice to prevent browning then add to the rest of the salad ingredients.

5. Remove the skin from the beetroot and cube into small pieces.

6. Place all the dressing ingredients in a screwtop jar, shake vigorously then toss the salad in the dressing.

Mille Feuille

Serves 20; 230 calories per portion

1 pint (600ml) skimmed milk
6 oz (175g) light brown Muscovado sugar
6 free-range egg yolks
1 oz (25g) gelatine or agar agar
6 tablespoonsful boiling water
¼ pint (150ml) double cream
4 drops vanilla essence
1 quantity wholemeal puff pastry (page 106)
1 jar 'no-added-sugar' raspberry jam

Filling (Bavarian Cream):

1. Place the milk in a saucepan to warm. Bring to simmering point but do not boil.

2. Whisk the sugar and egg yolks in a basin.

3. Sprinkle the gelatine or agar agar onto the water and stir to dissolve. Allow to cool.

4. Pour the warm milk onto the sugar and egg yolks, stirring all the time. Return to the pan and stir until mixture thickens to a custard, do not boil.

5. Remove from heat and leave to cool. When cool stir in the lightly whisked double cream and vanilla essence. Add the cooled setting agent when it is on the point of setting. Mix thoroughly.

Pastry:

1. Roll the pastry out thinly and cut into equal-sized oblongs to fit your baking tray; about 7 inches (17.5cm) by 3 inches (7.5cm) is the usual size of a mille feuille.

2. Lightly oil the baking trays and place the oblongs of pastry on them. Prick the pastry all over with a fork and glaze with beaten egg mixed with a little milk.

3. Bake at 425°F/220°C (Gas Mark 7) for about 10 minutes until risen and golden in colour. Cool on a wire baking tray before sandwiching together with Bavarian Cream and jam.

4. To sandwich, use three layers of pastry. Spread jam on the first layer then cover with a layer of cream. Repeat and top with a plain pastry layer. Use a sharp knife to cut individual portions from the mille feuille — about six per section.

Gooseberry and Hazelnut Fool

Serves 20; 90 calories per portion

3 lb (1.3 kilos) gooseberries

4 heads elderflowers

8 oz (225g) Quark or similar low-fat soft white cheese

2 oz (50g) clear honey

2 pints (1.2 litres) thick set natural yogurt

1 oz (25g) gelatine or agar agar dissolved in 6 tablespoonsful of water and cooled

8 oz (225g) toasted hazelnuts, finely chopped

1.   Wash and top and tail the gooseberries and place in a saucepan with enough water to cover them and add the elderflower heads. Cover and cook for about 20 minutes until soft enough to purée. Discard the elderflowers.

2.   Drain the gooseberries, reserving the juice and liquidize or press the gooseberries through a sieve.

3.   Pour the purée into a bowl with the cheese and honey and mix well.

4.   Add the yogurt and the setting agent and fold in the nuts, reserving a few for decoration along with a couple of nice gooseberry leaves.

6.

The Cheese and Wine Party

Cheese

Cheese is just one more victim of the modern food manufacturer's desire to increase shelf-life and ensure a uniformity of taste (or rather lack of taste) and appearance in a product that is increasing in popularity and, therefore, needs to be churned out as quickly as possible to meet the supermarket's desires for quick turnovers.

Before the last war it was possible to buy a large variety of real cheese made from un-pasteurized milk. Before that time there were many small farms and dairies producing local cheeses with the unique characteristics of their particular dairy herds, the flavours of their pastures and the characteristics of the atmosphere of the cellars, caves and cool buildings in which they were matured.

However, modern farming policies soon put a stop to all that and have succeeded in reducing British cheese to tasteless 'blocks'. In *The Great British Cheese Book*, expert Patrick Rance highlights the difference between traditional farmhouse cheese and factory block cheeses. He reports on a Milk Marketing Board blind tasting of two nine-month-old Cheddars in which unanimous preference was for the traditional clothbound cheese as opposed to the farmhouse block:

The Cheddar farms have been so swept along by the Board's block policy that in 1978-9, 77 per cent of their production was in this form. Of all the Cheddar made by English farm and creamery put together, only 2.4 per cent is the traditional kind which the tasters preferred.

However, there is some hope that more traditional cheeses will be produced due to public demand which has happily influenced the wider availability of wholemeal bread and real ale. Perhaps real cheese will follow.

The switch to increasing use of pasteurized milk for cheesemaking is bemoaned in France, the heart of European cheese production, but there are still raw cheeses available there and happily the *fromage fermiers* still line the roadsides, especially in the heart of Normandy, the home of the 2,000 brands of Camembert, and in neighbouring Brittany.

The widely held belief that pasteurized cheeses are somehow safer is misguided. Pasteurization may destroy bacteria which might cause the cheese to spoil but it also tends to demolish the elements responsible for cheese's flavour and unique characteristics — the very things that make a cheese high in quality.

Pasteurized cheeses are pretty well universally bland. It is probably these unfortunately enduring characteristics that have become responsible for the way the British use their cheeses. In most households the standard uses of cheese are for Welsh Rarebit, Macaroni Cheese, sandwiches, the occasional cheese salad or cheese and biscuits. The latter has come in for even more abuse from mass catering which has reduced this to processed sweaty yellow lumps of rubber, sealed in transparent plastic, with cellophane-wrapped yet stale-tasting biscuits and a regulation (paper wrapped) pat of melted (or frozen rock hard) butter.

It's no wonder we do not enjoy cheese like the French.

Unfortunately in Britain (unlike in France) we cannot usually select the best cheeses by knowing when the cows are being put out to pasture and then adding on the time it takes to make and mature the cheese to select the finest produce.

What we can do, if we live in a country area, is try to find a local producer of raw milk cheeses. If we live in towns we can try to shop in the specialist cheese shops which, if they are worthwhile, will offer only traditional farm-house cheeses. These can be recognized by their cheesecloth bindings or their wax coverings and they are in the traditional wheel shapes, not the notorious blocks.

They should be kept covered with their outer coatings until they are cut and the cut face of the cheese should look fresh, not shiny and cracked and hardened, nor sweaty with surface moulds or dirt from a surface left uncut for a day or two. If you do want a piece of cheese from a wheel with a surface so described the assistant should cut away the outer edge before cutting your slice.

If you are in doubt, ask to try a piece of the cheese and do not feel you have to buy it just because you have been given a taste. Buy only the quantity you want. There is no law to say you should have ½ lb (250g) or 1 lb (500g).

At home, cover only the cut surfaces with cling film; leave the rind or crust uncovered so it can breathe. Never store cheese in a plastic box which will make it sweaty and weepy. Cheese experts say the fridge is too cold and airless for cheese, which likes an almost humid atmosphere and the coolness of an old-fashioned larder. Ideally it should be in a temperature of between 50°-60°F (10°-15°C) and should lie on its longest cut side.

If you do store your cheese in a fridge always bring it out and remove the clingfilm, covering it with damp muslin, greaseproof paper or a thin damp teatowel and allow it to assume room temperature during the afternoon before a party. You will notice how its aroma and flavour develops as it warms back to life. Most people eat cheese while it is too cold to taste.

Cheese can be served as part of a meal or, as we shall see later, in the form of a cheese and wine party. There are several ways of serving cheese within a meal. To the *tyrophile* (Greek for one who loves cheese) the cheese is the crescendo of the meal and is the dessert. To others it comes after the main course and before a sweet dessert. Or it can happily follow the salad that follows the main course in some French meals or be served with salad after a main course.

As long as cheese has not been part of the main course it makes sense to serve it as part of the meal. To enjoy its true flavour it should be eaten on its own, in a small amount, or with bread. The wine that has accompanied the main course is usually acceptable with the cheese; however, if strongly flavoured cheeses are chosen a stronger wine might be offered. In wholefood terms it is probably preferable to offer cheese rather than a sticky or sugary dessert and it does provide a climax of taste to the meal (providing it does not follow curry or another highly spiced dish!).

The number of cheeses you offer as dessert is a matter of personal choice. Two is sufficient, but four may be preferred for a party. Try to choose cheeses that complement the main course and make them, as far as possible, seasonal. Without being pedantic you can point out to guests the milder cheeses which they might like to try first before the stronger varieties. Offer a variety of types of cheese on the cheeseboard. For instance, a soft cheese, a semi-soft and a firm variety (we often call our Cheddars, Cheshires etc., hard, but really hard cheeses are Parmesan and Romano etc.).

For a cheese and wine party a far wider selection of cheeses should be offered. With the wide variety available it should be possible to find something to suit everyone (unless they are allergic to cheese). Include familiar cheeses, but encourage guests to try something different rather than satiate their hunger on their personal favourites.

Label all the cheeses with their names and where they come from. They can be arranged in groups according to country of origin or they could perhaps more helpfully be put into groups according to their flavour so the guest who wants to get the most out of his or her tasting can work their way around from the mild to the pronounced flavours.

Instead of indiscriminately placing the bottles in a separate room, or in a jumble away from the cheese it is more fun to put bottles next to the cheeses you think your guests might like to try them with. The white wines can be kept cool in ice buckets and reds can be free-standing. The information can be put on the cheese label. For instance, 'Camembert, France, good with . . . worth trying with . . .'

Of course it's up to individuals to pick and choose as they want but often this kind of guidance is taken in the spirit of fun in which it is meant. Even if you do not like the suggestion your host has made at least you *know* from then on that you do not like Sauternes with Roquefort.

Part of the fun of tasting wines and cheeses is not to be a great connoisseur who can tell which side of the vineyard the grapes were picked from, but to know what you like and do not like and what likes and suits you.

You might also like to arrange fruit with cheese because a piece of cheese is often far nicer with a complementary fruit than it is with bread or biscuits for cheese. For instance:

- Blue Stilton is traditionally served with crispy celery. I think it is just as good with a very firm but juicy conference pear.
- White Stilton's beautiful crumbly texture (like Caerphilly) goes well with the softness of a ripe pear, perhaps the sweeter William pears.
- Mature English Cheddar is killed by pickles and onions, but it is enhanced by the crisp fresh flesh of a good dessert apple such as Worcester permain.
- Grapes, white or red, are, like wine, a natural accompaniment to most cheeses.

There is an enormous variety of cheese available in Britain so you will have to be disciplined about buying for a cheese and wine party. Availability in local shops will probably be the major deciding factor on how you make your final selection. Try to balance familiar cheeses with more unusual varieties. The excitement for most guests will be in trying varieties new to them.

Choose a selection that includes soft and hard cheeses and do not just use cheese made from cow's milk, goat and sheep cheeses are available or can be home-made — see recipes on pages 74-75, although it's unlikely that you will be able to get buffalo, ass, camel, mare, yak, zebra or reindeer cheese!

Soft cheese
Cottage cheese might sound a little boring, but

for any slimmers at your party it will be a Godsend because cheese is extremely high in calories and saturated fats. Cottage cheese is made from skimmed milk. It can be home-made to avoid additives (see page 75) and flavoured with chopped vegetables like peppers, onions, cucumbers, celery, or nuts, grapes and herbs of choice.

Caboc is a cream cheese coated with oatmeal, which tastes buttery but does not keep well. Goes well with oatcakes and flavoured savoury biscuits (see recipes on pages 71-72).

Curd cheese is usually sold as full-fat, but medium- and low-fat varieties are available. Generally has a slightly sour taste and is used in cheesecakes, but can be flavoured as for cottage cheese.

Quark, or similar low-fat soft white cheese such as *fromage blanc* can be bought plain or ready-flavoured with herbs, vegetables, fruit and horseradish. It can be home-made or bought plain and flavoured as desired in the same way as the cottage cheese. It is nice moulded into small rounds with the outside coated in ground pepper or chopped vegetables, or green peppercorns, or halved and seeded grapes pressed into the outside. It looks lovely arranged on vine leaves and is deliciously low in calories.

Boursin is a very popular cheese from Normandy made from cow's milk and flavoured with *fines herbes* or covered with peppercorns. It is very high in fat (70 per cent) and consequently it is probably preferable either to make your own soft cheese and flavour or use the above low-fat soft white cheeses. It's also cheaper.

Processed cheese and cheese spreads do not have a place on the connoisseur's or whole-fooder's cheese board because they are made from hard cheeses that have been melted down and re-moulded using emulsifiers and possibly artificial flavourings. They are usually made from off cuts and second rate hard cheese that would not sell on its own merits.

Wines which suit these light, creamy-flavoured cheeses are slightly dry French whites such as Pinot or Sylvaner from Alsace or a Gros Plant Muscadet, slightly cheaper than Muscadet Sur Lie and not quite so dry. Or try Soave (Italian), Vinho Verde (Portuguese), or a French rosé from Anjou or Provence. Dry English wine can also be drunk with these cheeses.

Soft rind cheeses
Brie is probably the best known of the French soft white rind cheeses. It has a white rind with a creamy-coloured flesh. Both are edible. It is usually sold as wedges cut from a large round, but can be bought in wedges packed in paper lined foil or plywood wedge-shaped boxes. Its best to buy from the whole cheese, when you can see if it is white and chalky (too immature) or runny and smelling faintly of ammonia (too mature). Buy when it is immature and store to preferred maturity. Good idea to buy a week before the party and store in a cool and airy place outside the fridge. *Wines:* try a French flowery bouquet from Touraine such as the *blanc fumé* from Pouilly or an Alsace Riesling or Traminer.

Camembert is another well-known French white rind cheese which no cheese and wine party is complete without. Usually bought as a whole small cheese, it is yellower in colour than Brie and stronger when mature.

Both Brie and Camembert are lower in calories than the harder varieties and are less fatty (40-45 per cent) and so preferable for health reasons. They are also less salty than some of the white rind French cheeses such as Neufchatel, or the brine-washed Pont l'Evêque and the Italian Taleggio. *Wines:* as for Brie, but a mature Camembert is good with fruity red wines of the Rhône, Bordeaux and Burgundy.

Soft pressed cheeses

These are again good buys because they are lower in calories and saturated fat than the harder cheeses.

Port Salut and St. Paulin are probably the most familiar with their distinctive bright orange rind and pale yellow cheese with small holes. They have a fat content of 45 to 50 per cent and are velvety in texture with a slight smell of lactic fermentation. *Wines:* light French white wine from Touraine or the Loire and the flowery German wines from the Rhine, including Liebfraumilch.

Bel Paese from Italy is another, similar, cheese with a yellow wax rind and pale yellow cheese. Made from cow's milk it is pressed and has a mild flavour, slightly more distinctive than Port Salut. *Wines:* whites from Alsace or the Loire will go well with Bel Paese or, as it is Italian, light reds such as Valpolicello.

Semi-hard cheeses

Danbo, Samsoe, Elbo and *Fynbo* come from Denmark and are all similar in appearance with yellow rinds (except Danbo, which is red), pale yellow cheese, and firm texture with small holes. They are mild-tasting and flavour matures with age. *Wine:* as for Edam and Gouda, but you could also try the German dry wine from Franconia.

Edam is probably the most famous of the Dutch cheeses. Its distinctive round shape and red wax coating over firm yellow cheese have made it popular, as has its mild flavour and its ability to keep well. It has also become popular as part of slimmer's diets because it has a fat content of 30-40 per cent and a pleasant flavour.

Gouda is similar to Edam, except that it has a yellow rind and is a little less fully flavoured, but still with a firm texture and holes. *Wine:* rosés from Anjou and Provence or Portugal make good companions as do light red wines like Beaujolais.

Jarlsberg from Norway has much larger holes than the previous semi-hard cheeses and has a bright yellow rind and pale yellow cheese. It is very smooth and firm in texture with a slightly sweet taste. *Wines:* the sweeter wines from the Rhine such as Rhinehessen, Rhinegau or general 'quaffing' wine like Liebfraumilch, will match the sweetness.

Tilsit is from Germany and also has a yellow rind covering yellow cheese. The holes are small and the texture is firm with a slightly sharp taste. *Wines:* try a dry wine from Burgundy, (not an expensive Chablis!) or even an English white wine.

Hard, crumbly cheeses

These are the typically British cheeses that, if made in their traditional way are full of flavour and very individual.

Cheddar is the most widely available cheese and makes up two thirds of the cheese eaten in Britain. Don't bother to buy the processed, mild or block varieties because they are not worthy of a place on the cheese board, or in cooking. Choose a mature English Cheddar made by the traditional farmhouse method. It is firm and varies in colour from pale to deep yellow as it matures. It has a close texture and is matured for months or even years. It is not particularly crumbly. *Wines:* the strong tang of a mature Cheddar needs to be matched with a full bodied red such as a Spanish Rioja or a French red Burgundy. A red Californian, like a Zinfandel, or a Chilean or Argentinian red from the Cabernet Sauvignon grape, also make good companions.

Caerphilly is a white cheese that is naturally crumbly and semi-soft for a hard cheese! It has a close and moist texture with a faintly salty or acidic flavour and a smooth white mould rind. *Wines:* softer wines like German Liebfraumilch or a French rosé from Anjou or a light French red from the Côte de Beaune.

Cheshire is supposedly the oldest of the popular British cheeses and it comes in white, red and blue varieties. In the north of England the white is the commonest variety, and is loose and crumbly in texture with a hint of a saltiness. The red variety may be slightly smoother and is coloured with a natural vegetable dye called annatto (also used in Red Leicester). The blue variety has an open texture and a creamy taste. *Wines:* light reds from Beaujolais or Italian Valpolicello make good companions for Cheshire as do good red table wines.

Derby comes in two varieties. The better known is Sage Derby which is yellow in appearance with a green marbling caused by the added sage leaves. Popular as a Christmas cheese it has a strong flavour of sage and is difficult to match to a wine. The ordinary Derby is pale in colour, ranging from white to creamy, with a mild taste and firm, moist texture. *Wines:* the strong Sage Derby can stand up well to a Chianti or a full Bordeaux. The milder white cheese is nice with a spicy Gewürztraminer from Alsace or the cheaper Traminer.

Double Gloucester is the stronger more acidic version of Single Gloucester. The latter is pale in colour (like a golden straw wine) with a smooth close texture. It has almost disappeared now, except in certain parts of Gloucester, but the Double Gloucester is still very popular. *Wines:* these old-fashioned cheeses deserve old fashioned wines like Bordeaux or a Hungarian Bull's Blood, but the more modern wines like

Côtes de Roussillon will go well with its close texture.

Lancashire is a white, soft and crumbly cheese used more for cooking than as a dessert cheese. Like Derby, Leicester and Double Gloucester it is made only in its native county and is eaten young. It has a mild but distinctive flavour. *Wines:* to bring out its best, match Lancashire with distinctive wines like Hermitage or Côte Rôtie from the Rhône.

Leicester is another cheese coloured with annatto and, along with its deep orange colour, it has a flaky, granular texture and a medium-strong flavour. *Wines:* another cheese that goes well with Rhône wines and also with the cheaper Bordeaux, as well as Portugese reds from Dão.

Stilton is often referred to as the King of English cheeses. It is made only in Leicestershire, Nottinghamshire and Derbyshire using traditional methods. White Stilton is crumbly with a delicious, slightly sour flavour. Blue Stilton is creamier with a salty, rich and creamy flavour. It is very strong when mature and is definitely an acquired taste. Blue cheeses are made by introducing a mould to the cheese and allowing it to make the cheese blue as it matures. There is considerable research into the safety of moulds in foods and many authorities think that the toxins produced by the moulds could be harmful to health; even in cheeses that have been traditionally enjoyed for centuries. *Wines:* Blue Stilton is traditionally served with a ruby port. Try it with a fine Burgundy or an Italian Barolo. For those who like sweet wines, it has to be Sauternes. White Stilton is better with whites from Burgundy or dry English and Loire wines.

Wensleydale has its origins in the monasteries of Yorkshire. White Wensleydale is sold young and has a close texture with a mild flavour. The blue veined variety is close and soft with a creamier taste and texture. *Wines:* soft wines from Rhinehessen and Rhinegau or the more fragrant Alsace wines like Sylvaner and Riesling go well with white Wensleydale, but reds do more to enhance the blue variety — lighter reds like Italian wines or French Vins du Pays.

Whey cheeses

Gjetost is made from goat's milk and is brown and comes in an oblong block. It is made in Norway and has a very strong, distinctive taste. *Wine:* a difficult cheese to suggest a wine for because of its very distinctive flavour. Try the cheese first to see if you like it, then perhaps select a dry red of your choice.

Ricotta is made from whey with added milk. It is white and soft-textured, similar to cottage cheese, but with a distinctive, slightly sweet flavour. It does not keep well and goes sour quickly. *Wine:* has to be Italian; light and refreshing white Frascasti or red Valpolicella.

Blue cheeses

For reasons already outlined these cheeses are avoided by some people who feel that the moulds may be injurous to health. They certainly are not 'fresh' cheeses and the essence of healthy eating is to choose fresh and vibrant foods. However, for those who feel a cheeseboard is not complete without a blue cheese those lower in fat content are:

Bleu d'Auvergne, creamy coloured with blue veins and small holes and a smooth texture and tangy taste.

Roquefort, made from ewe's milk and very white with blue veins and a smooth texture and strong tangy flavour.

Danish Blue, soft white crumbly cheese with blue/black veins and some holes. Tastes strong, tangy and salty.

Pipo Crem, with a brownish rind and a pale yellow cheese showing blue veins. It is soft and creamy in texture and mild for a blue cheese so it may suit those unused to strong Stilton flavours.

Wines: Rouissillon wines like Corbières or the burnt tastes of the reds from the Côtes-du-Rhône. Alternatively try a light and fruity Beaujolais to contrast with the blue taste, or a rosé from Provence.

Vegetarian cheese

It seems a contradiction in terms to talk about vegetarian cheese, but it refers to the rennet used to curdle the milk, producing the solids that make cheese. Normally animal rennet, made from the stomach of calves, is used, so many vegetarians prefer to use cheese made from non-animal rennet. Vegetarian rennet is produced from an extract of figs which has the ability to curdle milk in the same way that animal rennet does. Lactic acid and bacteria can also be used to curdle the milk to make cheese. There is a wide range of the most popular English cheeses made with vegetarian rennet.

Organically produced cheese is not available on a wide scale, only from small local producers. But some small scale cheesemakers have hopes for such cheese production in the future as demand for it increases.

There is also a vegetarian alternative to Parmesan cheese. This is a Swiss cheese called Geska which is made from skimmed cow's milk to which blue meliot, a mountain herbs is added. This herb, like the extract from figs, is able to turn the milk to curds and whey. Geska is apparently very hard, with a distinctive flavour. I have not tried it.

Not everyone can enjoy cheese because a substance in it called tyramine (the amine of the amino acid tyrosine) causes a reaction. It stimulates the sympathetic system and can cause a large rise in blood pressure. In most people tyramine found in food is destroyed by monoamine oxidases, but in some people this reaction is faulty and in others the use of certain drugs for depression prevents the reaction and results in headache, nausea, dizziness, severe high blood pressure and, very rarely, cerebral haemorrhage or heart failure.

Wine

You don't have to be an expert to enjoy wine but a little knowledge will enable you to recognize the wines you like and give a good idea about the ones to choose to accompany particular foods for parties, when eating out, or just for your own pleasure.

It is also useful to have the opinions of experts who are able to taste many different wines which it would be difficult for most of us to find the time or money to do. Of course everyone has their own taste (there are people who like kippers and custard!) but following the guidance of experts will enable you to make a wise choice and not waste your money.

Often, the health conscious person will wonder whether they should be drinking wine. Generally, it is regarded as an aid to relaxation, provided it is drunk in moderation, and medical practitioners recommend not more than two glasses per day. Dry white wine is the best choice for the health conscious because it is lighter and devoid of some of the proteins found in heavier red wines, like Chianti, that can cause hangovers, even in moderate consumption. These proteins are similar to those that cause allergic migraine reactions in cheese and some other foods. Dry white wine also contains less sugar than sweeter wines and is therefore lower in calories.

Some people prefer organically grown wine because there is less sulphur dioxide powder, which is used to dress vines against mildew and also added during the making of some wines to stop the fermentation of the yeast when the wine has reached the desired alcohol level. Bentonite is also used to clear much wine, but organic producers prefer to use traditional methods, employing egg white to speed the clearance previously left to time in traditional wine making. Organically grown wine also avoids the use of asbestos filtration which some wine makers use instead of adding sulphur to filter out the yeast. Traditional wine growers use the pressed grape skins as fertilizers for the vines, but others may use chemical fertilizers which are not used to produce organic wine.

There is one English variety of organically grown wine, available from the Pine Ridge vineyard in Robertsbridge, Sussex. This year (1984) the owner Roy Cook hopes to produce between 3,000-4,000 bottles of his light, medium-dry white wine, produced from a variety of German grapes but mainly the Reichensteiner grape.

Organically produced wine is also available from France and is usually sold as 'natural wine'. Germany produces a lot of organic wine, but not much is imported into Britain.

Generally when drinking wine with a meal it is usual to allow about ½ bottle per guest. One 70-75cl bottle will provide six glasses of wine. If you are offering more than one wine it is a good idea to start with the white wines or the youngest red and progress to the red and on to the oldest red. This is sensible because the whites and younger wines have a more subtle flavour, which the palate is more receptive to if it hasn't been hit by a strong flavour.

It is becoming more fashionable now to finish a meal with a sweet dessert wine like a Sauternes or Barsac but these are expensive wines and they are an acquired taste. It is easier to use the main course wine throughout the cheese course and match a cheese to it if that is preferred instead of dessert (see cheese section).

For a cheese and wine party it is probably pointless to buy a lot of expensive wines, unless you have many keen wine tasters among your friends, because with all the chatter and noise it is difficult to concentrate on the wines and they may not be appreciated. It is fun to suggest particular wines that will go with particular cheeses (see page 60).

White wines should be chilled for serving to make them more refreshing; generally the sweeter they are the more chilled they should be. A cool cellar is the ideal place to chill them. Red wines are served at room temperature. Ideally they should stand for 24 hours before serving to bring them to room temperature. If they have been brought in from a cold store don't stand them in front of an open fire or an electric fire. It is better, if necessary, to put them near a radiator where the air will warm the wine, not direct heat. Some light red wines like Beaujolais can be served chilled, as can tawny port if that is being offered with cheese.

Wines can be decanted and they certainly look very attractive in some decanters. The point of decanting wines is to remove the deposit from fine old wines and to give these red wines a chance to breathe. When wine is bottled it uses the oxygen in the bottle for its development. If it is being drunk a bit young, as most wines are, decanting them gives them a boost of oxygen a couple of hours before they are served which can 'mature' them and improve them. Decanting also gets rid of any odd smells the wine may have developed in the bottle. This is particularly possible with older red wines and Sauternes which release sulphur.

The following is a very brief guide to help recognize the main wines that are readily available in Britain and to assist in finding a wine you think you may like or would be suitable for a particular occasion.

Germany

German wine is the most popular general drinking wine in Britain and *Liebfraumilch* the most widely known of these wines. If you like this soft, sweet and rather indistinctive wine you may find that you will soon tire of it, so it is helpful to know just what else is available to make your choice from.

German wine law is very strict and divides wine into three quality grades. The lowest grade is *Tafelwein* which is ordinary table wine that need only attain five per cent natural alcohol before it has sugar added. It can be made from a blend of wine from anywhere in the EEC. *Deutscher Tafelwein* must conform to a strength of 8.5 per cent alcohol and be made from German wine only. The next grade up is *Qualitatswein (QbA)* which must come from a particular region, from certain grape varieties and attain a 'must' weight which results in it having a natural alcohol level of 7.5 per cent before it is sugared to bring it up to 9-9.5 per cent alcohol. It also carries a test number *(pfüfungsnummer)* and may have the name of the 'cooperative' (*Grosslage*) of vinegards or the region (*Bereich*) where the grapes were grown. *Qualitätswein mit Prädikat (QmP)* is the top grade of wine which is not allowed to have added sugar. Instead, the 9.5 per cent alcohol (or more) must be achieved with sugars naturally present in the grapes. This is of particular interest to those who want to avoid wines with added sugars.

Within this top quality *QmP* classification are further grades for wines made with grapes that have attained even higher 'must' weights and are therefore of a higher natural sugar content. This is achieved by leaving the grapes to mature for longer until, in the case of the very top quality wine *Trockenbeerenauslese* they are attacked by *edelfäul (Botrytis cinerea* or 'noble rot') which shrivels the grapes like raisins, reducing the water and concentrating the sugars. They are, in order of superiority, *Kabinett, Spätlese, Auslese, Beerenauslese* and *Trockenbeerenauslese*.

Wine law is also strict about the types of grapes used and these are the only vines allowed, by the German government, to be planted: Riesling, Silvaner, Müller-Thurgau, Ruländer, Spätburgunder and Portugieser.

Wine is grown in the following areas, whose names will be recognized as those of the popular wines. The name Hock is used to describe wine from the Rhine and probably derives from the village of Hochheim in the area called Rheingau which is said to produce the Rhine's finest wines and contains some of the most famous German vineyards. The wines are flowery, fruity and mature and long lived for white wines.

Neighbouring Rheingau is Rheinhessen, one of the largest areas of Rhineland which produces a light, soft, sweetish wine which makes up the bulk of wine that goes to produce the popular Liebfraumilch. Any other wine that is 'with pleasant character' from Rheinpfalz, Nahe or Rheingau and made from Riesling or Müller-Thurgau grapes can go into the mild, semi-sweet Liebfraumilch. Wines from Rheinpfalz (Palatinate) and Nahe are lighter and slightly less sweet than the other Rhine wines and are beginning to approach the crisper wines of the Mosel and Saar and Ruwer.

Mosels are mostly made from the characteristic Riesling grape that produces a lighter more refreshing wine, drier and crisper than the Hocks. The popular Piesport-Michelsberg comes from the middle of the Mosel region.

Different from the usual golden wines of Germany in their fluted bottles, is the Steinwein, a generic term for the wine from Franconia, bottled in shapes more like the popular Portuguese Mateus Rosé. It is less delicate and sweet and a much stronger and drier wine, made mainly from the Silvaner

grape rather than the Riesling.

France

France offers a far wider variety of wine than Germany and very briefly the main wine areas that we encounter in Britain are *Alsace, Bordeaux, Burgundy, Champagne, Loire, Côtes-du-Rhône* and more latterly *Côtes de Roussillon* and *Languedoc*.

The *Code du Vin* is the French law designed to protect these areas that have consistently produced wines of high quality. The top grade of wine is *Vins d'Appellation d'Origine Controlée*, seen on labels as A.O.C. or A.C. and known for short as *Appellation Controlée*. This indicates that the wine is a good quality representation of, for example, a Bordeaux wine. The second group is known as *Vins Délimités de Qualité Supérieure*, seen as V.D.Q.S. on the label. These are wines that have earned a reputation for their general quality rather than individual characteristics of A.C. wines.

Alsace is an area of France around Strasbourg that was once part of Germany. Consequently the wines have German characteristics and they are bottled in the slim bottles associated with Rhine wines. They are dry, white wines often with a flowery or spicy bouquet and they are classified by the type of grape from which they are made.

Hence vins d'Alsace labels will also give a grape name. They are Silvaner, a light soft dry wine; Pinot Blanc/Gris, a soft but less dry wine; Riesling, considered by many to be the best Alsace grape, very dry and crisp and aromatic; Gewürztraminer, a very distinctive spicy grape with a musky perfume; Traminer, similar but less distinctive than the Gewürztraminer and the Muscat, another aromatic dry wine with a distinctive muscat grape taste.

Bordeaux is the wine known to many British

as claret. It has, from the Middle Ages, been the most popular of French wines with the British and many Britons are involved in the châteaux of Bordeaux. In 1855 the best 62 red wines were classified into *crus* (growths) known as the *Crus Classés* (classified growths), of which there are five. From the *Premiers Crus* to the *Cinquièmes Crus* the wines are château bottled and include the world famous wines from Chateau Lafite, Latour and Margaux.

It is the *Bourgeois* growths, outside the *Cru Classés* which provide the wine for the majority of us. The châteaux here are unnamed and the wines take their names from the main A.C. districts of Bordeaux or Bordeaux Supérieur and the sub-divisions of these areas such as, for red wines, Médoc, Haut Médoc, Saint-Emilion, Pomerol, Côtes de Fronsac, Graves etc., and similarly for white wines, Graves, Sauternes, etc. However, within these sub-divisions there are areas with their own A.C. for instance, Saint-Estèphe, Pauillac, Margaux in the Haut Medoc area, Cérons in Graves and Barsac in Sauternes.

The wines of Bordeaux are generally full bodied but lighter and drier than the wines of Burgundy. They are also lower in alcoholic strength than Burgundy wines. Sugaring the wine is not allowed, except in very bad years. Wine does vary in quality from year to year, hence the declaration of vintages.

Burgundy is sometimes called the King of Wine. It is velvety, and fuller in flavour and slightly sweeter than the Bordeaux wines and it matures quicker. Over the years the vineyards have become fragmented and consequently some, such as the Clos de Vougeot (*Clos* or *Domaine* being the Burgundy equivalent of a château), have 60 growers each producing wine of differing quality under the same name.

Generally the label will have the name of the village, such as Gevrey-Chambertin, together with the term *Premier Cru* which is part of Burgundy's A.C. definition. There is further confusion with the practice of adding the name of the most famous vineyard in the area to the name of the village, resulting in examples such as wine from Aloxe being called Aloxe-Corton or wine from Nuits being called Nuits-Saint-George. For interested potential connoisseurs it is necessary to memorize the names of the main villages and avoid the hyphenated varieties.

Most wines from Burgundy found in Britain are under the label of the shipper or *négociant* of the area who selects good wine from that area. Many of the Burgundy *négociants* are in the Beaune area (another famous name on wine labels).

The main areas of Burgundy are Chablis, one of the most famous dry white wines in the world, clean and crisp with a slight greenish tinge; Côte de Nuits, mainly red with more body than Côte de Beaune which is better known for fine white wines. Côte Chalonnaise, Beaujolais and Mâconnais have their own A.C. Within Beaujolais the village names to look out for are Brouilly, Moulin-à-Vent, Morgon and Fleurie.

Beaujolais wines are lighter than clarets, drunk younger and not so highly sought after by the French who prefer the more substantial wines of the Côte d'Or and are happy for the English to have their annual Beaujolais Nouveau races for instant quaffing of the young wines. Beaujolais is served slightly chilled and may pleasantly surprise those who do not like the heavier red wines.

Champagne is a name protected by the French wine laws and allowed only for wine produced by the *méthode champenoise* in and near the Champagne *départment* (county) of Marne. The sparkle is derived by natural fermentation which takes place in the bottle. It is a costly, long and difficult process. Champagne may be vintage or non-vintage. The degree of sweetness is indicated on the label as brut/extra dry/extra sec for the driest, sec/dry for the slightly sweeter, followed by demi-sec/demi-doux, and doux being the sweetest. The British and Americans are the largest importers of champagne, the British preferring the driest and the Americans the sweetest.

The Loire is the longest river in France and most of its wines are V.D.Q.S. Anjou is best known for its rosé wine and the white of Saumur, both of which are light and refreshing and good buffet or outdoor wines. Probably the best known of the Loire wines is Muscadet, which refers to the name of a grape and not an area or vineyard. The official names for the *départments* using the A.C. for Muscadet grapes are Muscadet de Sèvre-et-Maine, Muscadet and Muscadet des Coteaux de la Loire. They are crisp wines with a delicate flavour that goes well with most foods but is especially good with shellfish and oysters or fish.

Another province of the Loire is Touraine which include the popular white wines of Sancerre and Pouilly (not to be confused with the famous Pouilly Fuissé white wine from the Mâcon in Burgundy) known as Blanc Fumé because of its distinctive and attractively smoky bouquet from the Sauvignon grape.

The Rhône is a vast river running through south-eastern France. As the popularity of wine has increased in Britain the prices of Bordeaux and Burgundy wines have increased and so more wine is now being imported from the Rhône, where good bargain buys can still be found. As the Loire produces mainly white wine so the Rhône produces mainly reds.

The general classification of wines from this area is Appellation Côtes-du-Rhône which covers most of the communés producing red,

white or rosé wine in the area's six counties; these are the cheapest wines. There are some communes in the southern part that have the specific appellation, Côtes-du-Rhône-Villages and there is another smaller area of distinction A.C. Coteaux du Tricastin.

The better wines come from three areas — Côte Rôtie, Hermitages and Châteauneuf-du-Pape. The first two are very dark wines, but the burnt taste of the heat of the south becomes more predominant with wine from Châteauneuf-du-Pape, which incidentally has nothing to do with a château but is the name of an area. These wines are often compared to the heavyweight Burgundies and Châteauneuf-du-Pape has the highest minimum strength of any French wine at 12.5 per cent alcohol.

Other wines from the south, Rouissillon and Languedoc are also growing in popularity. The four A.C. areas of Roussillon are Maury, Côte d'Agly, Rivesaltes and Banyuls and Banyuls Grand Cru. These are mainly heavy dessert wines with a velvety texture, known as *vins doux naturels* because some of their grape sugar has been prevented from fermenting by the addition of alcohol, turning them into fortified wine. There are many V.D.Q.S. wines from the midi region around Corbières in Languedoc which are lighter and more refreshing and are good to drink young.

Italy
Italy has recently set about the classification of its extensive wines and has a three tier system. The *Denominazione Semplice* is for the equivalent of table wine; *Denominazione de Origine Controllata* sets specific grapes for regions awarded D.O.C., plus ensuring traditional methods, limited yields, proper ageing and adequate records. The top classification is *Denominazione Controllata e Garantita* for wines within these broader areas.

To date there are four regions that have been awarded the top classification; they are Barolo, Barbaresco, Vino Nobile di Montepulciano (the name of both grape and town from Tuscany) and neighbouring Brunello di Montalcino, both just outside the heart of Chianti country.

The main areas are Piemonte, which contains the pride of Italian reds Barolo from the Nebbiolo grape, described by Hugh Johnson in his definitive *World Atlas of Wine* (Mitchell Beazley, 1977) as 'suggestion of truffles, a touch of tar, a positive note of raspberry'. Barboresco is slightly drier than Barolo and Nebbiolo is failed Barolo that is sold under the grape name. Barbera is a very dark and acidic red wine and Grignolino is a lighter, almost sweet wine. Asti Spumanti, from the Muscat grape, also comes from the same region and is the equivalent of French *vin mousseux*.

Some of the best known Italian wines are from the hills around Verona which produce Soave Simple or the more expensive (and superior) Soave Classico, a light dry pale wine which can accompany most foods. Valpolicella comes from the same area and is a red wine with a bright red colour, drunk young. Stronger versions, with added red wine from specially dried grapes, are called Reciolo but Bardolino is more to most people's taste, being a very light, almost rosé, young red wine.

The most universally acclaimed of the Italian wines is Chianti, the red wine from Tuscany in central Italy. Chianti Classico comes from a central zone in the heart of Chianti country and is often bottled in straw-covered flasks. It has unfermented must of dried grapes added after fermentation which is responsible for the slight 'prickle' in the wine. Some Chianti Riserva is aged in oak before bottling in Bordeaux-style bottles rather than straw-covered flasks.

The white wines from Tuscany are also famous. Orvieto from Umbria is well loved as a dry or medium-sweet white wine that is versatile enough to accompany many foods, as is Frascati which is slightly more fully flavoured with a drier taste.

Other wine regions

There are, of course, many more wines from many countries worthy of note and interest but beyond the scope of this chapter. For those who have been disappointed by cheap blended *Spanish* wines try the excellent reds from the Rioja region which have been aged in oak barrels before bottling — for 2-3 years for ordinary wine and up to 10 years for Rioja Reservas. They are tawny in colour and soft and smooth from the ageing. Among the whites from Rioja are some excellent light table wines and softer drinking wines.

Portugal is better known for its port (as Spain is for its sherry) but it has recently grown in popularity with its light Vinho Verde wine from Minho. Made from immature grapes it is very dry with a characteristic 'green' tinge referred to in its name. The best wines are to be tasted in Portugal because they are slightly sweetened with added sugar before being exported to Britain.

Bull's Blood from *Hungary* is still a good buy for those who want to put down a bottle for a few years. It is best aged for 10 years and is a strong wine when drunk young. There are also many excellent white Riesling wines from Hungary, for those of us who cannot afford the world-famous Tokay dessert wines.

America in particular has caught the British imagination with its Californian wines, which are classified by grapes. Different areas specialize in different grapes and some of them use the names of French wines such as Burgundy to indicate the type of wines they are producing. There are about 17 different grape varieties, so have fun tasting and discovering your favourite.

Home-made cheeses, biscuits and breads

The following recipes might make the basis of a cheese and wine party using home-made soft cheeses and crunchy home-made wholemeal biscuits.

The biscuits offer different flavours to complement the different cheeses and they can also be eaten on their own. They can be used either with home-made or bought cheese, and they avoid the usual chemical additives found in biscuits made commercially to go with cheese. They are also higher in fibre, being made from wholemeal flour.

There are also recipes for breads; a basic wholemeal loaf and a rye flour bread which is closer in texture than a wholemeal bread. These are excellent bases for a wholefood plough-man's lunch and are very useful, everyday recipes.

High Bake Oatcakes
Makes 20; 66 calories per biscuit
(Illustrated opposite page 97)

8 oz (225g) medium oatmeal

2 oz (50g) wholemeal flour

1 teaspoonful baking powder

2 oz (50g) unsalted butter or soft vegetable margarine

Boiling water to mix

1.   Mix together the oatmeal, flour and baking powder.

2.   Melt the fat in a saucepan and stir into the dry ingredients.

3.   Gradually add enough boiling water to make a soft dough.

4.   Turn onto a lightly-floured surface and knead until firm enough to roll out into a rectangle.

5.   Trim the edges and cut into triangular oatcakes. Carefully lift onto a lightly-oiled baking tray and bake in a pre-heated oven at 400°F/200°C (Gas Mark 6) for 10-15 minutes.

Water Biscuits
Makes 24; 35 calories each portion

8 oz (225g) wholemeal flour

½ teaspoonful sea salt

1 oz (25g) unsalted butter or soft vegetable margarine

4 fl oz (120ml) boiling water

1.   Sieve the flour into a mixing bowl and add the salt.

2.   Rub in the fat until the mixture resembles breadcrumbs in consistency.

3.   Add the water to form a soft dough.

4.   Roll to ⅛-inch (3mm) thickness and cut into rounds with a 2½-inch (5cm) biscuit cutter. Place on a lightly-oiled baking tray and prick with a fork.

5.   Bake for 10 minutes in a pre-heated oven at 450°F/230°C (Gas Mark 8) until brown and crisp.

6.   Cool on a wire tray before serving. Store in an airtight tin when cold.

Sunflower Thins

Makes 20; 45 calories each

2 oz (50g) sunflower seeds
3 oz (75g) wholemeal flour
1 oz (25g) stoneground rice
2 tablespoonsful corn oil
2 tablespoonsful cold water

1.   Crush the sunflower seeds in a pestle and mortar.

2.   Mix together the flour, rice and sunflower seeds.

3.   Add the oil and water and work to a dough.

4.   Turn onto a lightly-floured surface and roll out. Cut into shapes and place on a lightly-oiled baking tray.

5.   Bake in a pre-heated oven at 375°F/190°C (Gas Mark 5) for 12 minutes. Leave to cool and crispen before using. Store in an airtight tin when cold.

Cumin Biscuits

Makes 20; 45 calories per biscuit

4 oz (100g) wholemeal flour
1 oz (25g) wheatgerm
1 tablespoonful cumin seeds
2 oz (50g) unsalted butter or soft vegetable margarine
1 free-range egg

1.   Sieve the flour into a mixing bowl and add the wheatgerm and the cumin. Mix thoroughly.

2.   Rub the fat into the flour until the mixture resembles breadcrumbs in consistency.

3.   Lightly beat the egg and add to the mixture to form a soft dough.

4.   Roll out on a lightly-floured surface and cut into rounds using a biscuit cutter of choice.

5.   Arrange on a lightly-oiled baking sheet and bake in a pre-heated oven at 350°F/180°C (Gas Mark 4) for 20 minutes until browned well.

6.   Allow to cool before using. Store in an airtight tin when cold.

Digestive Biscuits

Makes 15 biscuits; 40 calories per biscuit
(Illustrated opposite page 97)

2½ oz (65g) wholemeal flour
1½ oz (40g) oatbran and oatgerm
Pinch of sea salt (optional)
1½ oz (40g) unsalted butter or soft vegetable margarine
½ tablespoonful Demerara sugar
2½ fl oz (60ml) water to bind (approx.)

1.   Sieve the flour and mix in a bowl with the oatbran and oatgerm. Add the salt, if using.

2.   Rub the fat into the mixture until it resembles breadcrumbs in consistency.

3.   Stir in the sugar and bind with water until a soft dough is formed.

4.   Roll out to ¼-inch (5mm) thickness on a lightly-floured surface and cut into rounds using 2½-inch (6cm) cutters.

5.   Place on lightly-oiled baking sheet and bake for 20-25 minutes in a pre-heated oven at 350°F/180°C (Gas Mark 4) until browned. Allow to cool on a wire tray until crisp before

using. Store in an airtight tin when cold.

Wholemeal Bread

Makes 2 small loaves; 1015 calories per loaf

1½ lb (675g) wholemeal flour
½ teaspoonful sea salt (optional)
1 oz (25g) fresh yeast
1 vitamin C tablet, crushed
¾ pint (450ml) lukewarm water
1 tablespoonful corn or soya oil
Sesame or poppy seeds (optional)
Lightly beaten free-range egg for glaze

1.   Sieve the flour into a mixing bowl with the salt, if using.

2.   Crumble the yeast and vitamin C tablet into the water and stir in the oil.

3.   Pour onto the flour and work to a soft dough. Turn onto a lightly-floured surface and knead for 10 minutes.

4.   Place in lightly-oiled loaf tins or shape into plait or rolls and set on lightly-oiled baking tray. Cover and leave until doubled in size.

5.   Glaze with egg or milk and bake the loaves for 35-40 minutes in a pre-heated oven at 425°F/220°C (Gas Mark 7). (Rolls will need only about 20 minutes.) If liked, sprinkle the glazed tops of the loaves or rolls with sesame or poppy seeds.

Garlic Bread:
Use the same basic wholemeal dough but shape into a bagnat or French stick shape, slashing the top diagonally with a knife. Glaze and bake in the same way. When the loaf has cooled a little, split it open and spread the inside with fresh garlic crushed to a paste and mixed with unsalted butter.

Seed Bread:
Sprouted seeds can be added to the basic wholemeal dough for a moister and different-flavoured loaf. Try adding 4 oz (100g) of alfalfa to the above quantity of dough.

Rye Bread

Makes 2 small loaves; 1150 calories per loaf

12 oz (325g) rye flour
12 oz (325g) wholemeal flour
¾ oz (20g) fresh yeast
1 vitamin C tablet, crushed
¼ pint (150ml) lukewarm water
½ pint (300ml) natural yogurt or cultured buttermilk
1 tablespoonful molasses
1 tablespoonful corn or soy oil

1.   Sieve together the two flours into a mixing bowl.

2.   Crumble the yeast and the vitamin C tablet into the water.

3.   Make a well in the flour and pour in the yeast mixture and the yogurt, and stir in the molasses and oil. Mix to a dough.

4.   Turn onto a lightly-floured work surface and knead for 10 minutes. Place in a lightly-oiled baking tin, loaf tins or shape into rolls or plaits. Cover and leave to double in size.

5.   Glaze with lightly-beaten egg or milk and bake in a pre-heated oven at 425°F/220°C (Gas Mark 7) for 35 minutes. The loaves are cooked when they sound hollow if tapped on the base. Rolls will take only 20 minutes to cook. Allow to cool before serving.

Lemon Cheese

Makes about 4 oz (100g); 260 calories

1.   Heat 1 pint (600ml) milk to 102°F/40°C in a double saucepan, then remove from heat.

2.   Stir in the juice of a freshly-pressed lemon and leave for 15 minutes.

3.   Line a colander with muslin and stand colander over a bowl to catch the whey.

4.   Ladle the curd into the muslin and gather the corners of the cloth, tie with a piece of string.

5.   Leave to drain for about an hour then untie the cloth and scrape off the resulting cheese. Chill before use.

Yogurt Cheese

Makes 4 oz (100g); 200 calories unflavoured

This is known as *Lebnie* or *Lebna* in the East and is a deliciously thick cheese with a tangy yogurt flavour. Add chopped chives, or cucumber, or any herbs of choice.

1.   Use a fresh natural goat's milk yogurt and place 1 pint (600ml) in a double saucepan and heat to 102°F/40°C, when it should separate into curds and whey.

2.   Line a colander with muslin and proceed exactly as for Lemon Cheese.

Buttermilk Cheese

Makes 4 oz (100g); 150 calories

1.   Place 1 pint (600ml) buttermilk in a double saucepan and heat to 160°F/70°C stirring occasionally.

2.   Remove from heat and allow the curds to settle for a couple of hours.

3.   Place in a muslin-lined colander and proceed as for Lemon Cheese.

Lactic Goat's Cheese

Makes 4 oz (100g) cheese; 150 calories
(Illustrated opposite page 97)

1.   Pour 1 pint (600ml) goat's milk into a double saucepan and heat to 102°F/40°C.

2.   Remove from the heat and stir in 1 teaspoonful of lactic acid.

3.   Allow to settle for 20 minutes before spooning into the muslin-lined colander as for Lemon Cheese.

4.   Add freshly chopped herbs of choice and cover the outside with roughly crushed black peppercorns.

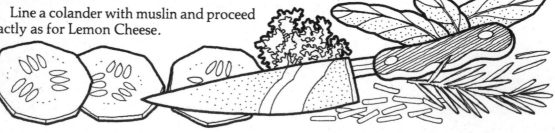

Cottage Cheese

2 pints milk (1.2 litres) makes 4-5 oz
(100-150g) cheese; 520 calories
(Illustrated opposite page 97)

Cottage cheese is a little more complicated to make than the previously described soft cheeses. It requires a cheese starter which can be bought from a health food shop. If you plan to make a lot of cheese you might invest in a *Fromagerer* which comes complete with a sachet of cheese starter. This machine is an incubator that contains a glass bowl and plastic colander. It plugs into the mains, but is very cheap to run.

To prepare the cheese culture:
1.   The cheese culture has to be activated from its freeze-dried form. To do this you need to sterilize two small bottles (such as tonic water bottles) in boiling water for 20 minutes.

2.   Then place ¼ pint (150ml) milk in each bottle and screw the top on loosely.

3.   Stand the bottles on a trivet in a saucepan of boiling water, cover with a lid and allow to boil for 30 minutes. Remove the bottles and screw down, leave to cool.

4.   Add half the contents of a sachet to each bottle in a sterile atmosphere, such as over steam from the saucepan (being careful not to scald yourself).

5.   Screw the tops on firmly and shake the bottles well. Place the bottles in the fridge until required.

6.   Before use, incubate the cultures for 18 hours in a warm place such as an airing cupboard. The incubation should be between 70°-80°F/21°-27°C.

Now you have the culture ready you can make the cheese. If this process seems tedious it might be possible to obtain some cheese starter from a local dairy creamery or agricultural college. Alternatively yogurt can be used because it has the requisite bacteria to turn the milk sugar into lactic acid which is part of the cheesemaking process and also develops the flavour.

To make the cottage cheese:
Refer to individual *fromagerer* instructions or use the following:

1.   Heat 2 pints (1.2 litres) cow's milk to 90°F/32°C (or 85°F/30°C for goat's milk) in a bowl over a pan of boiling water.

2.   Add 2 tablespoonsful cheese starter and either one junket tablet dissolved in water, or six drops of rennet. Stir well, cover and leave in a warm place for two hours.

3.   When the curd has set, cut through it with a knife, turn it with a spoon and cut again.

4.   Heat to 90°F/32°C (or 85°F/30°C) stirring all the time. Remove from heat and allow to stand for 10 minutes.

5.   Spoon into a colander lined with muslin. Gather the corners of the muslin, tie with string and hang the muslin up to drip for several hours.

6.   Remove from the cloth and chill.

Home-made cottage cheese is not lumpy like the commercially made product, which undergoes a special scalding treatment to make it granular. It is also 'washed' with single cream and this can be done to home-made cottage cheese for a richer flavour. Salt, or flavour with herbs, as required.

7.

Children's Parties

There is no specific formula for a successful children's party. They very much depend upon what is in fashion among children or the party your children last went to.

The vogue, whether it is for a disco or a Punch and Judy man, will be slavishly followed by children who want to be just like their friends and want their parties to be just like their friends' parties.

For those with smaller houses or flats it is often an idea to have an outing as the birthday treat, shared by some friends and followed by a short tea back at home. Some parents will prefer an outing followed by a birthday party at a burger bar or whatever type of fast food is in fashion, but don't be afraid to say no and have your type of food at home.

Paper plates and beakers and a matching paper cloth (to cover the plastic-covered dining room table) is a good idea and if the room is carpeted a plastic runner beneath the chairs and table may be essential . . . there's always one who will knock the juice, jam or whatever flying and leap out of the way only to tread it into the carpet.

In summer it's worth the effort to take the party _al fresco_ to a beach, or park or woods. They can burn up their energy outside and spill what they like on the grass. Prizes, too, for the one to collect up the most debris after the party!

Games are a good idea. There is still a lot of fun to be had from pass the parcel and musical chairs, but if they really insist on a disco instead then end the party with one; after they have finished with the food. Treasure hunts are good fun if you have a large garden, or can set one up in a nearby country spot. Even a trip to the swimming baths or ice rink before the party tea is a good idea.

Small cardboard party hats and streamers make good presents for the guests and a bag of fruit and nuts or a puzzle is a better present than the usual sweets. Home-made badges (cheaply bought in kit form) saying 'I've been to Peter's party' or similar messages make nice leaving presents or a novelty, token gift from the toy department of your local toy shop or department store. (I often stock up with novelties during Harrods sale or when they have a good selection at Christmas.)

Most people give children fruit squash to drink at parties but these drinks are usually a mixture of either sugar or an artificial sweetener with chemical colourings, flavourings and preservatives.

A better drink for children is real fruit juice, but because they tend to drink rather a lot it is best to dilute it almost half and half with water. If you make up the drink beforehand and place it in a jug they will think it is 'normal' squash.

Alternatively they could be offered bottled water. Sparkling water will have more novelty value for them and this could be used to dilute orange juice to make a sparkling orange drink, or any other fruit juice.

The food will be of secondary importance to most children who will be at the party for the fun of the games and to win any prizes and competitions. Make sure however that the food is prepared in advance and well hidden until you want it eaten. If the food is out on display it is difficult to persuade children not to touch it!

The recipes in this section are made from ingredients easily recognisable by children so they are not put off by unknown foods; many of them are not at all adventurous.

I remember going to a party as a child and being given baked beans on toast for tea. I had never eaten them before and told the hostess that 'I'm sorry, but we don't have baked beans'. Since then I've grown to quite like them . . .

Note: The parties are divided into three age groups: for five to eight year olds; nine to eleven year olds; and children of twelve and upwards. But first are two cakes to suit any party.

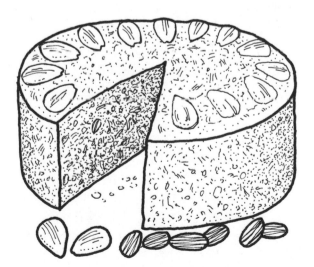

Birthday Fruit Cake
Serves 12; 130 calories per slice

This recipe is for an eggless fruit cake. It is deliciously tasty and very useful for those who are on an eggless diet. It does not rise as much as an ordinary fruit cake, but it is especially high in fibre and low in fat. Despite these virtues it has been given the thumbs up by fruit cake fan Charlotte who is 7!

2 oz (50g) unsalted butter
½ pint (300ml) skimmed milk
4 oz (100g) wholemeal flour
2 teaspoonsful baking powder
4 oz (100g) oatbran and oatgerm
4 oz (100g) raisins
2 oz (50g) currants
1 oz (25g) almonds, finely chopped
½ teaspoonful grated nutmeg

1. Melt the butter in a saucepan with the milk.

2. Sieve the flour and baking powder into a mixing bowl.

3. Stir in the oatbran and oatgerm, dried fruit and nuts. Rub fruit through the flour to ensure it is separated and evenly coated. Grate in the nutmeg and stir.

4. Add the butter and milk and mix to a soft dough.

5. Place in a lightly oiled 8 or 9-inch (20-23cm) cake tin and smooth the top.

6. Bake at 350°F/180°C (Gas Mark 4) for 1 hour or until an inserted skewer comes out clean.

Birthday Gateau

Serves 10; 140 calories per slice
(Illustrated opposite page 80)

3 large free-range eggs
3 oz (75g) clear honey
4 oz (100g) wholemeal flour
2 tablespoonsful carob powder
1 jar *Whole Earth* blackcurrant jam

1.   Whisk together the eggs and honey until pale in colour and thick and ropey in consistency.

2.   Sieve the wholemeal flour with the carob powder and fold into the whisked eggs with a metal spoon.

3.   Pour into a lined 8-inch (20cm) cake tin.

4.   Bake in a pre-heated oven at 350°F/180°C (Gas Mark 4) for 25-30 minutes until firm and springy to the touch.

5.   Remove from oven and leave until cold before using a palette knife to cut the gateau into three layers.

6.   Spread a generous amount of the jam between each layer of the cake before reassembling, reserving some for the top and sides of the cake.

Five to Eight Year Olds

Cheese or Marmite Twists
'Sausages' on Sticks
Vegetable Sticks
Alphabet Sandwiches

Party Mice
Fruit Jellies
Real Fruit Ice Lollies

Zoo Biscuits

Cheese or Marmite Twists

Serves 18; 48 calories per twist

Children like savoury snacks. To get away from the commercial crisps and savoury biscuits which are high in salt and flavouring make a selection of cheese straws and twists in different shapes and sizes.

1 quantity basic pastry (page 118)
2 oz (50g) cheese *or* yeast extract (e.g. *Marmite*)
Beaten egg or milk

1.   Add grated cheese to pastry, or flavour pastry with *Marmite*.

2.   Roll out and cut into thin fingers. Either leave as strips or make twists of pastry.

3.   Glaze with egg or milk and bake at 400°F/200°C (Gas Mark 6).

Alphabet Sandwiches
(Illustrated opposite page 81)

If your children's friends are fussy eaters and not used to wholemeal bread you can either give in and make some white sandwiches for the party or you can perhaps interest them in 'brown' bread by making one side of some sandwiches white and the other side brown.

Personalized sandwiches cut to the child's initials may be enough to sway the balance in favour of wholemeal bread. Cut each sandwich into the letter of your guests' initials, for instance if you have a James Brown at the party cut a J and a B, and so on. Alternatively you could cut the sandwiches into letters to make up the words Happy Birthday.

Finger sandwiches are popular with children, too. For fillings choose a variety of the following:
- yeast extract
- grated cheese
- mashed banana
- peanut butter
- mashed hard-boiled free-range egg together with any grated root vegetable of choice
- mustard and cress
- shredded lettuce or chopped watercress

They are fiddly, but if you have the patience to look after children this should be a doddle!

Vegetable Sticks

It's surprising how many children have never been offered a raw vegetable. Popular among 'sophisticated' adults as *crudités* these may also catch the imagination of children! Just before the party chop some carrots, cucumber, peppers, celery, courgettes, parsnips, or any vegetable of choice, into thin, even-sized sticks and place them on the party table within easy reach.

Sausages on Sticks

Children will have probably encountered the sausage-on-a-stick syndrome at other parties and may therefore want them at their own party. This doesn't have to mean the supermarket cocktail sausage that is full of preservatives, colouring and lots of fatty meat. Health food shops offer a selection of frankfurter-style sausages that are usually tinned and made from vegetable protein. Lightly grilled to brown them they can be cut up and stuck on a cocktail stick in a downturned halved grapefruit. Cubes of cheese and pineapple (although boring to adults) come in for the same treatment and are better than sticky cakes and buns.

Party Mice

I remember being enthralled by tales of the elaborate creations as centrepieces to regal buffets told by the Master Baker at a series of classes on Continental Patisserie I once attended. During one lesson when we made choux pastry swans we heard about the 'lake' our teacher had created as a centre to a buffet. The choux pastry swans swam on a lake of blue jelly among marzipan and fondant water lilies! A much simpler version can be made by filling a shallow dish with jelly (see page 80) and making mice using halved pears. The pears are placed on top of the jelly and they are given almond ears, currant eyes and a sultana nose.

Fruit Jellies

These are always more fun if made in the waxed paper party plates available from stationers and supermarkets. You don't have to make them from the rubbery cubes of jelly that contain colouring and flavouring, they can be made quite simply from fruit juice and a setting agent like gelatine or agar agar. For children reluctant to eat fruit on its own fruit set in jelly sometimes seems to take on another identity.

Use any fruit except pineapple which has an enzyme in it that dissolves gelatine. Cooked or tinned pineapple (it has been heat treated) may be used.

The most widely available brand of gelatine is *Davis* gelatine which can be bought in 2 oz (50g) packets containing five sachets, each enough to set 1 pint (600ml) of liquid, or more economically in 8 oz (225g) packs of loose powdered gelatine. Three level teaspoonsful of gelatine sets 1 pint (600ml) liquid.

Agar agar is available from health food shops where it may be packed in tubs from the manufacturer or packed by the shop. Usually the tubs have setting instructions on the labels but generally three level teaspoonsful will set 1 pint (600ml) of liquid. Agar agar and other vegetable setting agents, are preferred by vegetarians because gelatine is made from animal bones and hooves. Try the following combinations of fruit and jelly:

- Red grape juice with black grapes (seeded) in the jelly.
- White grape juice with green seeded or seedless grapes in the jelly.
- Apricot juice and apricot halves.
- Red grape juice and strawberries or raspberries.
- Apple juice and strawberries.
- Orange juice and satsuma or mandarin segments.
- Grapefruit juice and green grapes.
- Blackcurrants in red grape or blackcurrant juice.
- Redcurrant juice with blackcurrants.

Soft fruits can be used to make their own juice instead of using commercially prepared juice. Black, red or white currants can be cooked in a little water. The juice from the fruit will run and this can then be set. Raspberries are also suitable and so are blackberries.

The fruit juice or juice from cooked or puréed fruits can have water added to make it go further or to dilute the taste a little as in the case of some commercially prepared fruit juices, Fruit juice concentrates (not squashes and other soft drinks) may also be used to make jellies.

Remember always to add the setting agent to the liquid — not the other way round. It should dissolve quickly when sprinkled onto very hot liquid and stirred. If it does not completely dissolve, stand the cup with the gelatine or other setting agent and liquid in a pan of hot water and continue stirring over a low heat, but do not boil. If the liquid sets before you are able to use it, it can be re-dissolved by the same method.

If the jelly needs sweetening stir a tablespoonful of fructose or clear honey into the hot gelatine/agar agar mixture.

Opposite: A Children's Party. Birthday Gateau (page 78); Banana Rabbit (page 84).

Zoo Biscuits

Makes 36 animals; 56 calories per biscuit

4 oz (100g) unsalted butter or soft vegetable margarine
3 oz (75g) clear honey
1 free-range egg, beaten
8 oz (225g) wholemeal flour
1 teaspoonful baking powder
4 oz (100g) chopped or ground nuts

1.   Cream the fat and honey together until light and fluffy.

2.   Beat in the egg.

3.   Fold in the flour, sieved with the baking powder.

4.   Stir in the nuts and lightly knead the mixture on a lightly-floured surface until it can be rolled out.

5.   Stamp out the biscuits using zoo animal cutters and carefully lift onto a lightly-oiled baking tray.

6.   Bake in a pre-heated oven at 350°F/180°C (Gas Mark 4) for 15 minutes. Pack in an airtight tin when completely cold.

Opposite: A Children's Party.
Clockwise from apples: Vegetable Burgers (page 82); Alphabet Sandwiches (page 79); Fladbury Biscuits (page 84); Toasted Sandwiches (page 83).

Nine to Eleven Year Olds

Celery Boats and Cucumber Cups
Vegetable Burgers
'Sausage' Rolls
Coleslaw
Cheese Flapjacks
Toasted Sandwiches
(savoury and sweet)

Banana Rabbit
Fladbury Biscuits

Celery Boats and Cucumber Cups

Instead of using the usual full-fat cream cheese to make celery boats, try either a low-fat curd cheese which can be piped into pretty swirls or rosettes along the lengths of celery, or use cottage cheese, Quark or similar low-fat soft white cheese flavoured with finely chopped vegetables such as cucumber, peppers or herbs. Some children may not like the chopped vegetable or herb varieties so make a selection of each. To prepare the vegetables, cut the celery sticks into about three (after washing them well) and pipe the mixture into the 'boats'. For the cucumber cups cut 1 inch (2cm) pieces of cucumber, unpeeled, and carefully scoop out the central pippy flesh leaving enough flesh at the base to form a 'cup'. Pipe a rosette of cheese, or cheese with chopped herbs and vegetables, into each.

Vegetable Burgers

Serves 10; 200 calories per portion
(Illustrated opposite page 81)

Television, school friends and advertising are all bound to affect children. At an age when they want to do the same as their friends they will probably also want to eat the same as them. You can make beefburgers (for recipe see page 177) but if you prefer to stick to vegetable sources of protein you could buy several packets of *Vegeburger* mix, either herb or chilli flavoured, and serve with wholemeal home-made or bought baps and salad. But it may be more economical to make your own burgers using nuts and grains.

| 2 large onions |
| 1 clove garlic (optional) |
| 1 dessertspoonful corn or soya oil |
| 6 oz (175g) cooked weight brown rice |
| 6 oz (175g) ground walnuts |
| 4 oz (100g) ground almonds |
| 4 oz (100g) wholemeal breadcrumbs |
| 2 carrots, grated |
| 2 free-range eggs |
| 1 tablespoonful tomato purée |
| 1 tablespoonful Worcestershire sauce |
| 2 teaspoonsful dried basil |

1. Finely dice the onions and crush the garlic. Cook over a low heat in the oil until transparent, but not brown.

2. Mix together in a bowl the rice, nuts, breadcrumbs and carrots. Stir in the onion.

3. Lightly beat the eggs and add half the mixture to the nut mixture together with the tomato purée, Worcestershire sauce and basil. Mix until a soft dough is formed that will hold

together in burger shapes. Add more egg if necessary.

4. Place the burgers in a large grill pan and grill for 10 minutes either side. Alternatively, brush a large frying pan with a smear of oil and fry, turning once.

'Sausage' Rolls

Like the burgers, sausage rolls will be something children have encountered at other parties. They can be made using a vegetable-based filling with either shortcrust wholemeal pastry (page 87) or, if you have the time or are making a large batch, with puff pastry (page 106). The filling can be made with any packet of savoury vegetable protein mix from a health food shop or you could use one of the vegetable burger recipes in this, and other chapters.

Coleslaw

Serves 10; 95 calories per portion

A home-made coleslaw goes well with both the burgers and the 'sausage' rolls and the children in this age group should be familiar with it — either home-made or from the supermarket.

This version will, of course, be without the preservatives, colourings and sugar of the supermarket versions.

2 lb (900g) white cabbage

1 lb (450g) carrots

2 eating apples

Juice of 1 lemon

4 sticks celery

4 oz (100g) raisins or sultanas

Freshly ground black pepper

¼ pint (150ml) cold-pressed safflower mayonnaise

1. Shred the cabbage into a bowl.

2. Grate the carrots and dice the cored, but not peeled, apples. Toss immediately in the lemon juice.

3. Finely slice or dice the celery.

4. Mix all the ingredients together well. Cover in fridge until needed.

Cheese Flapjacks
Makes 14; 125 calories

Cranks, the health food restaurant, introduced a cheese version of their favourite flapjacks and found they were very popular with children. This is a variation on their theme.

8 oz (225g) rolled oats

3 oz (75g) soft vegetable margarine

4 oz (100g) mature Cheddar cheese, grated

1 teaspoonful ready-made stoneground mustard

Freshly ground black pepper

¼ pint (150ml) natural yogurt

1 free-range egg, beaten

1. Place the oats in a large mixing bowl.

2. Melt the margarine in a saucepan.

3. Stir the cheese and margarine into the oats together with the seasoning, yogurt and egg.

4. Press into a lightly-oiled 8-inch square cake tin and bake in a pre-heated oven at 350°F/180°C (Gas Mark 4) for 25-30 minutes until golden brown.

5. Remove from oven and place tin on a cooling tray. Cut into slices while hot, but do not remove from tin until cold.

Toasted Sandwiches
(Illustrated opposite page 81)

These are very easy to prepare and can be a good way of getting children to eat vegetables if they are reluctant. A very small amount of good strong cheese can flavour a mixture made up with sweet corn, chopped or sliced tomatoes, peppers, grated carrots or any other vegetables. The novelty value is also good and the different shapes make them fun for children.

There is no need to butter the outside of the bread to make it brown during toasting. It browns well without this. The moisture created by the ingredients cooking inside the bread, and from the bread itself means it's not necessary to butter the inside of the bread either, but this is a matter of personal choice.

Teacakes and malted fruit loaves can also be toasted. For a children's party you could try:

Savoury:
● Grated mature Cheddar cheese with lots of tomato and sweetcorn.
● Grated mature Cheddar cheese with lots of apple slices and some sultanas.
● Tuna fish with sweetcorn and cubed red or green peppers.

- Cold, left-over vegetables, flavoured with curry spices or home-made safflower mayonnaise.
- Baked beans with some chopped onion.
- Edam cheese, grated with lots of pineapple.
- Soft white cheese with chopped fresh vegetables and/or herbs.
- Hard-boiled free-range eggs with a little mayonnaise and chopped spinach.

Sweet:
- Chopped dates and apple in wholemeal bread.
- 'No-added-sugar' marmalade and orange segments in wholemeal bread.
- Diced walnuts with chopped dates and orange segments in wholemeal bread.
- Tea cake filled with cake crumbs moistened with fruit juice.
- Any chopped soft fruit of choice with natural yogurt in tea cake.
- 'No-added-sugar' jams with their matching fresh fruit in teacake or malt loaf.
- Mashed banana with nutmeg and orange juice in malt loaf.
- Fruit purées with chopped dried fruit in teacake.

Banana Rabbit

Serves 12; 60 calories per portion
(Illustrated opposite page 80)

1 oz (25g) gelatine or agar agar
¼ pint (150ml) orange juice
6 ripe bananas
Juice of 1 lemon
½ pint (300ml) natural yogurt

1.   Heat the orange juice and sprinkle on the setting agent. Stir until dissolved and allow to cool.

2.   Place the bananas, lemon juice and yogurt in a liquidizer and blend.

3.   When the gelatine is on the point of setting add it to the liquidizer, blend again and pour into a rabbit-shaped mould (or individual party dishes).

4.   Place in fridge to set and chill.

Fladbury Biscuits

Makes 18; 60 calories per biscuit
(Illustrated opposite page 81)

3 oz (75g) wholemeal flour
½ teaspoonful baking powder
3 oz (75g) Demerara sugar
3 oz (75g) rolled oats
3 oz (75g) unsalted butter or soft vegetable margarine
1 tablespoonful milk
1 tablespoonful honey

1.   Sieve the flour and baking powder into a bowl. Stir in sugar and oats.

2.   Heat the butter, milk and honey in a saucepan. Pour onto oat mixture and mix thoroughly.

3.   Roll into small balls using the palms of your hands and place 4-inches (10cm) apart on a lightly-oiled baking tray. Flatten slightly with the back of a fork.

4.   Bake for 25-30 minutes in a pre-heated oven at 325°F/165°C (Gas Mark 3). Cool.

Twelve Years Upwards

Pitta Bread Sandwiches
Bridge Rolls
Crudités and Dips
Party Pasties
Féta Cheese Pizza

Red Fruit Yogurt Whip
Date or Apricot Slice

Bridge Rolls

If serving the pitta breads alongside the salads you might like to halve some home-made or bought wholemeal bridge rolls (page 73 for wholemeal bread recipe) and top with a delicious mixture of tuna fish liquidized with sieved cottage cheese, paprika and freshly ground black pepper on a bed of lettuce or mustard and cress. Finely chopped hard-boiled free-range eggs mixed with safflower mayonnaise and freshly ground black pepper placed on a bed of mustard and cress are also good party choices for older children or teenagers.

Pitta Bread Sandwiches

These make an interesting change from ordinary sandwiches. They can be served either ready-filled and standing in a deep sided basket or dish or they can be cut in half, ready, and placed beside a selection of salads on the table.

Fillings or Salads:
● Beansprouts mixed with watercress and orange segments and chopped spring onions.
● Sliced tomatoes with black olives, crispy lettuce, onion rings and (optional extra) anchovy fillets.
● Cooked chickpeas with crispy lettuce, diced cucumber and alfalfa sprouts, flavoured with cumin and fennel seed mixed into mayonnaise.
● Grated red cabbage with diced beetroot, tomatoes and grated carrot.

Crudités and Dips

For this age group it should be safe to introduce crudités with soft dips without too much risk to the carpet from uncoordinated grabs. Try one dip based on a soft cheese and another based on yogurt. You could also use cocktail and cheese biscuits or Cheese or Marmite Straws (page 118).

Crudités

Prepare a selection of any seasonal vegetables. Make it a balanced mixture by using some leaf vegetables such as cabbage, one or two root vegetables like carrots or parsnips and more exotic choices like chicory, cucumbers, fennel and brightly coloured vegetables like peppers. Cauliflower florets are useful and so are whole mushrooms. Chard, Chinese lettuce and celery can also be used. Arrange the vegetables in small glasses or around the dips with the biscuits.

Soft Cheese Dip
400 calories in total

1 lb (450g) soft cheese such as Quark or a home-made variety (chosen from pages 74-75)

1 small bunch spring onions

6 oz (175g) button mushrooms

2 teaspoonsful paprika

1.   Place the cheese in a mixing bowl.

2.   Clean the onions and, using kitchen scissors, snip them finely into the cheese.

3.   Slice the mushrooms very thinly and add to the dip.

4.   Stir in the paprika.

Green Yogurt Dip
700 calories in total

½ pint (300ml) thick natural yogurt

½ pint (300ml) soured cream

½ cucumber

2 sprigs fresh mint

4 oz (100g) cold cooked fresh garden peas

1.   Mix the yogurt and cream together thoroughly.

2.   Dice the unpeeled cucumber very finely and add to the mixture.

3.   Wash and dry the mint. Snip very finely and stir in with the garden peas.

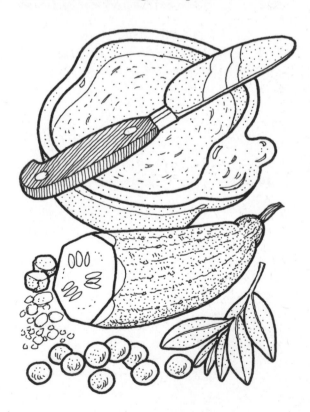

Party Pasties

Makes 12 small pasties; 170 calories each

Small Cornish pasties, or larger ones cut in half, can be used for a children's buffet. Any variety of seasonal vegetables can be used for the filling together with a cooked grain such as Scotch barley (not pearl barley which is partially refined) or rice or buckwheat. If not using a grain, make potato the basis of the filling. Partly cook the vegetables and mix with white sauce to moisten before filling the pastry and baking.

Pastry:

8 oz (225g) wholemeal flour
4 oz (100g) soft vegetable margarine
Water to mix

1. Rub fat into sieved flour and mix to a soft dough with water.

2. Roll out on a lightly-floured surface and cut out circles about 3 inches (7.5cm) in diameter.

Filling:

1 onion, diced
1 leek, diced
1 carrot, finely grated
1 dessertspoonful full corn or soya oil
4 oz (100g) mushrooms, sliced
6 oz (175g) cooked-weight barley, or
6 oz (175g) cooked boiled potatoes, diced
1 tablespoonful wholemeal flour
1 dessertspoonful concentrated vegetable stock (or a vegetable stock cube) in ¼ pint (150ml) water

1. Place the onion, leek and carrot in a saucepan with the oil and sauté gently for 5 minutes.

2. Stir in the mushrooms and barley or diced potatoes and continue to cook for another 5 minutes.

3. Stir in the flour and add the stock. Continue stirring for a couple of minutes until the mixture has thickened.

4. Place a spoonful of filling in each pastry circle and pull the edges up to meet in the middle above the filling. Pinch together and brush with egg wash.

5. Bake in a pre-heated oven at 400°F/200°C (Gas Mark 6) for 20 minutes. Serve hot or cold.

Féta Cheese Pizza

Serves 10; 170 calories per portion

This pizza can be made in a Swiss-roll tin and cut into squares for a children's party, rather than being made on a pizza plate and cut into pieces that might be too large for junior portions. First line the tin with greaseproof paper lightly-oiled on both sides or with silicone baking paper.

Dough:

1 lb (450g) wholemeal flour
½ oz (12g) fresh yeast
½ pint lukewarm water
25g vitamin C tablet, crushed
1 teaspoonful corn or soya oil

1. Sieve the flour into a mixing bowl.

2. Crumble the yeast into the water with the vitamin C tablet and add the oil.

3. Make a well in the centre of the dough and add the liquid.

4. Make a soft dough and turn onto a lightly-floured surface and knead for 5 minutes.

5. Return to the bowl and cover. Leave to rest for 10 minutes, while the topping is made.

Topping:

3 shallots, diced
1 green pepper, diced
2 sticks celery, thinly sliced
1 carrot, grated
1 dessertspoonful corn or soya oil
14 oz (400g) tin tomatoes
Freshly ground black pepper
1 dessertspoonful tomato purée
4 oz (100g) féta cheese

1. Place the shallots, pepper, celery and carrots in a saucepan with the oil and cook over a gentle heat until the shallots are transparent, but not browned.

2. Stir in the tomatoes and the purée and break up the tomatoes with the back of a wooden spoon. Allow the liquid to reduce a little.

3. Add a little freshly ground black pepper.

4. Roll out the rested dough into a rectangle to fit the prepared Swiss-roll tin, allowing the dough to go a little way up the sides of the tin, to contain the pizza topping.

5. Pour over the topping from the saucepan and spread evenly.

6. Crumble the cheese over the top and bake in a pre-heated oven at 400°F/200°C (Gas Mark 6) for 30-40 minutes. Serve hot or cold.

Red Fruit Yogurt Whip

Serves 6; 80 calories per portion

½ oz (12g) gelatine or agar agar
½ pint (300ml) red grape juice
4 oz (100g) strawberries, raspberries or blackberries
½ pint (300ml) natural yogurt

1.   Heat the fruit juice in a saucepan and pour into a cup.

2.   Sprinkle the setting agent onto the very hot liquid and stir to dissolve. Leave to cool.

3.   Place the chosen fruit in a mixing bowl and pour over the cooled fruit juice.

4.   When the jelly is on the point of setting, whisk in the yogurt and pour into a mould or individual serving dishes or party paper plates.

5.   Place in fridge to set and chill.

Date or Apricot Slice

Makes 24; 125 calories per slice

Apricots can be used instead of dates and the flesh of two oranges may be used in place of the apple. Less water is needed to reduce this to a pulp because the oranges are very juicy.

12 oz (325g) rolled oats
6 oz (175g) unsalted butter or soft vegetable margarine, melted
2 tablespoonsful Demerara sugar
1 teaspoonful cinnamon
8 oz (225g) pitted dates
8 oz (225g) cooking apples
¼ pint (150ml) water

1.   Place the rolled oats in a mixing bowl and add the melted fat, mix thoroughly and stir in the sugar and cinnamon.

2.   Place half the oat mixture in the base of a lined Swiss-roll tin and press down lightly.

3.   Place the dates in a saucepan with the apple which has been sliced but not peeled. Add the water and cook to a pulp.

4.   Spread the resultant date purée on top of the oats and top with the rest of the oat mixture. Pat down flat.

5.   Bake in a pre-heated oven at 350°F/190°C (Gas Mark 4) for 35-40 minutes until golden brown. Makes a delicious dessert when warm, served with natural yogurt.

8.
A Christening Lunch
and High Tea

Catering for a Christening may mean either one or two sets of parents travelling some distance. As Christenings are usually on a Sunday it is nice for both sets of parents to come to the children's home, admire the grandchild to be Christened and enjoy a lunch together, rather than meeting outside the Church for hurried greetings before the service.

The family party can be joined later by the godparents and other guests for a Sunday High Tea or buffet with the Christening cake.

This lunch is simple to prepare and serve and some of the components, such as the tomato sauce, the Coeur à la Crème and its sauce, can be made the night before.

There is a summer buffet or high tea and a winter buffet too. Both include salads using seasonal ingredients and the summer buffet makes use of strawberries, which can be substituted later in the season with raspberries.

The winter buffet can be served either hot or cold, and the food can be made in advance and reheated in the oven before serving if the day is cold. Quantities are for 12 in the buffet recipes which will cater for immediate family and godparents.

Christening Lunch

Asparagus Mousse

Chicken Spinach Parcels

*Coeur à la Crème with
Sauce and Fresh Fruit*

5.   Dissolve the gelatine in the water and leave to cool slightly.

6.   Add the cheese to the sauce and place the sauce and the asparagus in a liquidizer. Blend until smooth.

7.   When the sauce and the gelatine are cool pour the gelatine into the sauce.

8.   Whisk the egg white until stiff but not dry.

9.   Fold the egg white into the sauce when it is on the point of setting and pour the mousse mixture into six small wetted moulds. Place in fridge to set for a couple of hours.

Asparagus Mousse
Serves 6; 75 calories per portion

15 oz (425g) tin asparagus
1 tablespoonful unsalted butter
1 tablespoonful wholemeal flour
½ pint (300ml) skimmed milk
Freshly ground black pepper
¼ teaspoonful paprika
½ oz (12g) gelatine or agar agar
2½ fl oz (75ml) boiling water
2 tablespoonsful Parmesan cheese
1 free-range egg white

1.   Drain the asparagus.

2.   Place the butter and flour in a saucepan over a gentle heat and stir to make a roux. Cook the mixture for 2 minutes.

3.   Gradually add the milk, a little at a time and stirring between additions to prevent lumps forming.

4.   Season the sauce with the pepper and paprika.

Chicken Spinach Parcels
*Serves 6; 250 calories per portion; 320
calories with pasta
(Illustrated opposite page 96)*

6 boned free-range chicken breasts
8 oz (225g) fresh spinach
Nutmeg, freshly grated

1.   Skin the chicken breasts, if they are not already skinned.

2.   Blanch the spinach in boiling water for a minute. Remove and separate the leaves to drain.

3.   Sprinkle the chicken breasts with a small amount of freshly ground nutmeg and wrap each in the spinach leaves.

4.   Place in the base of a lightly-oiled ovenproof dish and cover with tomato sauce.

5.   Cook in a pre-heated oven at 350°F/180°C (Gas Mark 4) for 30 minutes.

6.   If liked, remove the chicken breasts and thicken the sauce with arrowroot.

Tomato Sauce:

2 shallots, diced

½ oz (12g) unsalted butter

12 fl oz (340ml) canned tomatoes

Bouquet garni (3 parsley stalks, bayleaf, sprig thyme wrapped in butter muslin)

1 stick celery, diced

1 orange, the pared rind of half and all of the juice

Freshly ground black pepper

5 fl oz (150ml) dry sherry

1 teaspoonful arrowroot slaked with 1 tablespoonful water

1. Sauté the shallots in butter, but do not allow to brown.

2. Add the tomatoes, bouquet garni, celery, orange rind and juice and pepper. Cover and cook for 20 minutes. Break up tomatoes with back of spoon.

3. Pour sauce through a sieve, pressing out all juice from pulp.

4. Stir in the sherry.

Note: Serve the chicken with either wholemeal or *verde* noodles boiled until *al dente* and tossed in a small amount of unsalted butter and freshly chopped basil or, if unavailable, parsley. Allow 3 oz (75g) dry weight per portion.

Coeur à la Crème

Makes 6; 64 calories each or 100 including fruit and sauce
(Illustrated opposite page 96)

8 oz (225g) low-fat soft, white cheese such as Quark

8 oz (225g) cottage cheese, sieved

2 free-range egg whites

1 lb (450g) raspberries, blackcurrants or blackberries

1. Place the two types of cheese in a mixing bowl and beat together.

2. Whisk the egg whites until stiff but not dry. Fold 2 tablespoonsful of egg white into the mixture to lighten it.

3. Fold the rest of the egg white into the mixture and pour or spoon into prepared coeur à la crème moulds. To prepare the moulds, line six small ceramic heart-shaped moulds, which have holes in the base, with a layer of butter muslin and place the moulds on a tray which will fit inside the fridge. (The moulds need to stand on a tray because they will produce a little liquid as they drain and set.)

4. Press half the soft fruits through a sieve or liquidize, and pour into a jug as a sauce. Leave the remainder of the fruit whole and place some on each plate with a Coeur à la Crème. Offer sauce separately.

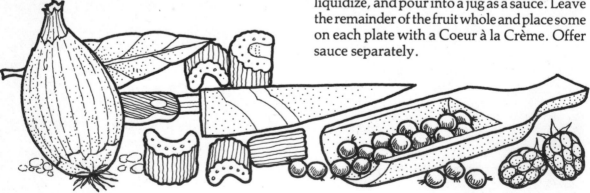

**Summer Christening
High Tea**

*Cucumber Sandwiches
Sardine Sandwiches
Summer Salad
Cheese Board*

*Strawberry Gateau
Exotic Strawberry Salad*

Christening Biscuits

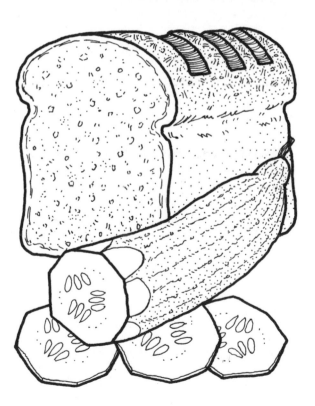

Cucumber Sandwiches
*Makes four small sandwiches per guest;
190 calories per portion*

1 large wholemeal loaf

4 oz (100g) unsalted butter or soft vegetable margarine

1 cucumber

1.   Slice the bread thinly, but do not remove crusts.

2.   Butter one side of the slices.

3.   Thinly slice the cucumber and place on one side of the bread. A cheese plane makes super-slim slices of cucumber, or a slicing attachment on a food processor does the job in seconds.

4.   Place the second slice on top of the sandwich and cut into four.

5.   Cut some of the sandwiches into triangle, in which case the two slices will make four sandwiches. Alternatively cut the double slice into three strips for finger shaped sandwiches. It is nice to have a selection of both.

Sardine Sandwiches
Makes one round of four small sandwiches per guest; 190 calories per portion

1.   Make as for Cucumber Sandwiches but replace cucumber with two cans of sardines in olive oil.

2.   Drain and then mash the sardines finely with a fork.

3.   Wash and trim a bunch of watercress and use as filling with the sardines.

Summer Salad

Serves 12; 120 calories per portion with dressing

2 large Webb's lettuce
½ cucumber
1 bunch radishes
6 tomatoes
1 bunch watercress
1 bunch spring onions

Dressing:

4 tablespoonful olive oil
1½ tablespoonful cider vinegar
Freshly ground black pepper
1 teaspoonful dry or ready-made mustard

1.   Wash the lettuce and tear the outer leaves into manageable strips. Cut the heart of each lettuce into six small sections. Place the loose leaves in the base of the serving dish.

2.   Thinly slice the cucumber, but do not peel.

3.   Wash the radishes and cut into quarters.

4.   Wash the tomatoes and cut into quarters.

5.   Wash and trim the watercress and spring onions. Break the cress into small sprigs. Chop the onions into small pieces using kitchen scissors.

6.   Arrange the salad ingredients in an attractive 'wheel' on the bed of salad, alternating groups of each vegetable around the dish.

7.   Offer salad dressing in a separate jug. To make, place all ingredients in a clean screwtop jar and shake vigorously.

Note: It is often best not to dress a salad when you have a family group, as older members of the family might prefer to have their salad vegetables without dressing. Try to defer the making of the salad as long as possible because it will not keep 'fresh' and crispy for long.

Cheese Board

With the salad offer a selection of cheese. For 12 people a 6 oz (175g) slice of each of the following will be sufficient:

- Mature English or Irish Cheddar
- Brie
- Red Leicester
- Caerphilly
- Double Gloucester
- Plus a small bowl containing 4 oz (100g) of soft goat's cheese flavoured with herbs, or any home-made cheese (see recipes on pages 74-75).

Strawberry Gateau

Serves 6; 190 calories per portion

1½ oz (40g) unsalted butter or soft vegetable margarine
3 oz (75g) wholemeal flour
2 oz (50g) clear honey
3 free-range eggs
8 oz (225g) low-fat soft white cheese
8 oz (225g) strawberries
2 tablespoonful 'no-added-sugar' strawberry jam

1. Line an 8-inch (20cm) cake tin with lightly oiled greaseproof paper or silicone baking paper. Heat the oven to 375°F/190°C (Gas Mark 5).

2. Melt the fat in a saucepan over a low heat. Remove from heat.

3. Sieve the flour and stand in a warm place.

4. Place the honey and eggs in the bowl of an electric food mixer and whisk until pale in colour and thick and ropey in consistency. Alternatively, place in a basin over a bowl of hot water if whisking by hand.

5. Fold in the sieved flour using a metal spoon.

6. Add the melted fat by pouring it down the side of the bowl and fold in with a metal spoon.

7. Pour into the prepared cake tin and bake until firm and set; about 25 minutes. Allow to cool and cut in half, horizontally using a palette knife.

8. Mash 4 oz (100g) of the strawberries with a fork and beat into the cheese. Spread the mixture in the centre of the cake and place the top in position.

9. Spread the top of the cake very thinly with the jam using just enough to hold the strawberries in position on top of the cake. To decorate, halve the strawberries and place them in concentric circles with the cut side uppermost.

Exotic Strawberry Salad
Serves 6; 65 calories per portion

Many people prefer plain strawberries in a bowl to eat either on their own or with single cream offered separately in a jug. But this recipe is for those who fancy something a bit different.

8 oz (225g) fresh strawberries
3 kiwifruits
½ ripe melon, preferably rock melon
Orange juice (optional)

1. Hull the strawberries and slice from the top to the point.

2. Thinly peel the kiwifruit and cut into slices horizontally.

3. Use a Parisienne cutter and cut balls from the flesh of the melon.

4. Mix all the fruits thoroughly and serve in a glass fruit salad bowl.

5. If you prefer a salad in a juice mixture, pour a glass of orange juice over the fruit.

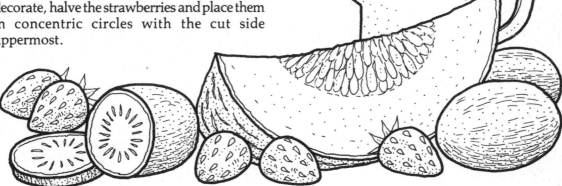

Christening Biscuits

Makes 36 biscuits; 65 calories per biscuit

12 oz (325g) wholemeal flour

1 teaspoonful mixed spice

2 free-range eggs

4 oz (100g) unsalted butter or soft vegetable margarine

2 oz (50g) Demerara sugar

4 oz (100g) currants

5 fl oz (150ml) skimmed milk

1. Sieve together the flour and spice.

2. Separate the eggs, whisking the whites until stiff but not dry.

3. Cream together the fat and sugar until pale and fluffy in texture.

4. Add the egg yolks to the fat and sugar mixture. Stir in the currants.

5. Stir in the flour and milk. Fold in the whisked egg whites.

6. Roll out the biscuit dough on a lightly floured surface and cut out using a medium-sized fancy edged cutter.

7. Place biscuits on a lightly-oiled baking tray and bake at 350°F/180°C (Gas Mark 5) for 20 minutes.

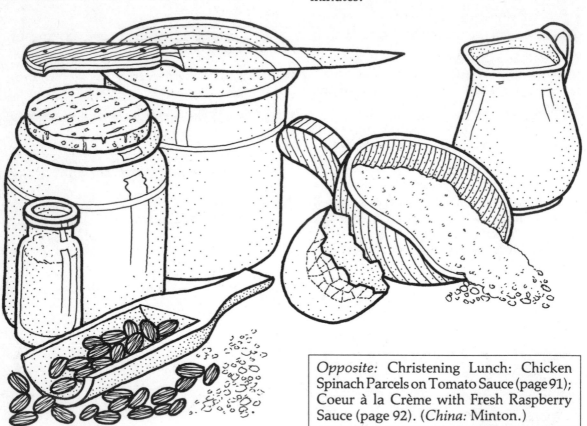

Opposite: Christening Lunch: Chicken Spinach Parcels on Tomato Sauce (page 91); Coeur à la Crème with Fresh Raspberry Sauce (page 92). (*China:* Minton.)

**Winter Christening
High Tea**

Hot Cheese Scones
Hot Onion Tarts
Winter Salad

Hot Fruit Salad

Apple Cake
Toasted Teacake

Hot Cheese Scones

Makes 12; 119 calories per scone

8 oz (225g) wholemeal flour
2 teaspoonsful baking powder
1 teaspoonful dry mustard powder
½ teaspoonful cayenne pepper
2 oz (50g) polyunsaturated margarine or unsalted butter
4 oz (100g) mature Cheddar cheese, grated
Generous ¼ pint (150ml) skimmed milk

1.   Sieve the flour into a mixing bowl with the baking powder, mustard and cayenne pepper.

2.   Rub the fat into the flour until the mixture resembles breadcrumbs in consistency.

3.   Stir in the grated cheese.

4.   Gradually blend in the milk, using a fork, until the mixture is soft and pliable.

5.   Place the dough on a lightly floured surface and roll out to about ¾-inch (2cm) thickness.

6.   Cut the scones with a plain or fancy edged cutter and glaze the tops with milk or beaten egg before placing on a lightly-oiled baking sheet.

7.   Bake in a pre-heated oven at 425°F/220°C (Gas Mark 7) for about 12 minutes until golden-brown and an inserted skewer comes out cleanly.

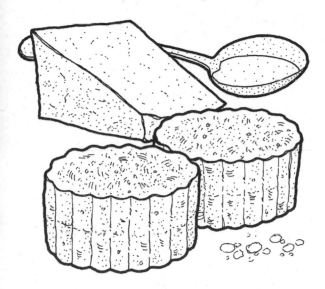

Opposite: Recipes from the Cheese and Wine chapter provide the cheeseboard for the Christening High Tea. *From the top:* Lactic Goat's Cheese with Pepper (page 74); Oatcakes (page 71); Digestive Biscuits (page 72); Cottage Cheese with Herbs (page 75).

Hot Onion Tarts

Makes 12 individual tarts in 3½-4-inch (8-10cm) tins; 280 calories per tart

Pastry:

1 lb (450g) wholemeal flour
8 oz (225g) soft vegetable margarine
1 free-range egg yolk
Water to mix

1. Sieve the flour into a mixing bowl and rub in the margarine until mixture resembles breadcrumbs in consistency.

2. Lightly beat the egg yolk with a few tablespoonsful of water and stir into the flour to make a soft dough, adding more water as necessary.

3. Turn onto a lightly-floured surface and roll out pastry. Line the lightly-oiled tartlet tins and place a piece of greaseproof or silicone paper in each. Weigh it down with baking beans and bake in a pre-heated oven at 400°F/200°C (Gas Mark 6) for 10 minutes.

4. Remove from oven. Remove paper and beans and fill with onion mixture. Return to oven for a further 20-25 minutes until mixture is set and golden brown on top.

Filling:

12 oz (325g) onions, finely diced
1 green pepper, de-seeded and diced
1 dessertspoonful corn or soya oil
4 oz (100g) mushrooms, diced
2 free-range eggs, beaten
½ pint (300ml) natural yogurt
4 oz (100g) cottage cheese, sieved

1. Place the onions and pepper in a saucepan over a moderate heat with the oil and cover. Sweat for 5 minutes, stirring once or twice for even cooking.

2. Add the mushrooms and continue cooking while the eggs, yogurt and cheese are mixed together.

3. Stir the vegetables into the cheese mixture and pour into the prepared pastry cases.

Winter Salad

Serves 12; 75 calories per portion

Juice of 1 lemon
1 small white cabbage, shredded
4 large carrots, grated
8 sticks celery, diced
1 Bramley cooking apple, diced
1 red-skinned eating apple, diced
4 oz (100g) sultanas or raisins
1 large onion, diced
¼ pint (150ml) cold-pressed safflower oil mayonnaise
Freshly ground black pepper

1. Use the lemon juice to dress the vegetables as soon as they are cut to prevent browning and vitamin loss.

2. Mix all the ingredients together in a large bowl and toss in the mayonnaise and seasoning.

Hot Fruit Salad

Serves 12; 100 calories per portion

2 pints (1.15 litres) water
2 tablespoonsful clear honey
1 teaspoonful cinnamon
1 teaspoonful nutmeg
4 cloves
8 oz (225g) dried apricots
4 oz (100g) dried peaches
4 oz (100g) muscatel raisins
Juice of 1 lemon
1 lb (450g) cooking apples
4 fresh cooking pears

1.   Place the water, honey and spices in a saucepan and bring to boiling point.

2.   Place the dried fruit in a saucepan with enough cold water to cover, bring to the boil and drain, throwing away the water. This will remove any mineral oil that may be on them.

3.   Add the dried fruit and the lemon juice to the spiced water and cover. Simmer for 25 minutes.

4.   Wash and core the apples and pears, but do not peel. Slice and add to the fruit for the last 15-20 minutes.

5.   Serve hot. Offer natural yogurt separately.

Apple Cake

Serves 12; 165 calories per slice

1 lb (450g) cooking apples
12 oz (325g) wholemeal flour
2 teaspoonsful cinnamon
1 teaspoonful ground cloves
1 teaspoonful baking powder
4 oz (100g) unsalted butter
¼ pint (150ml) milk
1 teaspoonful lemon juice
1 large free-range egg
2 tablespoonsful clear honey

1.   Wash and core the apples and slice, without peeling, into a saucepan with 4 tablespoonsful cold water. Cook over a low heat until soft enough to purée. Allow to cool a little.

2.   Sieve the flour and spices into a mixing bowl with the baking powder.

3.   Rub in the butter.

4.   Measure out the milk and add the lemon juice to sour it.

5.   Lightly beat the egg and honey into the milk and pour onto the flour. Add the warm apples and beat the cake well.

6.   Pour into a lined cake tin and bake in a pre-heated oven at 350°F/180°C (Gas Mark 4) for 45 minutes to 1 hour until golden-brown and an inserted skewer comes out clean.

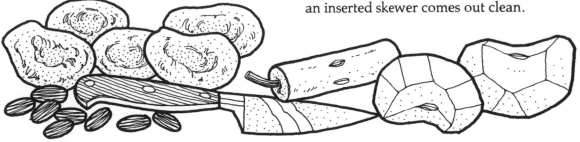

Toasted Teacakes

Serves 12; 140 calories per portion

1 lb (450g) wholemeal flour
1 teaspoonful mixed spice
3 oz (75g) mixed dried fruit
½ pint (300ml) skimmed milk
½ oz (12g) fresh yeast
1 vitamin C tablet, crushed
Free-range egg, beaten with little milk

1.   Sieve the flour and spice together into a mixing bowl.

2.   Stir the dried fruit into the flour.

3.   Warm the milk slightly and crumble in the yeast and the vitamin C. Leave to stand for 5 minutes.

4.   Stir the yeast mixture into the flour and add the egg, leaving enough egg to glaze the tops of the teacakes.

5.   Mix to soft dough and turn onto a lightly floured surface and knead for 5 minutes. Return to bowl, cover and leave to rest for 10 minutes.

6.   Return dough to work surface and knead again. Form into 12 roll shapes and place on a lightly-oiled baking sheet. Cover and leave to rise until doubled in size (about 40 minutes).

7.   Glaze when risen and bake in a pre-heated oven at 425°F/220°C (Gas Mark 7) for 20-25 minutes. Before using, cut in half and toast, then spread with 'no-added-sugar' jam or a little honey.

9.

Christmas Entertaining

The recipes in this section are designed to provide something for everyone at Christmas, whether they are vegetarians or non-vegetarian, and also something a little different from the usual Christmas fare.

There is no set Christmas meal because most families have their own Christmas tradition, but there are suggestions for different ways of serving the turkey, if that is what you choose for Christmas.

A deliciously light and attractive Turkey Terrine will make an imaginative change from roast, stuffed turkey (although this is a very nice dish). The Savoury Mille Feuille (layers of wholemeal puff pastry and turkey sauce) makes an excellent buffet dish and is an unusual way of using the leftovers. Part of it can be made in advance.

If you are thinking of serving turkey, it is worth considering a free-range bird because it is less likely to contain drug residues, such as hormones used to promote growth in poultry, or antibiotics.

Ask around your local butcher's, poulterer's and fishmonger's a few weeks before Christmas because free-range birds are popular but quite scarce and they will need to be ordered in advance.

Game, like poultry, is also lower in fat than most meats and less likely to contain any drug residues. The flavour of pheasant, partridge, grouse and guinea fowl is distinctive and it is probably best to try them before you order them for a special meal in case you do not like them.

For the vegetarians there are Nut Croquettes with a chestnut sauce, which makes a change from the usual nut roast. They can be served with Parsnip Ramekins and sprouts.

At Christmas, many people who do not usually entertain invite friends to their home for a drink. Remember not to ply Christmas visitors with heavy spirits or cocktails (unless that is what they want) but offer a choice of wine, or perhaps a mulled wine. Dry white wines and sparkling wines are also acceptable to those who do not usually drink much.

Always offer something to eat with a drink and make the nibbles and titbits appetizing (see Chapter 10 for extra ideas). Open sandwiches are different from the usual sandwiches and they are quick and easy to assemble.

The tartlets for the Curry or Mackerel Tartlets can be made in advance and stored in an airtight tin to be filled when required over the Christmas break.

Other things that can be made in advance of the Christmas rush are the mincemeat, Marinated Herrings, and the Christmas Cake. For those who do not like a rich fruit cake (and for children in particular) there is a light Carob Yule Log and some Swedish heart-shaped biscuits which are traditionally hung on the Christmas tree in Scandinavian countries; a better idea that the chocolate novelties sold in Britain!

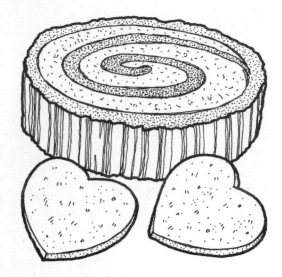

Open Sandwiches

(Illustrated opposite page 113)

Smorgasbord, or open sandwiches, always look attractive, fresh and appealing. During the rich fare of Christmas they will be a welcome treat for visitors a little tired of mince pies, turkey vol-au-vents, turkey sandwiches . . . That is not to say that you cannot use turkey in them, but they are a chance to get away from the usual presentations.

There is more than one way to make an open sandwich. Starting with the base there are several types to choose from:

wholemeal bread	original Ryvita
rye bread	wholemeal crispbreads
other grain breads	wholemeal biscuits

Even those who have not travelled to Scandinavia will be aware of the perennial popularity of Norwegian prawns on a bed of lettuce with some tomato mayonnaise and a slice of lemon. Also popular among the Swedes, Danes and Norwegians are cold meats, smoked sausages, salamis and pâtés, but there are other toppings that offer fewer additives. Try some of these combinations for a start:

- A bed of sliced tomatoes topped with rollmop herring and onion rings.
- Cooked smoked Finnan haddock mixed with safflower mayonnaise and topped with slices of avocado dressed with lemon juice.
- Sardines with sticks of celery and twists of lemon.
- Low-fat soft white cheese mixed with fresh herbs and topped with a couple of prawns.
- Thin slices of Edam cheese (it's lower in fat than other hard cheeses like Cheddar) topped with slices of apple dressed in lemon juice.
- Try Edam topped with fresh pineapple slices.
- Hard-boiled free-range eggs with a couple of anchovy fillets and cress are delicious.
- Make an instant coleslaw with apple slices dressed with lemon juice, grated carrot and sultanas topped with safflower mayonnaise.
- Even thin slices of Cheddar-type cheeses with home-made chutney are good.
- For a grander effect, asparagus spears with twists of lemon and a prawn or two.
- Piped rosettes of low-fat cheese topped with watercress are impressive too.
- Cavair or lumpfish roe go very well with beetroot and soured cream.

Nut Croquettes with Chestnut Sauce

Serves 6; 250 calories per portion;
350 calories including sauce

2 onions, diced
6 oz (175g) pecan or walnuts, ground
4 oz (100g) wholemeal breadcrumbs
8 oz (225g) cooked millet, mashed
2½ fl oz (75ml) natural tomato ketchup
2 teaspoonsful oregano
Freshly ground black pepper
1 free-range egg, beaten with little water

1.   Sauté the onions with a smear of oil for 5 minutes.

2.   Stir into the onions the rest of the ingredients (except the egg) and cook, stirring continuously, for another 5 minutes.

3.   Remove from heat and place in a bowl. Add the egg and bind the mixture together. Form into 6 croquettes and lightly fry in a smear of oil until golden-brown. Serve hot with Chestnut Sauce poured over and lightly steamed broccoli.

Chestnut Sauce:

1 tablespoonful unsalted butter or soft vegetable margarine
1 tablespoonful wholemeal flour
½ pint (300ml) vegetable stock or skimmed milk
1 teaspoonful cayenne pepper
8 oz (225g) cooked and puréed chestnuts
¼ pint (150ml) single cream or yogurt

1.   Make a roux with the butter and flour and gradually add the stock, stirring continuously to prevent lumps forming.

2.   Season with cayenne pepper and stir in the chestnut purée.

3.   When heated through add the cream or yogurt and remove from heat to pour over croquettes.

Parsnip Ramekins

Serves 8; 190 calories per ramekin

2 lb (900g) parsnips
8 oz (225g) mature English Cheddar cheese, grated
6 oz (175g) wholemeal breadcrumbs
¼ pint (150ml) skimmed milk (optional)

1.   Scrub the parsnips and peel if necessary. Roughly chop and boil or steam in a small amount of water until just cooked.

2.   Mix together 2 oz (50g) of cheese and 2 oz (50g) of breadcrumbs, and place on one side.

3.   Mash or liquidize the parsnips in the cooking water, if any is left. Add the milk, if required, to make a soft mixture.

4.   Stir in the rest of the cheese and breadcrumbs and place the mixture in lightly-oiled ramekin dishes.

5.   Top each dish with a layer of the breadcrumb mixture and bake at 350°F/180°C (Gas Mark 4) for 20 minutes until golden-brown on top.

Vegetarian Scotch Eggs
Makes 4; 250 calories per egg

4 free-range eggs, hard-boiled

1 free-range egg, beaten

4 oz (100g) ground hazelnuts

2 tablespoonsful 'no-added-sugar' tomato ketchup

2 teaspoonsful freshly chopped sage

Freshly ground black pepper

2 onions, grated or minced

1 tablespoonful sesame oil

2 oz (50g) wholemeal breadcrumbs

1.   Shell the hard-boiled eggs and place on one side with the beaten egg.

2.   Mix together the rest of the ingredients to form a thick paste.

3.   Dip the eggs in the beaten egg and mould the paste around them.

4.   Place on a lightly-oiled baking sheet and bake at 375°F/190°C (Gas Mark 5) for 20 minutes, turning once. Allow to cool before serving.

Note: Scotch eggs are traditionally deep fried. This adds a lot of calories to a dish already quite high in fat from the oil and eggs. Baking them in the oven produces just as good results without the oiliness of deep frying.

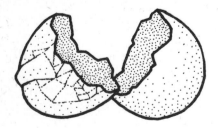

Savoury Tartlets
25 calories per tartlet

Make a quantity of pastry (from page 98) and line 18 small tartlet tins 1½-2 inches (4-5cm) in diameter. Bake them blind and when cold fill with the following fillings:

Creamy Mackerel Filling:

1 smoked mackerel

4 oz (100g) cottage cheese

Juice of ½ lemon

Freshly ground black pepper

Blade of mace, finely ground

1.   Flake the fish from the bone and skin.

2.   Sieve the cottage cheese and mix with the fish.

3.   Add the lemon juice and season to taste. Fill the tartlets.

Curry Filling:

4 oz (100g) cooked lentils

1 tablespoonful tahini

4 oz (100g) tofu

1 tablespoonful ground cumin

1.   Mash the lentils with the tahini to a smooth paste.

2.   Drain all the whey from the tofu and stir into the lentils.

3.   Season with cumin, adding more if preferred.

Avocado Filling:

1 avocado pear
Juice of ½ lemon
2 oz (50g) shelled prawns
2 oz (50g) safflower mayonnaise
Freshly ground black pepper

1. Mash the pear to a smooth paste with the lemon juice.

2. Drain the prawns and stir into the avocado with the mayonnaise.

3. Season to taste.

Braised Meatballs and Vegetables

Serves 6; 195 calories per portion

Meatballs:

1 lb (450g) minced steak
2 oz (50g) wholemeal breadcrumbs
1 onion, minced or grated
1 free-range egg
1 teaspoonful allspice
Freshly ground black pepper

Vegetable base:

6 sticks celery
2 carrots
1 large onion
1 dessertspoonful vegetable oil
¾ pint (450ml) vegetable stock
1 teaspoonful lemon juice
Freshly ground black pepper

1. Stir together all of the meatball ingredients. Form into balls. Lightly sauté.

2. Scrub the celery and cut into 1-inch (2.5cm) pieces.

3. Scrub the carrots and slice thinly. Finely dice the onion.

4. Sauté the vegetables in the oil for 3 minutes.

5. Place the vegetables in an ovenproof dish and pour over the stock, lemon juice and seasoning.

6. Place the meatballs on top of the vegetables and stock and bake in a pre-heated oven at 400°F/200°C (Gas Mark 6) for 40 minutes.

Note: For a better quality mince it is best to buy steak and trim off all the fat before mincing it at home. This ensures you are getting meat without any fillers or preservatives (though butchers do have to declare the use of additives). Meatballs are a part of a traditional Scandinavian Christmas and they make a welcome change from turkey and a healthier alternative to roast pork and hams.

Savoury Mille Feuille

Serves 12; 415 calories per person

Wholemeal Puff Pastry:
Wholemeal puff pastry is difficult to work with and it will not give the same light, puffy results as white flour pastry. However, it does make an extremely light and crispy pastry with a delicious flavour. Butter must be used, both for its flavour and its ability to help trap air. Adding a little lemon juice to the initial dough will help make it elastic and easier to use. Frozen wholemeal puff pastry is now available in some supermarkets and delicatessens.

7 oz (200g) wholemeal flour
7 oz (200g) unsalted butter
2 teaspoonful lemon juice
2½ fl oz (75ml) cold water

1. Sieve the flour into a mixing bowl and rub in 2 oz (50g) of the butter.

2. Make a well in the centre and add the lemon juice and enough water to form a stiff dough. Cover and leave to stand for 10 minutes.

3. Place the remaining butter on a lightly floured surface and flatten it into a rectangle by hitting with a rolling pin.

4. Roll the dough out into a rectangle shape twice as long as the butter and a couple of inches wider.

5. Place the butter on top of one half and fold the pastry over, sealing the edges with a rolling pin. Cover and place in the fridge for 15 minutes until the butter hardens.

6. Remove from fridge and roll into a long thin oblong. Fold the bottom third up and the top third down and press the edges together with a rolling pin.

7. Turn the pastry one turn to the left so that open folds are now facing you and roll again into a long strip. Repeat the folding. Cover and leave in the fridge for 15 minutes.

8. Repeat this rolling and folding twice more. After the final rolling, cover and leave to rest again before rolling out for use.

9. To make Mille Feuille slices and bake the pastry, see the instructions in the Mille Feuille recipe on page 56.

Note: It is important to cover the pastry each time it is rested to prevent it drying out and a crust forming on the surface.

Filling:

1 lb (450g) cooked turkey
1 large onion, diced
2 sticks celery, diced
2 carrots, diced
1 tablespoonful vegetable oil
2 oz (50g) unsalted butter or vegetable oil
2 oz (50g) wholemeal flour
½ pint (300ml) milk or good vegetable or turkey stock
Freshly ground black pepper
1 teaspoonful ready-made wholegrain mustard

1. Flake the turkey finely into a bowl.

2. Place the onion, celery and carrot in a saucepan with the fat and sauté gently for 10 minutes.

3. Stir in the flour and cook until the mixture is thick.

4. Gradually add the liquid, stirring all the time to prevent lumps forming.

5.   Season with pepper and mustard and pour over turkey. Mix thoroughly and place half the mixture on top of one sheet of puff pastry.

6.   Top with a second sheet of puff pastry and add the remaining turkey mixture. Place the final layer of puff pastry on top.

12 herring fillets or 6 whole fish
2 oz (50g) sea salt
1 pint (600ml) water
6 shallots
2 carrots
2 slices fresh horseradish root
1 teaspoonful whole allspice
1 teaspoonful black peppercorns
1 teaspoonful mustard seeds
2 bay leaves
1 pint (600ml) white wine or cider vinegar mixed with ¼ pint (150ml) water and 1 tablespoonful Demerara sugar

Marinated Herring
250 calories a fillet

Sild (or marinated herrings) are a popular part of Swedish and Danish cuisine. They are served all year and come in different sauces including brine, tomato, mustard, horseradish and others. At Christmas a large amount of sild is prepared to use during the holiday with salad or as part of the smorgasbord (cold table) and on open sandwiches with rye breads or crispbreads. Made a week or so in advance these are very handy for as an instant snack for visitors. They can also be served as a starter to a meal with hot boiled potatoes, garnished with fresh dill, or with wholemeal crispbreads. Many Scandinavian cooks prefer to use salted herring which they soak for 24 hours before use, but a healthier, less salty version is to soak the herring fillets overnight in a small amount of salt. Prepare about a week before Christmas.

1.   If using fresh fish, gut, discard the heads and fillet. Rinse thoroughly under cold water.

2.   Place fish in a shallow dish and sprinkle with the salt. Cover with water and leave to soak overnight.

3.   Next day rinse thoroughly and pat fish dry on kitchen paper. Cut into 1-inch (2.5cm) pieces.

4.   Finely dice the shallots and carrots and grate the horseradish.

5.   Place layers of fish pieces, vegetables and spices in clean *Kilner* jars and pour over the vinegar solution. Store in the fridge for a week before use.

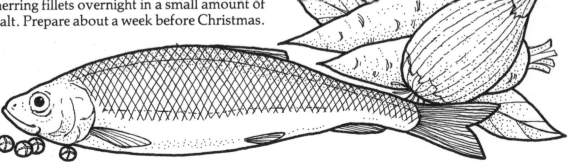

Turkey and Asparagus Terrine

Serves 8; 210 calories per portion

4 boned turkey breasts
1 lb (450g) fresh spinach
15 oz (400g) tin asparagus
3 free-range egg whites
7 oz (200g) Quark or similar low-fat soft white cheese
Freshly ground black pepper
Pinch of ground mace

1. Mince the turkey meat and place in a mixing bowl.

2. Blanch the spinach in boiling water for two minutes. Drain, separate the leaves and allow to cool.

3. Lightly oil a large bread tin and line with the spinach leaves, allowing some to hang over the top of the tin. (These will be folded around over the top of the filling to envelope it.) Reserve a few leaves to place on the top.

4. Drain the asparagus.

5. Whisk the egg whites until stiff.

6. Beat the cheese into the turkey and season with pepper and mace.

7. Fold a couple of tablespoonsful of egg white into the mixture to lighten it, then quickly fold in the rest of the whites.

8. Place a layer of turkey mousse in the base of the tin and top with a couple of rows of asparagus running the length of the tin. Place another layer of mousse on top, followed by more asparagus and finally the rest of the mousse.

9. Fold the spinach leaves over the top of the mousse and place the reserved leaves on the top.

10. Bake standing in a baking tray of hot water in a pre-heated oven at 425°F/220°C (Gas Mark 7) for 40 minutes.

11. Remove from oven and allow to become cold before carefully turning out of tin. Chill before serving with hot buttered wholemeal tagliatelle.

Russian Salad

Serves 15 as an accompaniment; 85 calories per portion

8 oz (225g) cold cooked potatoes
8 oz (225g) cold cooked carrots
4 oz (100g) cold cooked peas
4 small cold cooked beetroot
8 oz (225g) cold cooked cauliflower
4 oz (100g) roasted cashew nuts
1 tablespoonful chopped fresh parsley
Freshly ground black pepper
Juice and rind of ½ lemon
¼ pint (150ml) safflower mayonnaise

1. Dice all the cooked vegetables (except the peas!) and place in a mixing bowl.

2. Stir in the nuts, parsley and seasoning.

3. Mix thoroughly with the mayonnaise and place on a serving dish or press lightly into a mould and set in the fridge for a couple of hours before unmoulding carefully.

Satsuma Cheesecake

Serves 8; 250 calories per person
(Illustrated opposite page 112)

Instead of leaving the satsumas on the sideboard to gather dust during Christmas use them to make this deliciously juicy cheesecake. I prefer to cut away all the skin from the segments but this is fiddly and you may prefer to leave the segments in their skins.

Base:

6 oz (175g) wholemeal digestive biscuits, crushed
2 oz (50g) soft vegetable margarine, melted

Filling:

8 oz (225g) low-fat curd cheese
2 free-range eggs, separated
¼ pint (150ml) soured cream
2 tablespoonsful honey
½ oz (12g) gelatine or agar agar
½ pint (300ml) boiling water
4 satsuma oranges, peeled and segmented or mandarins tinned in fruit juice

1. Mix the biscuits with the melted margarine and press into the base of a lightly-oiled, loose-bottomed 8-inch (20cm) flan case. Place in fridge to chill.

2. Beat the cheese together with the egg yolks then stir in the soured cream. Ensure mixture is smooth. Stir in honey.

3. Sprinkle the gelatine onto the water and stir to dissolve. Allow to cool before adding to creamed mixture.

4. Whisk the egg whites until stiff. Fold 2 tablespoonsful into the creamed mixture to lighten it, then add the remainder, folding in with a metal spoon.

5. Place three of the segmented satsuma oranges in the base of the prepared biscuit cake. Pour the cheese mixture on top and place in the fridge to set.

6. Decorate with the reserved satsuma segments just before serving (and some grated orange rind, if liked).

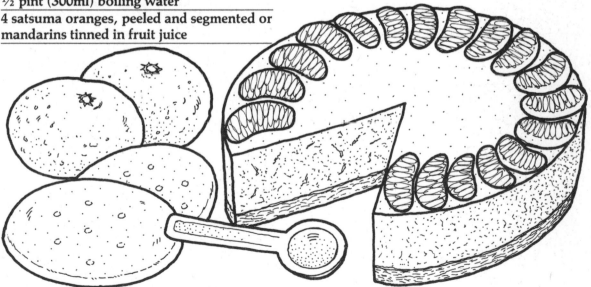

Lemon Mincemeat

Makes 5 × 1 lb (450g) jars; 640 calories per pound (450g)

8 oz (225g) cooking apples
Juice and rind of 2 lemons
6 oz (175g) raisins
6 oz (175g) sultanas
6 oz (175g) currants
4 oz (100g) almonds
2 oz (50g) candied lemon peel (optional)
1 tablespoonful brandy

1.   Wash and mince the cored apples and mix with the juice and rind of the lemons.

2.   Add the cleaned raisins, sultanas, currants and finely chopped, but not blanched, almonds.

3.   Stir in the lemon peel and brandy and pot in clean, dry jars. Store in the fridge.

Note: This mincemeat has no suet or sugar, two of the traditional ingredients that allow mincemeat to be preserved for a long time. For this reason it is best to keep the mincemeat in the fridge, where it will keep for about six weeks. It can also be made a couple of days before use, unlike the suet and sugar mincemeat which needs about four weeks to mature before use. Use to make mince pies in the same way as usual (illustrated opposite page 112) or use in the following recipe.

Mincemeat and Apple Plait

Serves 10; 225 calories per portion

1 lb (450g) wholemeal flour
1 teaspoonful cinnamon
½ pint (300ml) warmed milk
½ oz (12g) fresh yeast
1 vitamin C tablet, crushed
1 teaspoonful clear honey
1 lb (450g) Lemon Mincemeat
1½ lb (675g) cooking apples
Juice of 1 lemon

1.   Sieve the flour and cinnamon into a mixing bowl.

2.   Warm the milk and crumble in the yeast, vitamin C tablet and the honey and leave to stand for 5 minutes.

3.   Stir the milk into the flour and work to a soft dough. Turn onto a slightly floured work surface and knead for 5 minutes.

4.   Return to bowl and cover. Leave to stand for 10 minutes.

5.   While dough is resting core the apples and slice, but do not peel. Toss in lemon juice to prevent browning. Place in a saucepan with 4 tablespoonsful of water and cook gently for 5 minutes to slightly soften. Drain.

6.   Roll the dough out thinly to a long strip about 18 inches (45cm) by 8 inches (20cm). Spread the mincemeat down the centre of the strip and place the apples on top.

7.   Cut the dough at 1-inch (2.5cm) intervals from the outside edges to the filling. Bring the strips alternately up over the dough and pinch into place.

8.   Glaze with beaten egg or milk and carefully lift onto a lightly-oiled baking sheet. Cook in a pre-heated oven at 400°F/200°C (Gas Mark 6) for 30 minutes.

Swedish Christmas Biscuits

Makes 36 hearts; 20 calories each
(Illustrated opposite page 112)

2 oz (50g) clear honey

2 oz (50g) Demerara sugar

2 oz (50g) unsalted butter or soft vegetable margarine

1 level teaspoonful each of ground ginger, cinnamon and cloves

4 tablespoonsful single cream

1 rounded teaspoonful baking powder

8 oz (225g) wholemeal flour

1.   Melt the honey, sugar and butter together over a low heat. Add the spices.

2.   Remove from heat and stir in the cream.

3.   Sieve the baking powder and flour together into a mixing bowl and stir in the melted ingredients.

4.   Work the dough on a lightly-floured board until it can be rolled out to ¼-inch (.5cm) thickness.

5.   Cut out heart-shaped biscuits and place on lightly-oiled baking tray. Cook in a pre-heated oven at 450°F/230°C (Gas Mark 8) for 10 minutes.

Mulled Wine

Serves 8; 80 calories a glass

Pared rind of 1 lemon

1 bottle red wine of choice

2 tablespoonsful Demerara sugar

½ pint (300ml) water

1 teaspoonful cloves

1 teaspoonful ground cinnamon

1 teaspoonful ground nutmeg

1.   Scrub the lemon well and peel off the rind with a potato peeler. Blanch for 1 minute.

2.   Place the wine and the rest of the ingredients, together with the lemon rind, into a stainless steel or glass saucepan and gently heat to boiling point.

3.   Lower heat and simmer for 5 minutes.

4.   Strain through a double layer of butter muslin lining a sieve, and pour into a punch bowl or jug.

Carob Yule Log

Serves 8; 120 calories per portion
(Illustrated opposite)

3 free-range eggs
3 oz (75g) clear honey
3 oz (75g) wholemeal flour
1 tablespoonful carob powder
1 tablespoonful hot water
8 oz (225g) Quark or similar low-fat soft white cheese
2 teaspoonsful decaffeinated coffee, dissolved in a little water
2 teaspoonsful carob powder
A little yogurt to thin filling, if necessary

1.   Whisk the eggs and honey together until pale in colour, and thick and ropey in consistency.

2.   Sieve together the wholemeal flour and carob powder and fold into the whisked mixture using a metal spoon.

3.   Add the hot water and turn into a paper-lined and lightly-oiled Swiss-roll tin and bake at 425°F/220°C (Gas Mark 7) for 12 minutes until cooked and springy to the touch.

4.   Remove from oven and turn upside down onto a piece of greaseproof or silicone baking paper on a work surface.

5.   Remove the paper from the roll and trim the edges. Roll up with the clean piece of paper inside the roll. Allow to cool.

6.   Mix together the cheese, coffee and carob powder, adding yogurt if the mixture is too stiff.

7.   When the roll is cold unroll and spread with half the mixture before re-rolling and spreading the rest on top of the log. Make a bark pattern using the back of a fork.

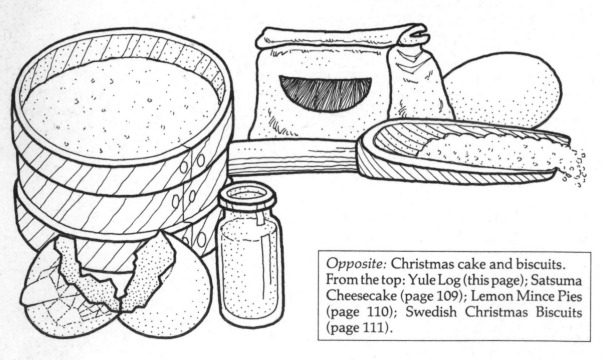

Opposite: Christmas cake and biscuits. From the top: Yule Log (this page); Satsuma Cheesecake (page 109); Lemon Mince Pies (page 110); Swedish Christmas Biscuits (page 111).

Christmas Cake

Serves 35-40 slices; 225-200 calories per slice
(un-iced and without marzipan)

12 oz (325g) wholemeal flour
2 teaspoonsful mixed spice
1 teaspoonful ground nutmeg
1 teaspoonful ground cinnamon
1 teaspoonful ground cloves
4 oz (100g) ground almonds
1 lb (450g) currants
1 lb (450g) raisins
1 lb (450g) sultanas
8 oz (225g) mixed peel
4 oz (100g) almonds
12 oz (325g) soft vegetable margarine
Rind and juice large lemon
8 free-range eggs
2½ fl oz (75ml) brandy

1. Lightly oil a 10-inch (25cm) cake tin and line with greaseproof paper, oiled on both sides. Pre-set oven to 300°F/150°C (Gas Mark 2).

2. Sieve the flour and spices into a mixing bowl and stir in the ground almonds. If the raisins are very large, chop them into smaller pieces. Mix the dried fruit in with the flour and spices, coating the fruit thoroughly.

3. Roughly chop the almonds (they need not be blanched), and blend in with the fruit and flour.

4. Cream the margarine together with the lemon rind and beat in the eggs.

5. Stir the margarine and egg mixture into the flour, then add the juice of the lemon and the brandy. If the mixture is not soft and moist add a little milk.

6. Spoon cake mixture into the prepared tin and level the top. Bake, below the centre of the oven, for 1½ hours then reduce the heat to 250°F/120°C (Gas Mark ½) for a further 3 hours. If the cake is browning too much place a triple layer of greaseproof paper over the top. The cake is done when an inserted skewer comes out cleanly.

7. Leave to cool before removing from tin. When completely cold the cake can be wrapped in fresh greaseproof paper and foil and stored in an airtight tin for up to 6 weeks before Christmas.

8. Decorate with marzipan made from raw cane sugar or dried fruit and nuts glazed with 'no-added-sugar' jam.

Opposite: Open Sandwiches (page 102) make an ideal Christmas buffet, but are perfect for many other occasions, too. (*Tray:* Altraco, made in France. *Pie slice:* Harrod's Thistle.)

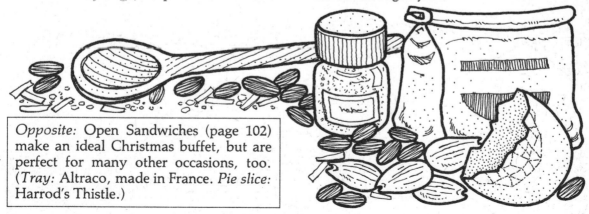

10.

Cocktail Party Snacks

Worldwide, hospitality involves giving visitors something to eat, even a token slice of cheese in Scandinavia or a biscuit in Britain. Nowadays it is more usual to greet new people with 'You must come over for a drink', but it can be difficult on these occasions to know what to serve with it.

Most people prefer to nibble at something while they are drinking and talking. It gives them something to do with their hands and stops them reaching for the cigarettes (if you allow smoking in your home!).

To keep the occasion simple and informal it is a good idea to provide food that can be eaten with the minimum of fuss, either straight from hand to mouth or with just a plate and serviette.

Savoury foods are traditionally served with drinks and the recipes in this chapter avoid the excessively salty nuts and crisps that are popular on such occasions, and which are so high in calories. They also avoid the additives needed to keep fatty crisps from going rancid and the monosodium glutamate added to many cocktail nuts and biscuits to give them flavour. There is also a whole range of other flavourings, colourings and preservatives used in these foods.

Rather than use these products, start out with tasty wholefood ingredients and put together an attractive platter of one or two of the 'nibbles' from the recipes in this chapter. Some can also be used as starters. All are simple and quick to make, though they do take a little more effort than opening a bag of crisps!

Cheese Doughnut Rolls

Makes about 30 small rolls;
75 calories each

| 1 lb (450g) wholemeal flour |
| 1/2 oz (12g) fresh yeast |
| 1/2 pint lukewarm water |
| 1 teaspoonful sunflower oil |
| 1 vitamin C tablet, crushed |

Filling:

| 6 oz (175g) Caerphilly or other crumbly white cheese |
| 1 oz (25g) soft vegetable margarine |
| 1 free-range egg |
| 1/2 teaspoonful ready-made stoneground mustard |

1. Sieve the flour into a mixing bowl.

2. Crumble the yeast into the water and add the sunflower oil and crushed vitamin C tablet.

3. Leave the yeast mixture to stand for 5 minutes and pre-heat the oven to 400°F/200°C (Gas Mark 6). Lightly oil a baking tray.

4. Grate the cheese and mix well with the other filling ingredients.

5. Stir the yeast mixture into the flour and work together to make a dough. Turn out onto a lightly-floured surface and knead for 5 minutes. Cover and leave to rest for 10 minutes.

6. Knead the dough after it has rested and divide it into equal pieces to make the rolls. Place each piece of dough on the work surface and work into a roll shape by placing a cupped hand over the top of the dough and working in a circular motion to make the dough round.

7. Using the knuckles of two fingers and working with floured hands make a well in the centre of the rolls and place 1/2 teaspoonful of the cheese mixture inside. Pull the edges up over the filling and seal in a twist. Glaze with egg wash.

8. Place on baking tray and bake for 15-20 minutes. Serve hot or cold.

Tahini Tasties

Makes 16; 65 calories per portion
(Illustrated opposite page 129)

| 4 tablespoonsful wholemeal breadcrumbs |
| 1 tablespoonful crunchy peanut butter |
| 1 tablespoonful tahini |
| 2 oz (50g) flaked almonds |
| 1 free-range egg |
| 1 dessertspoonful corn oil |

1. Mix together the breadcrumbs, peanut butter and tahini using a fork to ensure it is thoroughly mixed.

2. Form mixture into small balls by rolling in the palms of lightly floured hands.

3. Dip the balls into beaten egg and then roll in the flaked almonds.

4. Place the oil in a frying pan and fry, turning, until golden-brown all over.

Herb Scones

Makes 10; 60 calories per scone

4 oz (100g) wholemeal flour
1 teaspoonful baking powder
1½ oz (40g) soft vegetable margarine
2 teaspoonsful freshly chopped sage, thyme, parsley, or other herb of choice
2½ fl oz (70ml) skimmed milk

1.   Sieve the flour into a mixing bowl with the baking powder.

2.   Rub the margarine into the flour until mixture resembles breadcrumbs in texture.

3.   Stir in the herbs and the milk and knead lightly until firm enough to roll out on a floured surface.

4.   Roll dough to about ½-inch (1cm) thickness and, using small scone cutters, cut out 10 mini-scones.

5.   Place on a lightly-oiled baking tray and brush the top of the scones with milk.

6.   Bake in a pre-heated oven at 425°F/220°C (Gas Mark 7) for 10 minutes. Serve hot or cold.

Variations:
Grated mature Cheddar or other cheese with a strong flavour could be used in place of herbs. Use 2 oz (50g) to the above mixture.

   Similarly, paprika could be used in place of herbs for a hot, spicy scone.

Pinwheel Sandwiches

Serves 8; 145 calories per portion for yeast extract, or 180 calories for peanut butter (Illustrated opposite page 129)

1 small wholemeal loaf
2 oz (50g) soft vegetable margarine
Marmite, Barmene, Tastex **or similar yeast extract** *or* **crunchy peanut butter**

1.   Slice the risen top off the loaf to make a rectangular block. Cut off the crusts.

2.   Carefully cut slices along the length of the loaf. Place the long, rectangular slices on a flat surface and either spread with margarine and yeast extract or peanut butter without the margarine.

3.   To make the pinwheels roll the narrowest edge of the slice away from you, pressing the bread gently but firmly to make it stick.

4.   Cut slices from the rolled up bread and lay them flat on a serving dish to reveal their pinwheel effect.

Variations:
Other fillings like *Tartex* vegetable pâté, taramasalata or a soft herb cheese could also be used.

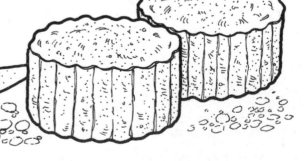

116

Taramasalata and Crudités

Serves 8; 75 calories per portion of taramasalata, 95 with crudités
(Illustrated opposite page 129)

4 oz (100g) smoked cod's roe
1 tablespoonful tomato purée
Juice of ½ lemon
2 oz (50g) unsalted butter, softened
2 oz (50g) wholemeal breadcrumbs
½ lemon, cut into wedges

Crudités:

2 sticks celery
4 carrots
½ bulb fennel
Red pepper
Cauliflower florets

1. Remove the outer skin from the cod's roe and mash roe in a mixing bowl.

2. Add the tomato purée and lemon juice and mix thoroughly.

3. Beat in the butter and breadcrumbs and place in a small bowl.

4. Arrange the crudités, cut to even lengths, around the bowl on a larger plate. Add some wedges of lemon from the remaining lemon half.

Olive Pâté Triangles

Serves 8; 114 calories per portion
(Illustrated opposite page 129)

Wholemeal bread
8 oz (225g) black olives
1 dessertspoonful olive oil
1 clove garlic, crushed

1. Cut eight slices from a large wholemeal loaf. Cut each slice into eight triangles.

2. Toast on both sides under the grill.

3. Remove the stones from the olives and place them, with the olive oil and garlic, in a liquidizer or blender. Blend to a smooth pâté.

4. Spread the hot toast with pâté and arrange on serving dish.

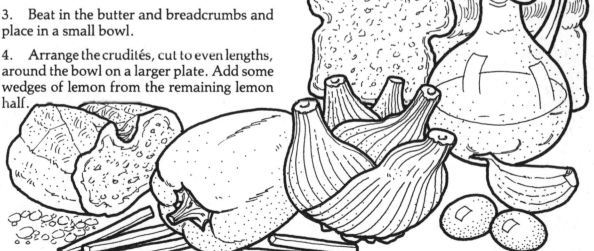

Cheese and Mustard Fingers
Makes about 12; 80 calories each
(Illustrated opposite page 129)

4 oz (100g) wholemeal flour

2 oz (50g) soft vegetable margarine

½ teaspoonful paprika

Skimmed milk to mix

2 teaspoonsful ready-made wholegrain mustard

2 oz (50g) finely grated mature English Cheddar cheese

Beaten free-range egg

1. Sieve the flour into a mixing bowl.

2. Add the margarine and rub in until the mixture resembles breadcrumbs in texture.

3. Stir in the paprika and mix to a soft dough with the milk.

4. Turn onto a lightly-floured work surface and roll the pastry out thinly into a long rectangle. Trim the edges.

5. Cut the rectangle in half lengthways and spread with the mustard. Sprinkle the cheese in a thin strip across the two widths, about 1-inch (2.5cm) in from the edge.

6. Fold the edge over the cheese and brush with beaten egg to make it stick. Cut off the two cheese fingers and repeat. Seal the two ends of the fingers by pressing together with a fork. This will also give a nice pattern.

7. Brush with beaten egg and bake in a pre-heated oven at 400°F/200°C (Gas Mark 6) for about 15 minutes until golden-brown.

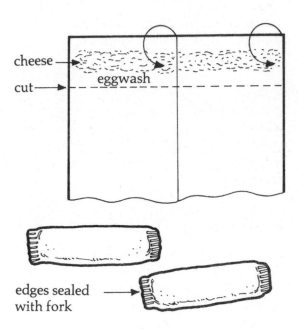

cheese

cut

eggwash

edges sealed with fork

11.

Coffee Mornings

Coffee mornings seem to be going out of fashion, probably because very few people have the time to attend them. However, they are still used for fund-raising events and often mothers get together, with their children, over a cup of coffee. Then there are home selling parties, such as _Tupperware_, jewellery, make-up and others that might require a small amount of food preparation, and these recipes would be useful for those occasions too.

If it is a coffee morning, remember that coffee does not have to be full of caffeine to be tasty. Excellent decaffeinated coffee beans can be bought and ground at home for use in percolator or filter. Ready-ground decaffeinated coffee is also available from several manufacturers and the _Rombout_-style coffee filters are also available in decaffeinated coffee.

Herbs teas or China tea with lemon can also be offered, and for the summer iced coffee is delicious.

The recipes in this section are slightly sweet because that is the type of food usually offered for 'elevensies' with coffee, but you could always use sandwiches or snacks from other chapters.

The recipe for scones does not use sugar, they are sweetened with the dried fruit and spices, and stuffed dried fruits like apricots and prunes make a good alternative to sticky sweets and biscuits. The biscuit recipe is low in sugar and seedcake is flavoured with spices. Gingerbread is traditionally a sticky texture but this version cuts down on a lot of the sugary ingredients.

Iced Coffee

Make a percolator full of decaffeinated coffee the night before the party. Allow to cool then carefully pour into a glass jug or similar container that will fit in the fridge. Be careful not to pour in any dregs. Cover the top of the jug and leave overnight in the fridge. Serve black straight from the fridge. It's delicious and very refreshing. Add skimmed milk for those who prefer white coffee.

Gingerbread

Serves 16; 155 calories per slice, unbuttered

4 oz (100g) soft vegetable margarine
4 oz (100g) molasses
2 tablespoonsful clear honey
4 oz (50g) Demerara sugar
12 oz (325g) wholemeal flour
2 level teaspoonsful ground ginger
1 level teaspoonful cinnamon
1 level teaspoonful baking powder
½ tablespoonful lemon juice
7½ fl oz (225ml) skimmed milk

1. Melt the margarine, molasses, honey and sugar together in a saucepan over a low heat.

2. Sieve the flour, ginger, cinnamon and baking powder together into a mixing bowl.

3. Pour melted mixture into flour and stir well.

4. Stir the lemon juice into the milk to sour it, then add to the batter.

5. Pour into slightly oiled 9-inch (23cm) cake

tin and bake in a pre-heated oven at 300°F/150°C (Gas Mark 2) for 1 hour until set and springy to the touch.

6. Allow to cool and cut into squares, which may be cut in half and buttered if preferred.

Sultana Scones

Makes 12; 100 calories each

8 oz (225g) wholemeal flour
1 teaspoonful mixed spice
1 teaspoonful baking powder
2 oz (50g) soft vegetable margarine
3 oz (75g) sultanas
½ tablespoonful lemon juice
¼ pint (150ml) skimmed milk

1. Sieve the flour, mixed spice and baking powder into a mixing bowl.

2. Add the margarine and rub in until the mixture resembles breadcrumbs in texture.

3. Stir in the sultanas.

4. Stir the lemon juice into the milk and add to the scone mixture.

5. Mix together to form a soft dough. Turn onto a lightly-floured work surface and knead lightly until the dough is able to be rolled out.

6. Roll out to a thickness of about ½-inch (1cm) and, using scone cutters, make 12 scones.

7. Place on a lightly-oiled baking tray and bake in a pre-heated oven 450°F/230°C (Gas Mark 8) for 10 to 12 minutes.

Old-Fashioned Seed Cake

Serves 10; 195 calories per slice

4 oz (100g) unsalted butter or soft vegetable margarine

5 fl oz (150ml) real ale

2 free-range eggs, well beaten

8 oz (225g) wholemeal flour

Grated nutmeg, plenty

Freshly pounded piece of mace

½ oz (12g) caraway seeds

Grated rind of ½ lemon

1. Place fat in a saucepan and soften over a low heat. Allow to cool.

2. Mix ales and eggs with the cooled butter.

3. Sieve flour and nutmeg into a mixing bowl and stir in the nutmeg and mace to taste. Add the caraway seeds and lemon rind.

4. Pour the liquid into the dry ingredients and mix thoroughly.

5. Spoon the mixture into a lightly-oiled loaf tin and bake at 350°F/180°C (Gas Mark 4) for 50 minutes or until an inserted skewer comes out clean.

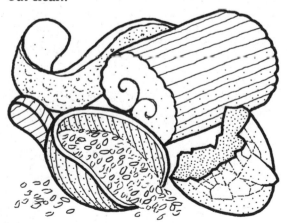

Stuffed Apricots

Makes 10; 52 calories each

10 large dried apricots

2 oz (50g) low-fat soft cheese

2 oz (50g) desiccated coconut

1. Wash the apricots and carefully remove the stones leaving the pocket in the fruit to be filled.

2. Mix together the cheese and the coconut and carefully spoon it into the apricots.

3. Place in *petit four* paper cases or arrange on a doily.

Stuffed Prunes

Makes 10; 54 calories each

10 large prunes, cooked

2 oz (50g) ground almonds

1 oz (25g) soft raw cane sugar

1 free-range egg white

Juice of ½ lemon

1. Carefully remove the prune stones leaving a pocket in the fruit to stuff.

2. Mix together the almonds, sugar, egg white and lemon juice and carefully spoon it into the prunes.

3. Place in *petit four* cases or arrange on a doily.

12.

The Coming of Age Party

A special birthday deserves a special meal and the menu recipes in this section cater for between 8-10 guests, to take in more members of the family (or friends) than would usually be catered for.

Catering for larger numbers also means catering for wider tastes. The main course is stuffed crêpes which can be prepared slightly in advance and heated through before serving. There is a vegetarian recipe or a chicken stuffing — either, or both, could be offered.

The meal starts with a classic Waldorf salad, which is popular and well known, so the less adventurous diners in the family need not feel put off. The crêpes can both be served with the Beansprout Salad which can be prepared a little in advance. However, if the family would prefer hot vegetables a selection of *saisonnière* (plateful of lightly cooked seasonal vegetables) would be ideal. Try to mix the types of vegetables, not all cabbage and cauliflower, and avoid potatoes because the crêpes provide enough carbohydrate and fibre.

There is an optional cheese course to the party. This can be either the delicious Cheese Ramekins or a cheeseboard, either of which can be served before or after the Raspberry Ring.

Choosing a wine for a larger party means taking into account more tastes. As there are two main courses it is an idea to offer either a white or a red, or even a rosé, and let the guests choose for themselves. However, because the non-vegetarian main course is based on chicken a white wine only could be served. If using white serve a good quality German wine (QmP) and also offer a dry white wine such as a French Muscadet or a white Burgundy, or a light Italian Frascati or Soave or a Portuguese Vinho Verde.

A red wine could be introduced for the cheese course (see Cheese and Wine chapter, pages 65-70) or it may be preferred to serve a sparkling wine throughout.

This section also includes a less formal menu for a hot buffet party for about 25 guests. This would be more suitable for a group of young people and could be served either formally seated around a table or as a buffet with chairs and sitting places available. A hot table would be useful for keeping the food warm, or a slow cooker could be used to keep the soup hot.

For a cold buffet use either the Christening, Bring a Bottle, Office Parties, Lunches or Wedding menus.

If this hot buffet is used for younger people it may be preferred to serve either fruit juice, mineral water or some beer or cider or a light white drinking wine.

Coming of Age Birthday Lunch

Waldorf Salad

Ratatouille Crêpes or
Chicken and Grape Crêpes
Beansprout Salad

Cheese Ramekins

Raspberry Ring

Waldorf Salad

Serves 8-10; 120 or 95 calories per portion

4 red skinned eating apples
Juice of a lemon
Head of celery
4 oz (100g) cottage cheese
2 tablespoonsful cold-pressed safflower mayonnaise
4 oz (100g) walnut pieces
Freshly ground black pepper
Lettuce

1. Wash the apples well. Quarter, core and thinly slice into a bowl containing the lemon juice. Toss regularly to ensure even coating of juice to prevent browning.

2. Wash and dice the celery and toss in the cottage cheese and mayonnaise.

3. Stir in the walnut pieces and pepper to taste.

4. Wash the lettuce and make a bed of lettuce either in individual serving dishes or a large serving dish. Place the celery and nut mixture in the centre and arrange the sliced apples around the outside in an overlapping arrangement.

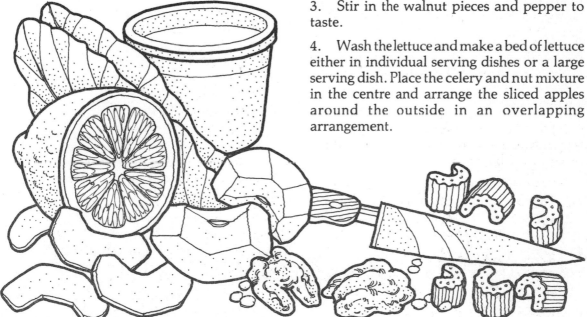

Crêpes

Makes 20 crêpes; 50 calories each

8 oz (225g) wholemeal flour
Pinch sea salt (optional)
2 free-range eggs
1 pint (600ml) skimmed milk

To make the batter:

1. Sieve the flour into a large bowl and add salt if using.

2. Beat the eggs together in a cup.

3. Make well in centre of flour and add eggs. Using a fork gradually stir in the flour nearest the centre, working towards the edge of the bowl. Add milk as the mixture becomes thicker.

4. Work slowly and thoroughly to avoid lumps developing in the mixture. If it does go lumpy whisk in a blender or liquidizer for a few moments.

5. When all the milk is added the liquid should have a consistency like single cream.

To make the crêpes:

1. Smear a heavy-based omelette or frying pan with a small amount of corn or soya oil and place over a high heat.

2. When the pan is hot add enough batter to coat the bottom of the pan by lifting and tipping the pan to evenly cover the base. A small jug is useful for this job.

3. Cook for a minute or two then turn the crêpe by slipping a palette knife beneath it and lifting. Cook the second side for a few seconds.

4. Remove the crêpe from the pan and place, folded in half, on a dish until ready to stuff.

Note: The crêpes should be very thin and have small pin-like holes in them if they are being cooked at the correct temperature. They can be frozen at this stage and defrosted later to be either warmed, or stuffed and heated through. To freeze, pack in polythene boxes with layers of silicone or greaseproof paper between the flat crêpes. This will keep the crêpes separate and allow either a few or several to be removed at once.

Ratatouille Crêpes

Filling for 20 crêpes. Serves 10;
105 calories per portion

2 aubergines
2 onions
2 cloves garlic
6 tablespoonsful olive oil
1 red pepper
1 green pepper
2 large courgettes
4 large ripe tomatoes
Freshly ground black pepper
2 oz (50g) Gruyère cheese

1. Wash the aubergines and slice into rounds. Plunge into boiling water and cook for 3 minutes. Remove and drain.

2. Peel and slice the onions and crush the peeled cloves of garlic. Add to the olive oil in a large, heavy-based saucepan which has a well-fitting lid.

3. Cook over a low heat for 5 minutes.

4. Add the drained aubergine to the pan and

continue to cook while washing and slicing the peppers, removing the seeds as you go. Add these to the pan and replace lid.

5. Wash and slice the courgettes into the pan. Stir the ratatouille well to ensure even cooking.

6. Wash the tomatoes and roughly chop before adding to the pan. Cover and cook over a low heat for a further 20 minutes.

7. Meanwhile set the oven to 350°F/180°C (Gas Mark 4) and lightly oil a large ovenproof dish.

8. Lay the prepared crêpes on a flat work surface and divide mixture equally between them. Roll up and place in the ovenproof dish.

9. When all the crêpes are piled in the dish, grate 2 oz (50g) Gruyère cheese over the top and place in the oven to heat through (about 10-15 minutes). Serve at once.

Chicken and Grape Crêpes

Filling for 20 crêpes. Serves 10;
180 calories per portion

3 lb (1.3 kilos) free-range chicken
1 lemon
Sprig of tarragon
1 tablespoonful wholemeal flour
1 tablespoonful unsalted butter or soft vegetable margarine
¼ pint (150ml) vegetable stock
1 teaspoonful ready-made stoneground mustard
6 oz (175g) green grapes, halved and de-seeded
2 oz (50g) flaked almonds

1. Wipe insides of chicken with a piece of kitchen towel and put the lemon and tarragon into the cavity. Place chicken in a pre-soaked chicken brick with a few tablespoonsful of water.

2. Cook at 375°F/190°C (Gas Mark 5) for 1 hour. The chicken is cooked when the juices released by inserting a skewer into the bird no longer run red.

3. Remove chicken from brick and when cool enough to handle shred flesh into a large bowl.

4. While the chicken is cooking, make a white sauce by stirring the flour and butter together in a heavy-based saucepan over a moderate heat to make a roux.

5. After cooking the roux for a couple of minutes by stirring continuously over the heat, gradually pour in the vegetable stock. (A bouillon cube will do for this purpose.) Stir all the time to prevent lumps forming.

6. Place sauce on one side until the chicken is cooked then thin the sauce with some of the juices released from the cooked chicken and add the mustard. The sauce should not be too thin.

7. Pour the sauce onto the shredded chicken in the bowl and stir in the grapes and almonds.

8. Place the prepared crêpes on a flat working surface and divide the chicken mixture between them. Either roll up or fold the edges over the mixture if there is too much to allow the crêpes to be rolled.

9. Place in an ovenproof dish and re-heat for 10-15 minutes at 350°F/180°C (Gas Mark 4).

Beansprout Salad

*Serves 8-10; 75 or 60 calories
per portion*

8 oz (225g) beansprouts
2 oranges
Bunch of watercress
2 oz (50g) cashew nuts
2 tablespoonsful sunflower oil
1 tablespoonful orange juice
Freshly ground black pepper

1.   Wash the beansprouts and drain.

2.   Peel and slice the oranges into rounds. Remove the pips from the orange slices.

3.   Wash the watercress and remove excess stalks and any yellowing leaves. Divide into small sprigs.

4.   Place the cashews under a grill and brown lightly on both sides.

5.   Place the sunflower oil, orange juice and pepper in a clean screwtop jar and shake vigorously.

6.   Toss the watercress in the dressing and place in the bottom of a serving dish. Stir in the beansprouts.

7.   Scatter nuts on top and arrange orange rings around the edge of the dish.

Cheese Ramekins

Serves 8-10; 210 or 170 calories per portion

1 wholemeal bread roll
¼ pint (150ml) skimmed milk
4 oz (100g) unsalted butter or soft vegetable margarine
4 oz (100g) grated Cheshire cheese
4 oz (100g) freshly grated Parmesan cheese
4 free-range eggs, separated
Freshly ground black pepper
½ teaspoonful freshly pounded mace

1.   Soak the roll in the milk, adding water if more is needed to cover.

2.   Place the butter in a saucepan and melt over a gentle heat, taking care not to brown the butter. Remove as soon as it has melted.

3.   Pre-heat the oven to 400°F/200°C (Gas Mark 6) and lightly oil or butter 8 or 10 ramekin dishes. Place them on a baking tray.

4.   Crumble the soaked bread into a mixing bowl.

5.   Pour the butter into the bread mixture and stir in the prepared cheeses. Beat in the egg yolks.

6.   Season with pepper and mace.

7.   Whisk the egg whites until stiff and holding peaks.

8.   Fold the egg whites into the cheese mixture and pour immediately into the ramekins which should be about two-thirds filled.

9.   Bake at once for 10-12 minutes until set and serve immediately.

Note: If using this as the cheese course for a party you can prepare up to stage 7 beforehand leaving the whites ready in the kitchen. Just return, whisk them and put the ramekins in the oven while the previous course is being finished.

Raspberry Ring

Serves 8-10; 105 or 85 calories per portion

4 tablespoonsful juice, from defrosting raspberries, or water
½ oz (12g) gelatine or agar agar
8 oz (225g) cottage cheese
¾ pint (450ml) thick-set natural yogurt
1 lb (450g) fresh or frozen raspberries
1 tablespoonful clear honey (optional)
8 oz (225g) fresh raspberries

1. Put the juice from defrosting raspberries, or water, into a cup and stir in the gelatine or agar agar. Stand the cup in a pan of boiling water and stir to dissolve the setting agent. Remove from heat and leave to cool.

2. Press the cottage cheese through a sieve into a large mixing bowl. Stir in the yogurt.

3. Press the raspberries through a sieve into a separate bowl. Discard the pips.

4. Stir the cooled gelatine mixture into the raspberry purée and carefully fold this into the cheese and yogurt mixture. Add the honey.

5. Pour into a wetted ring mould of 2 pint (1 litre) capacity and place in the fridge to set. Unmould before serving and fill the centre of the ring with fresh raspberries.

**Coming of Age Party
Hot Buffet**

*Fresh Tomato Soup
with
Hot Garlic Bread*

*Vegetable Goulash
with
Verde or Wholemeal Noodles*

Apricot Upside Down Cake

Tomato Soup

Serves 25; 30 calories per portion
(Illustrated opposite page 128)

1 lb (450g) onions
8 shallots
2 cloves garlic
8 oz (225g) carrots
6 lb (3 kilos) ripe tomatoes
2 oranges
6 pints (3.5 litres) water
Bouquet garni made with 2 bay leaves, 6 sprigs thyme and 8 parsley stalks tied in muslin
1 tablespoonful tomato purée

1. Peel and finely chop onions, shallots and garlic.

2. Place a little oil in large saucepan over a

moderate heat and add the onions, shallots and garlic. Cover and cook for 5 minutes.

3. Finely dice and scrub the carrots and add to the onion mixture.

4. Wash and chop the tomatoes roughly, reserving all the juice, and add to the pan. Cover and cook for another 10 minutes. Stir occasionally to ensure even cooking.

5. Squeeze the juice from the oranges and add to the pan. Peel the rind from one of the squeezed oranges and blanch for a minute in boiling water. Drain and add the rind to the pan.

6. Add the water, *bouquet garni* and tomato purée to the tomato soup and simmer with the lid off the pan for 20 minutes.

7. When cooked, remove *bouquet garni* and orange rind before either pressing through a sieve or liquidizing in small quantities.

8. Serve with hot garlic bread.

Hot Garlic Bread
Serves 25; 100 calories per portion

2 French sticks of wholemeal bread
4 oz (225g) unsalted butter
4 cloves garlic

1. Place the bread in a warm oven for 15 minutes to heat through.

2. Put the butter in a large mortar and pound until soft with a pestle.

3. Peel and crush the garlic cloves into the mortar using a garlic press. Stir well.

4. Remove bread from oven and split lengthways. Butter and wrap in white damask serviettes for serving.

Note: If your local baker does not make wholemeal French sticks make your own using the recipe on page 73 for wholemeal dough. Instead of using bread tins shape to a French stick shape, tapering the ends to points and make diagonal slashes on top of the loaf. Wash with beaten egg or milk before baking at the same temperature as the loaf. A French stick cooks quicker because it is not in a tin and the loaf is thinner — check after 20 minutes.

Opposite: Coming of Age Hot Buffet. Tomato Soup (page 127); Vegetable Goulash (page 129); Apricot Upside Down Cake (page 130); (*China:* Villeroy and Boch Maroir.)

Happy 21st
birthday

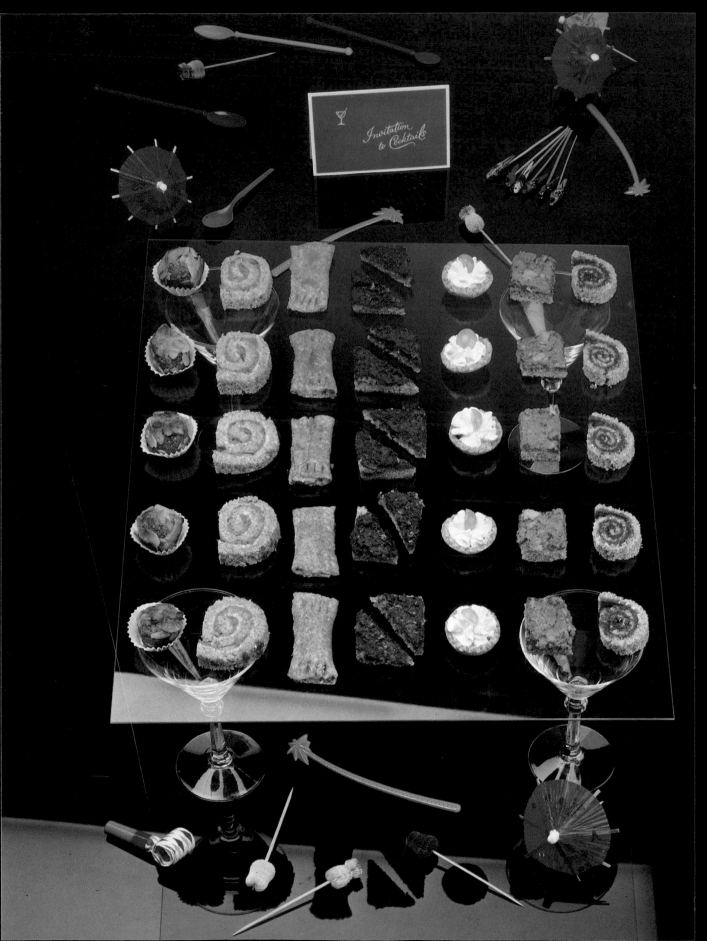

Vegetable Goulash with Noodles

Serves 25; 150 calories per portion
(Illustrated opposite page 128)

2 lb (900g) onions
2 cloves garlic
1 tablespoonful vegetable oil
1 lb (450g) carrots
1 white cabbage
2 lb (900g) ripe tomatoes
1 lb (450g) courgettes
5 pints (2.8 litres) water
3 tablespoonsful paprika
2 teaspoonsful caraway seeds
2 teaspoonsful marjoram
3 tablespoonsful unsalted butter or soft vegetable margarine
3 tablespoonsful wholemeal flour
5 oz (125g) tomato purée
1 pint (600ml) soured cream
3 lb (1.3 kilos) wholemeal or verde fettucine or tagliatelle

Opposite: These Cocktail Party snacks will suit any buffet party. *In rows, from left to right:* Tahini Tasties (page 115); Taramasalata Pinwheels (page 116); Cheese and Mustard Fingers (page 118); Black Olive Triangles (page 104); Savoury Tartlets (page 117); Taramasalata on Toast (page 117); Marmite Pinwheels (page 116).

1. Peel and dice the onions and garlic and place in a large saucepan with the oil. Cook, covered, over a low heat for 5 minutes stirring to ensure even cooking.

2. Scrub and slice the carrots into julienne strips. Add to the pan and continue cooking.

3. Shred the cabbage finely and add to the saucepan with the washed and roughly chopped tomatoes and sliced courgettes.

4. Stir well for a few minutes before adding the water, paprika, caraway seeds and marjoram. Cover and continue cooking for 5 minutes.

5. In a separate saucepan make a roux by stirring together the butter and flour. Cook over a low heat for a couple of minutes. Stir in the tomato purée.

6. Take a cupful of the liquid from the goulash pot and gradually add to the roux to make a thick sauce. Gradually add more liquid until the sauce is thin enough to pour into the main goulash pot without going lumpy. Stir the goulash while adding the sauce. Continue cooking, stirring from time to time, for another 15 minutes with the lid off the pan.

7. In another large saucepan bring plenty of water to the boil. As a general rule 1 lb (450g) of pasta should be boiled in 8 pints (4.5 kilos) of water. Unless catering-size pans are available this will mean cooking the pasta in several pans. Cook the pasta for 10-12 minutes until *al dente* (that is, cooked but still offering some resistance to the teeth when bitten).

8. Drain the pasta and place onto warmed serving dish(es).

9. Just before pouring the goulash onto the pasta stir in the soured cream. Serve at once.

Apricot Upside Down Cake

Makes three cakes, which serve 25;
250 calories per portion
(Illustrated opposite page 128)

8 oz (225g) unsalted butter

4 oz (100g) Barbados sugar

4 oz (100g) whole hazelnuts, lightly toasted

3 × 14 oz (400g) tins apricots halves in their own juice or in apple juice

1½ lb (675g) wholemeal flour

1 tablespoonful baking powder

6 oz (175g) unsalted butter or soft vegetable margarine

6 oz (175g) soft Muscovado sugar

3 free-range eggs

1½ tablespoonsful decaffeinated coffee dissolved in ½ pint (300ml) skimmed milk

1.   Beat together the butter and sugar and spread it over the bases of three 9-inch (23cm), lightly-oiled cake tins.

2.   Place the drained apricots in the base of the cake tins with the cut sides resting on the base of the tin. In the centre of each halved apricot place a hazelnut, and arrange the extra hazelnuts between the fruit halves.

3.   Pre-heat the oven to 350°F/180°C (Gas Mark 4).

4.   Sieve the flour and baking powder into a mixing bowl.

5.   Cream the butter and sugar together in another bowl until light and fluffy.

6.   Beat in the eggs one at a time adding a little of the flour if the mixture starts to curdle.

7.   When all the egg has been added fold in the flour and then mix in the milk and coffee mixture.

8.   Divide the mixture between the three prepared tins and bake for about 50 minutes until a skewer inserted into the cake comes out clean.

9.   Invert tin onto a serving dish. Offer with thick-set natural yogurt.

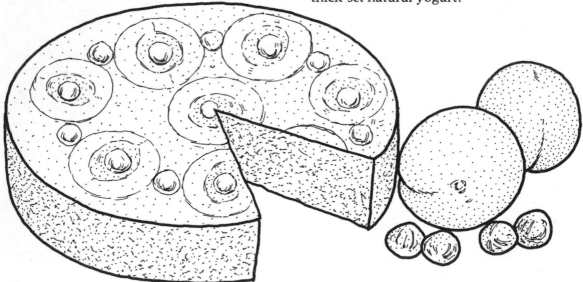

13.

Dinner Parties

Giving a dinner party for friends should always be something special. A smaller number of guests means you can often tackle more ambitious dishes and in a quieter atmosphere among friends a thoughtfully compiled menu can be better appreciated than in a noisy, larger group.

Attention to detail and presentation makes all the difference to a dinner party. Laying the table in an attractive way, with candles in the winter, or eating in the garden on a summer evening, is very special. Nice crockery and cutlery will make a lot of difference to the appearance of the food and pretty cloth or cloth/lace place settings on a wooden table are attractive.

If buying a dinner service it is best to stick to a very plain design, basically white or cream, because all food will be equally pleasant to look at when served from neutral colours. Brightly coloured crockery and highly elaborate patterns can often clash with food, and eye appeal is very important to its enjoyment.

A simply designed, classic cutlery service is a good investment. Silver plated cutlery is expensive, but extremely attractive. If choosing stainless steel there are some excellent designer sets, especially from Scandinavia, which will not date. Choose a cutlery with a good weight,

the better quality products are generally heavier, although high quality knives will often have a hollow handle, to prevent them tipping off the plate.

Glasses should match the style of crockery and cutlery. Generally modern designs go best together and traditional designs suit lead crystal or cut glass drinking glasses. A set of sherry or aperitif glasses and two sizes of wine glass, for white and red, are useful, together with champagne flutes or saucers if you drink a lot of sparkling wine. Lager glasses are not only useful for beer, they can also be used for long drinks such as fruit juices or non-spirit cocktails.

This chapter contains two dinner party menus for each season of the year. One in each section is cheaper and the other more expensive, but both use seasonal produce, and have three courses. Depending on the mood or occasion they can be served omitting one course, or you can swap the menus to suit your taste, but be careful not to end up with an unbalanced meal which, for instance, has eggs or pastry in more than one course. Make sure the courses contrast. The colours of the food can either contrast between courses or follow a similar theme through the meal.

There are wine suggestions with each menu,

but for more comprehensive notes from which to make your own choice see Cheese and Wine chapter.

When planning a dinner party make it easier for yourself by having one or more courses that can be either completely prepared or partially prepared in advance. Pastry can always be made and wrapped in clingfilm and kept in the fridge until just before use. Soups can be made in advance and reheated, and pâtés can be made and kept in the fridge to give plenty of time for preparing fresh fruits, salads and vegetables.

Mousses can be made earlier in the day and ices can be made whenever convenient a few days before the party; however, the fresher they are the better the aroma and taste.

It is particularly helpful to keep a record of which of your friends have been presented with which menu, especially if you eat with them on a regular, if spasmodic, basis. It may seem easy to remember, but menus and dates can easily be muddled if you don't make a note at the time. That's not to say they cannot be given the same

dishes again, but you will be able to keep them well apart and serve with different dessert or starter.

If serving soup as a starter it is not necessary to offer wine until the second course. Wholemeal bread with the soup is optional, as are croutons in the soup. A basket of freshly made or warmed rolls is often nice with winter starters. They can be cut in half for those with small appetites or, if preferred, sliced bread can be offered with butter in a separate dish; many people prefer unspread bread with soups, especially if they are watching their weight or the amount of fat they are eating.

Menus

Here are the seasonal menu suggestions with the dishes that can be made in advance asterisked. The more economical menu is in the left-hand column. There are also wine suggestions.

SPRING

I	II
Mushroom Soup*	Stuffed Artichokes
Braised Calves Liver	Seafood Timbale
Light Lemon Custards*	Gooseberry Crunch*
Wine: Beaujolais/ Frascati Superiore	Wine: Pouilly Fumé/ Gerwurztraminer

AUTUMN

I	II
Mackerel Pâté*	Avocado Salad
Bean Croquettes* Broccoli in Cashew Sauce	Cod Pie and Lemon Parsley Sauce*
Baked Spiced Pears	Apple and Orange Mousse*
Wine: Valpolicella/ Côtes-du-Rhône	Wine: Soave Classico/ English white wine

SUMMER

I	II
Stuffed Peppers*	Cold Cucumber Soup*
Lemon Guinea Fowl	Poached Turbot* Mushroom Puffs*
Cherry Clafoutis	Blackcurrant Sorbet*
Wine: Mosel/ Muscadet	Wine: Chablis/Sparkling white (méthode champenois)

WINTER

I	II
Jerusalem Artichoke Soup*	Asparagus Soup*
Turkey Croquettes	Pheasant with Apple and Red Wine
Dutch Apple Cake*	Almonds and Raisins*
Wine: Côte de Beaune/ Tavel Rose	Wine: Bordeaux/ Chianti Classico

SPRING I

Mushroom Soup

Serves 6; 95 calories per portion with cream

12 oz (325g) mushrooms
2 tablespoonful unsalted butter or soft vegetable margarine
2 tablespoonful wholemeal flour
1 pint (600ml) vegetable stock
½ teaspoonful freshly ground paprika
2½ fl oz (70ml) soured cream (optional)
Extra paprika for garnish

1.   Cook the mushrooms in boiling water for about 5 minutes.

2.   While the mushrooms are cooking stir the butter and flour together in a saucepan over a moderate heat to make a roux. Gradually add the stock to the roux, stirring all the time to prevent lumps forming.

3.   Drain the mushrooms, reserving the water which is added to the sauce. Season with the paprika.

4.   Put the mushrooms in a liquidizer and blend to a fine purée.

5.   Stir the mushroom purée into the sauce and bring back to the boil. Adjust seasoning. Just before serving swirl the cream on top of the soup, if using, and dust with another pinch of paprika. Serve immediately.

Braised Calves Liver

Serves 6; 280 calories per portion

2½ lb (2.2 kilos) calves liver, sliced thinly
3 bunches spring onions
1 oz (25g) unsalted butter
Freshly ground black pepper

1.   Wash the calves liver and leave to drain.

2.   Wash the spring onions and trim away any damaged parts. Cut into small pieces using kitchen scissors.

3.   Melt the butter in a heavy-based, tight-lidded saucepan that is large enough to accommodate all the liver.

4.   When the butter is melted, strew the bottom of the pan with a layer of the onions. Add a layer of liver and sprinkle with black pepper. Repeat layers until all the ingredients are used up.

5.   Replace the lid and leave to cook over a low heat in its own steam for about 15 minutes.

6.   Meanwhile, boil well-scrubbed new potatoes and French beans to serve with the liver.

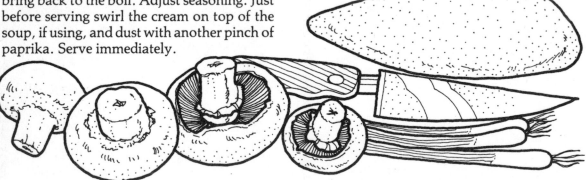

Light Lemon Custards

Serves 6; 135 calories per portion

1 pint (600ml) skimmed milk
1 lemon
4 free-range eggs
2 tablespoonsful vanilla fructose*

1.   Place the milk in a double saucepan with the grated rind of the lemon and stand over a low heat for about 15 minutes to infuse the flavour into the milk.

2.   Raise the heat and bring *almost* to boiling point then take it off the heat and pour into a basin containing the vanilla fructose. Stir to dissolve the sugar.

3.   Separate two of the eggs. Whisk the other two eggs well with the two separated egg yolks and when the milk has cooled pour it onto the eggs, stirring all the time.

4.   Return to the double boiler and stir over a low heat until the custard thickens. *Do not* allow the custard to boil or it will curdle and go lumpy. The custard will take about 10-15 minutes to thicken.

5.   Remove the thickened custard from the heat and allow to cool. To speed the cooling process pour into a cold basin and stand over ice or in a bowl of cold water.

6.   When the custard is cold, and just before serving, whisk the egg whites until stiff and fold into the custards.

7.   Pour into individual serving glasses or ramekins and decorate serving plates with laurel leaves.

*   To make vanilla flavoured fructose store the fructose with part of a vanilla pod in the jar in the same way as for vanilla sugar.

SPRING II

Stuffed Artichokes
Serves 6; 220 calories per portion

| 6 globe artichokes |
| 2 teaspoonsful salt |
| 4 oz (100g) wholemeal breadcrumbs |
| 2 oz (50g) anchovy fillets |
| 4 cloves garlic, crushed |
| 1 tablespoonful stoned black olives |
| 2 tablespoonsful freshly chopped parsley |
| Freshly ground black pepper |
| Juice of ½ lemon |
| ¼ pint (150ml) olive oil |
| 1 pint (600ml) water |

1. Soak the artichokes upside down in plenty of cold water with the two teaspoonsful of salt added. This is to remove all the dirt from between the leaves.

2. Remove them from the water and cut off the stalks and all the smaller outer leaves around the base of the artichokes.

3. Force open the centre of the artichoke and if the middle leaves come away easily remove them.

4. Place the breadcrumbs in a bowl.

5. Pound together the anchovies, garlic and olives and add to the breadcrumbs.

6. Stir the parsley and black pepper into the anchovy mixture. Add the lemon juice.

7. Place the artichokes in a large saucepan (or two smaller ones) and press small balls of the stuffing down between the leaves.

8. Drizzle the olive oil over the artichokes and add the water to the pan. Bring to the boil and cook with lids on the pans for about 45 minutes until leaves come away easily when plucked. Check towards end of cooking and top up water if necessary.

9. Serve at once, with an optional extra of vinaigrette dressing in which to dip leaves — for those not watching their weight!

Seafood Timbale
Serves 6; 350 calories per portion

| 8 oz (225g) brown rice |
| 1 clove garlic |
| 2 onions |
| 1 red pepper |
| Freshly ground black pepper |
| 1 tablespoonful corn or soya oil |
| 1 lb (450g) monkfish |
| 6 scallops |
| 12 oz (325g) squid |
| ¾ pint (450ml) vegetable stock |
| 1 tablespoonful wholemeal flour |
| 1 tablespoonful unsalted butter or soft vegetable margarine |
| 1 tablespoonful tomato purée |
| 2 oz (50g) peeled prawns |

1. Wash the brown rice and remove any grit and husks.

2. Peel and dice the garlic and onions. Wash and dice the red pepper.

3. Put the garlic, onion and red pepper in a large saucepan, in which the rice is to be cooked, with a tablespoonful of oil.

4.   Cover the pan and cook over a low heat for 5 minutes.

5.   Add the washed rice and stir well. Pour in boiling water and cover the pan. Cook over a medium heat. Check periodically to ensure the rice does not boil dry; it will need 2½-3 times its volume of water to cook.

6.   Cut the monkfish off the tail bone using a sharp knife and cube the fish.

7.   Wash the scallops and cut up if they are large. Wash the squid and slice it.

8.   Place the fish in the vegetable stock and bring to the boil. Simmer for 15 minutes.

9.   While the fish is cooking stir the butter and flour together in a separate pan to make a roux and cook for a couple of minutes.

10.   Stir in the tomato purée and add some of the liquid from the fish to thin the roux. When thin enough to pour, add it carefully, stirring all the time, to the fish mixture.

11.   Stir in the prawns and cook for a further 10 minutes.

12.   Pour the fish timbale onto a bed of cooked rice and serve immediately.

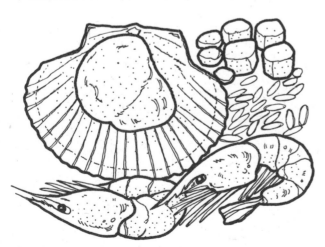

Cool Gooseberry Crunch
Serves 6; 335 calories per portion

8 oz (225g) digestive biscuits
2 oz (50g) unsalted butter or soft vegetable margarine
½ oz (12g) gelatine
4 tablespoonsful boiling water
1½ lb (675g) gooseberries
2 large heads elderflowers
½ pint (300ml) thick natural yogurt
1 tablespoonful clear honey (optional)

1.   Crush the biscuits to crumbs.

2.   Melt the fat in a saucepan over a low heat and stir into the biscuits. Press mixture into an 8-inch (20cm) flan dish or loose-bottomed flan tin. Place in the fridge to chill.

3.   Sprinkle the gelatine onto the water and stir to dissolve. Leave to cool.

4.   Wash the gooseberries and top and tail. Place them in a saucepan with just enough water to prevent them burning and add the elderflower heads. Cover and cook over a low heat until just cooked. Remove one-third of the gooseberries, keeping them whole. Remove the elderflower heads.

5.   Return rest to the heat and cook to a pulp. Remove from heat and purée.

6.   When cold, stir in the yogurt, gelatine and honey and place in the prepared flan dish. Return to the fridge.

7.   Top with the reserved whole gooseberries for decoration.

SUMMER I

Stuffed Peppers

Serves 6; 150 calories per person

3 large green peppers
6 oz (175g) wholemeal breadcrumbs
6 oz (175g) cooked brown rice
2 oz (50g) anchovy fillets
12 stoned black olives
2 tablespoonsful tahini
1 free-range egg
2 tablespoonsful freshly chopped parsley
3 small tomatoes

1.   Wash the green peppers and cut them in half vertically. Remove the seeds.

2.   Lightly oil a lidded ovenproof dish and arrange the halves in the dish.

3.   Mix together the breadcrumbs, rice, chopped anchovy fillets, and olives and bind together with the tahini and beaten egg. Stir in the parsley.

4.   Place one tomato half in the centre of each cut pepper, cut side uppermost, and spoon the stuffing in around the tomato.

5.   Pour ½ pint (300ml) boiling water around the peppers and bake in a pre-heated oven at 350°F/180°C (Gas Mark 4) for about 40 minutes.

Lemon Guinea Fowl

Serves 6; 400 calories per person

2 guinea fowl
4 slices wholemeal bread
2 onions, diced
4 sticks celery, diced
1 dessertspoonful corn oil
4 oz (100g) chopped hazelnuts
2 lemons, juice and grated rind
2 free-range eggs
Freshly ground black pepper

1.   Wipe the insides of the guinea fowl with kitchen paper.

2.   Crumb the bread and place in a mixing bowl.

3.   Sauté the celery and onion in the oil until transparent but not browned.

4.   Remove from the heat and stir into the breadcrumbs. Add the nuts and lemon rind and beat in enough egg to bind the stuffing.

5.   Stuff the birds and place them on a rack in a roasting tin.

6.   Baste birds with the lemon juice and pepper and roast for 1 hour in a pre-heated oven at 375°F/190°C (Gas Mark 5).

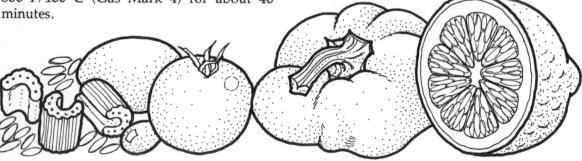

Cherry Clafoutis

Serves 6; 145 calories per portion

1½ lb (675g) fresh cherries
1 free-range egg
2 free-range egg yolks
3 rounded tablespoonsful wholemeal flour
¾ pint (450ml) skimmed milk
1 tablespoonful clear honey
1 tablespoonful Armagnac (optional)

1.   Wash the cherries. Cut them in half and pit them, place in base of a shallow lightly-buttered dish.

2.   Beat together the egg and egg yolks in a basin.

3.   Sieve the flour into the eggs and stir well.

4.   Gradually add the milk, beating between additions.

5.   Stir in the honey and brandy and pour over the cherries.

6.   Bake in a pre-heated oven at 425°F/220°C (Gas Mark 7) for 30 minutes until golden brown, risen and firm to the touch. Serve at once.

Note: This dessert is a deliciously French summer pudding. The cherries rise to the top in the pancake batter by the end of cooking and give a wonderful juicy flavour. Choose black, ripe juicy French cherries.

SUMMER II

Cold Cucumber Soup

Serves 6; 50 calories per portion

1 large cucumber, about 1¼ lb (550g)
4 oz (100g) low-fat soft white cheese
½ pint (300ml) natural yogurt
1 clove garlic, crushed
1 tablespoonful finely chopped mint
Freshly ground black pepper
½ pint (300ml) vegetable stock

1.   Wash the cucumber and roughly chop without peeling.

2.   Place the cheese and cucumber in a liquidizer and blend.

3.   Stir the cucumber purée into the yogurt and add the garlic, mint, pepper and stock.

4.   Chill thoroughly before pouring into individual serving bowls and garnishing each with a sprig of fresh mint.

Poached Turbot

Serves 6; 350 calories per portion

2¼ lb (1 kilo) turbot cut into 6 × 6 oz (175g) steaks (or fillets)

1½ pints (900ml) court bouillon

1.   Carefully cut turbot steaks and place them in a large ovenproof dish which has been lightly buttered.

2.   Pour over enough court bouillon to just cover the steaks and place in a pre-heated oven at 350°F/180°C (Gas Mark 4) to cook for 15-20 minutes.

Court Bouillon:

2 carrots

1 onion

2 sticks celery

2 shallots

1 bay leaf

3 parsley stalks

2 sprigs thyme

Juice of ½ a lemon

½ pint (300ml) dry white wine

1½ pints (900ml) water

6 black peppercorns

1.   Peel and finely chop carrots, onion, celery and shallots.

2.   Put all ingredients in a large saucepan. Cover and bring to the boil.

3.   Lower heat and simmer for 20 minutes. Remove from heat and allow to cool.

4.   Strain before use.

Mushroom Puffs

Serves 6; 150 calories per portion

Choux Pastry:

3 oz (75g) 85 per cent wholemeal flour

2 oz (50g) unsalted butter or soft vegetable margarine

¼ pint (150ml) water

2 free-range eggs, medium-sized

Egg or milk to glaze

1.   Sieve the wholemeal flour and pre-heat the oven to 425°F/220°C (Gas Mark 7).

2.   Melt the butter with the water in a saucepan over a moderate heat.

3.   Remove the melted butter and water from the heat and immediately add all the flour at once. Beat well until the mixture is soft and shiny and leaves the sides of the pan cleanly in one lump.

4.   Add one egg at a time to the slightly cooled pastry, beating well between additions.

5.   Spoon the pastry into a piping bag with a ½-inch (1cm) plain nozzle, and pipe 12 puffs onto a lightly-oiled baking tray.

6.   Lightly brush with beaten egg or milk and bake for 15-20 minutes until well risen and golden-brown. Insert a skewer into a ball to test if it is cooked. It will come out cleanly when cooked.

7.   If the pastry is not cooked, lower the heat to 350°F/180°C (Gas Mark 4) and cook for a further 5 or 10 minutes.

8.   Remove from heat and leave until cool enough to handle.

9.   Fill the balls with mushroom purée and

return to the oven in an ovenproof serving dish to heat through.

Mushroom Purée:

8 oz (225g) mushrooms
1 onion, diced
1 teaspoonful corn oil
½ oz (12g) wholemeal flour
½ oz (12g) unsalted butter

1.   Wash the mushrooms, chop and place in a saucepan with the onion and oil. Cover and cook for 15 minutes.

2.   Stir in the flour and butter to thicken the mixture. Remove from heat and blend to a smooth purée in a liquidizer.

3.   Place the purée in a piping bag as soon as it is cool enough to handle and, using an ⅛-inch (25mm) plain nozzle, fill the choux balls with the purée.

Blackcurrant Sorbet

Serves 6; 45 calories per portion

1 lb (450g) blackcurrants
2 tablespoonsful water
2 tablespoonsful fructose or clear honey
3 egg whites

1.   Strip the blackcurrants from their sprigs and wash them. Place in a saucepan with the water and cook over a gentle heat for about 5 minutes until the juices run from the fruit.

2.   Remove from the heat and press through a sieve, adding any juices from the pan to the purée.

3.   Stir the fructose or honey into the hot purée to dissolve. Then allow the purée to stand until completely cold.

4.   Turn the purée into an ice-cube or other shallow tray and put in the freezing compartment of the fridge or in the freezer and leave until nearly firm.

5.   Whisk the egg whites until they form stiff peaks, but are not dry.

6.   Place the freezing purée in a mixing bowl and break up with a fork. Carefully fold the egg whites into the blackcurrant purée and pour into a deeper container. Return to the freezer.

7.   To serve, scoop out balls of sorbet with an ice-cream scoop.

Note: If you have the time, sprigs of Iced Currants hung over the edge of the sorbet dish will give a very special effect. To ice the currants, whisk the whites of two eggs and mix with ¼ pint (150ml) of iced water. Place a fine layer of icing sugar on a work surface. First dip the bunches of currants into the egg white and water mixture, then into the icing sugar. Lay them on sheets of greaseproof paper for about 4 hours, when the sugar will crystallize the fruit.

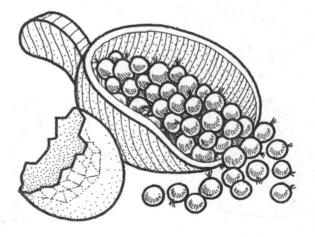

AUTUMN I

Smoked Mackerel Pâté
Serves 6; 400 calories per portion

2 smoked mackerel
Blade of mace
3 oz (75g) unsalted butter
8 oz (225g) curd cheese
Freshly ground black pepper
1 lemon
A few sprigs of parsley
12 thin slices wholemeal bread

1. Flake the fish from the bones and skin into a bowl.

2. Pound the mace in a pestle and mortar then add to the mackerel and work well in.

3. Beat the butter to soften it and work into the mackerel.

4. Sieve the curd cheese and add to the mackerel mixture.

5. Add a few twists of black pepper and a few drops of lemon juice and mix well.

6. Pile into a serving dish and garnish with freshly chopped parsley.

7. Toast the bread and cut each slice into quarters. Keep warm until ready to serve.

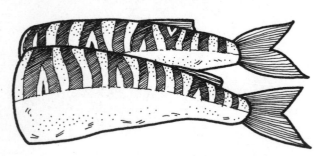

Bean Croquettes
Makes 6; 225 calories per portion

6 oz (175g) black-eye beans, soaked overnight
4 oz (100g) brown rice
4 oz (100g) buckwheat
1 onion, diced
2 cloves garlic, crushed
1 teaspoonful corn or soya oil
8 oz (225g) mushrooms
1 teaspoonful cayenne pepper
1 teaspoonful allspice, ground
Piece of mace, pounded
1 free-range egg, beaten
Toasted wholemeal breadcrumbs

1. Place the soaked beans in boiling water and cook for 30-40 minutes. Drain.

2. Cook the rice in twice its volume of water for about 30 minutes. Drain.

3. Cook the buckwheat in twice its volume of water for 15 minutes. Drain.

4. Place the onion and garlic with the oil in a large saucepan. Cover and cook over a moderate heat for 5 minutes.

5. Wash and roughly chop the mushrooms and add to the onion. Cover and cook for 10 minutes.

6. Place the beans and mushroom mixture in a liquidizer and blend to a purée.

7. Pour into a mixing bowl and stir in the rice, buckwheat and the spices.

8. Shape bean mixture into 6 large croquettes, dip in beaten egg and roll in breadcrumbs.

9. Lightly fry croquettes in corn or soya oil,

turning once or bake at 350°F/180°C (Gas Mark 4) for 20 minutes.

Broccoli in Cashew Sauce

Serves 6; 270 calories per portion

1 lb (450g) broccoli
2 oz (50g) cashew pieces
½ pint (300ml) yogurt
4 oz (100g) ground cashews
¼ pint (150ml) single cream
1 free-range egg yolk

1. Wash the broccoli and divide into florets. Steam over a small amount of boiling water for 7 to 10 minutes, until cooked but still firm.

2. Heat a cast iron skillet or frying pan without fat in it and toss in the cashew pieces. Brown on all sides and remove from the heat.

3. In a saucepan, gently heat the yogurt and ground cashew nuts, but do not boil.

4. Whisk the cream and the egg yolk together in a mixing bowl. Pour the warmed yogurt onto the cream and stir well.

5. Return to the pan and stir over a low heat until slightly thickened.

6. Drain the broccoli and arrange on a serving dish. Pour over the cashew sauce, and sprinkle with toasted nuts.

Baked Spiced Pears

Serves 6; 90 calories per portion

6 pears, choose Conference or a hard cooking variety
1 lemon
4 cloves
4 whole allspice
1 tablespoonful Demerara sugar
1 tablespoonful pear liqueur (optional)

1. Wash the pears and halve leaving the stalks on. Do not peel but carefully remove the core. If the pears are very large quarter them.

2. Place the pears in an ovenproof dish and almost cover with water.

3. Add the rind of the lemon and the juice of half the lemon.

4. Add the spices and sugar and liqueur and place in a slow oven 300°F/150°C (Gas Mark 1) for 1½ to 2 hours.

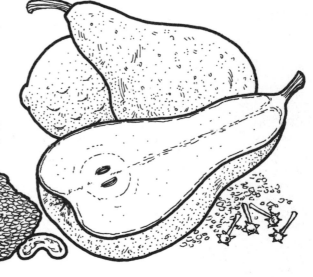

AUTUMN II

Avocado Salad

Serves 6; 240 calories per portion

2 grapefruits

5 fl oz (150ml) soured cream

Freshly ground black pepper

2 oz (50g) toasted cashew nuts

3 large ripe avocado pears

Paprika

1. Peel the grapefruit and remove the pith. Using a serrated knife, cut into segments and remove the skin from each segment. Cut the grapefruit over a bowl to catch the juice.

2. Put the segments in the bowl with the juice and stir in the cream, black pepper and nuts.

3. Halve the avocados and remove the stones. Pile the filling on top immediately and dust with paprika.

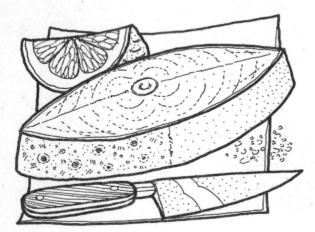

Cod Pie

Serves 6; 275 calories per portion

Pie Crust:

4 oz (100g) wholemeal flour

2 oz (50g) unsalted butter or soft vegetable margarine

Grated rind of ½ lemon

Water to mix

1. Sieve the flour into a bowl and add the fat. Rub in until the mixture resembles breadcrumbs in texture.

2. Stir in the lemon rind and add water to mix to a soft dough.

3. Turn out onto a lightly-floured board and roll to the circumference of your pie dish and set aside.

Filling:

2 lb (900g) cod

1 oz (25g) unsalted butter

½ teaspoonful grated nutmeg

1 blade of mace, pounded

½ pint (300ml) Court Bouillon (page 140)

Egg wash or milk to glaze

1. Remove the skin and bones from the cod and cut into small pieces. Place in the bottom of the lightly-buttered pie dish.

2. Dot the butter on top of the cod and sprinkle over the nutmeg and mace.

3. Pour over the stock.

4. Cover the top of the dish with a pie crust. Crimp the edges of the pastry around the pie and cut out small fishes to stick on for decoration. Egg wash the pie and bake in a pre-

heated oven at 350°F/180°C (Gas Mark 4) for 40 minutes.

Lemon and Parsley Sauce

340 calories in total

1 tablespoonful wholemeal flour
1 tablespoonful soft vegetable margarine
½ pint (300ml) skimmed milk
Grated rind of ½ lemon
3 tablespoonsful finely chopped fresh parsley
Freshly ground black pepper

1.   Stir the flour and fat together in a saucepan over a moderate heat to make a roux. Continue cooking for 2 minutes.

2.   Gradually stir in the milk to make a sauce. Stir continuously to prevent lumps forming in the sauce.

3.   When all the milk has been added stir in the lemon rind and the parsley and season to taste with pepper. Offer separately.

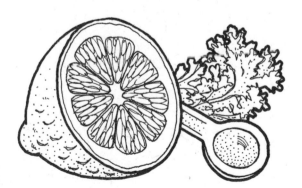

Apple and Orange Mousse

Serves 6; 45 calories per portion

1 lb (450g) apples
1 tablespoonful clear honey
½ oz (12g) gelatine
2 free-range eggs, separated
4 tablespoonsful orange juice
1 orange

1.   Wash the apples and core but do not peel. Slice into a saucepan with a few tablespoonsful of water and cook over a low heat until the apples are soft and mushy.

2.   Remove from heat and purée the apples in a liquidizer or press through a sieve. Stir in honey, if using.

3.   Sprinkle the gelatine into a cup containing the orange juice and place in a pan of boiling water. Stir to dissolve the gelatine, remove from heat and leave to cool.

4.   Carefully peel the orange removing all peel and pith and slice into thin rounds, removing pips from the slices.

5.   Line the sides of a pudding basin with the slices of orange. The basin should be lightly oiled, to help the oranges stick to the sides and also to facilitate unmoulding.

6.   When the apple purée has cooled, whisk the egg whites until stiff but not dry and fold into the purée.

7.   Immediately pour the purée into the basin and place in the fridge to set.

8.   Unmould before serving.

WINTER I

Jerusalem Artichoke Soup
Serves 6; 40 calories per portion

2 lb (900g) Jerusalem artichokes
Juice of 1 lemon
1 large onion, diced
Bunch parsley tied with string
1 pint (600ml) vegetable stock
¾ pint (450ml) skimmed milk
Freshly grated nutmeg
Freshly ground black pepper

1.   Peel the artichokes and place immediately in cold water acidulated with the juice of a lemon to prevent browning.

2.   Roughly chop artichokes and place in a large saucepan with onion and parsley. Ensure the parsley is tied by the stalks so it can be easily removed.

3.   Cover with stock, place lid on saucepan and simmer for 20-30 minutes until tender.

4.   Remove parsley and sieve or liquidize the artichokes and onion.

5.   Return to pan, stir in milk and season to taste. Reheat and serve.

Turkey Croquettes
Serves 6; 185 calories per portion

8 oz (225g) cold turkey
2 shallots, diced
1 teaspoonful corn or soya oil
2 carrots, grated
6 oz (175g) chestnuts, cooked and mashed with a little milk
2 free-range eggs, beaten
4 oz (100g) toasted wholemeal breadcrumbs

1.   Very finely dice the left-over turkey into a bowl.

2.   Place the shallots in the oil and cook over a low heat until they are transparent.

3.   Stir in the carrot and cook for a few more minutes.

4.   Remove from heat and stir into the turkey. Beat in the mashed chestnuts and half the egg; form into croquettes.

5.   Dip in the rest of the beaten egg and roll in the breadcrumbs before lightly frying or grilling for about 20 minutes, turning to prevent over-browning. Alternatively, bake in a moderate oven, 350°F/180°C (Gas Mark 4) for 20 minutes.

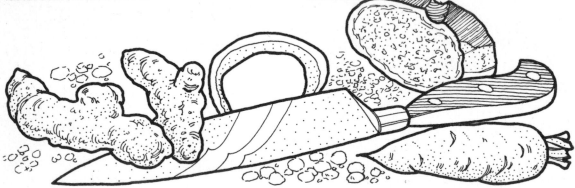

Dutch Apple Cake

Serves 6; 450 calories per portion

8 oz (225g) wholemeal flour
1 teaspoonful baking powder
5 oz (150g) unsalted butter or soft vegetable margarine
2 free-range eggs, separated
Juice of 1 lemon
2 lb (900g) cooking apples
18 dried apricots, soaked overnight
4 oz (100g) raisins
1 teaspoonful cinnamon
2 oz (50g) ground almonds

1. Make the pastry by sieving the flour and baking powder into a mixing bowl and rubbing in the fat until the mixture resembles breadcrumbs in consistency.

2. Lightly beat the egg yolks and add to the pastry with a tablespoonful of lemon juice. Bind to a soft dough.

3. Roll out on a lightly-floured board and line a lightly-oiled spring-sided cake tin (about 9-inches/23cm) with the pastry. Roll remainder ready for use as lid.

4. Wash and core the apples but do not peel. Slice into a saucepan with a few tablespoonsful of water and start cooking over a low heat for 5 minutes, stirring to ensure even cooking. Drain.

5. While the apples are cooking, boil the apricots in another pan for about 5 minutes. Drain.

6. Fill the prepared pastry case with layers of apple and apricots and raisins.

7. Mix together the spice and ground almonds and sprinkle on top.

8. Brush the edges of the pie with egg white and place the pastry lid in position. Glaze with egg white and bake in a pre-heated oven at 350°F/180°C (Gas Mark 4) for 45-50 minutes.

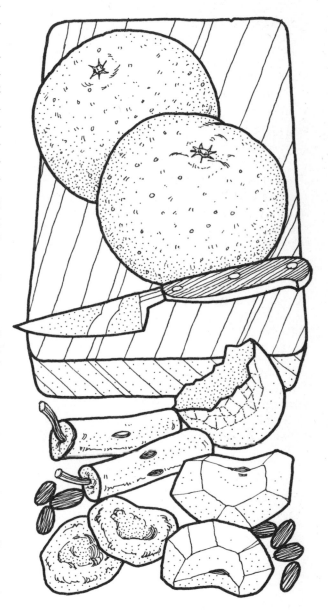

WINTER II

Asparagus Soup

Serves 6; 200 calories per portion

1 lb (450g) asparagus
1 pint (600ml) water
1 pint (600ml) good vegetable stock or chicken stock
2½ fl oz (75ml) dry white wine
6 thick slices of wholemeal French stick
Unsalted butter

1. Untie the bundle of asparagus and scrape the stalks, working away from the head, to remove any stringy parts. Place asparagus in a saucepan and cover with the water. Bring to the boil and cook for 12 minutes. (The asparagus does not need to be cooked in an asparagus kettle because the heads are removed and the rest left to cook.)

2. Remove from the heat, drain (reserving the liquid) and cut the heads from the stalks. Reserve the heads and return stalks and water to the pan to cook for another 10 minutes.

3. Strain the asparagus again and add the cooking water to the stock. (Reserve the stalks for use in a salad or quiche.) Return to the heat and add the wine. Allow to boil and, just before serving, drop in the reserved heads to re-heat.

4. Meanwhile toast the slices of bread on both sides. Butter one side and place in the bottom of individual serving bowls. Pour the soup over the bread and serve immediately.

Pheasant with Apple and Red Wine

Serves 6; 370 calories per portion

2 pheasants
1 bay leaf
1 carrot, diced
1 onion, quartered
2 oz (50g) unsalted butter
3 onions, diced
3 cooking apples
1 leek
4 oz (100g) wholemeal breadcrumbs
6 oz (175g) mushrooms
½ pint (300ml) red wine

1. Joint the pheasants into leg and breast joints.

2. Place the carcases in a large saucepan with the bay leaf, carrot and onion. Cover with water and bring to the boil. Lower the heat and simmer for 30 minutes.

3. Brown the pheasant joints using half the butter.

4. Sauté the onions in a separate pan.

5. Wash the apples and core but do not peel. Grate into the onions and stir well. Cover and continue to cook on a very low heat.

6. Thoroughly wash the leek and slice into the apple and onion mixture. Add breadcrumbs.

7. Lightly butter the sides and base of a large, heavy-based cast iron saucepan or casserole and place the apple mixture in the base. Lay the pheasant joints on top with the whole mushrooms. Pour over the wine and cover with well-fitting lid that will keep the steam in the pan.

8.   Cook on top of the stove, or in the oven at 375°F/190°C (Gas Mark 5), for 30 minutes.

9.   Strain the pheasant carcase stock and when the joints have been cooking for 30 minutes pour in ½ pint (300ml) of stock. Bring to boil and allow to reduce with the lid off for 20 minutes. The vegetables will have dissolved to a delicious thick sauce to spoon over the pheasant.

Almonds and Raisins

When fresh fruit is expensive and out of season during winter a dish of nuts and raisins makes a seasonal dessert. Choose large, stoned muscatel raisins. Arrange a mixture of shelled almonds and raisins on a glass dish or, if using almonds in their shells, place the raisins on a separate dish.

Filberts could be offered in place of almonds. These can be piled high on a glass cake stand for a good effect. Alternatively new season walnuts could be used. Dried figs and dates can be prettily arranged on doilys or glass dishes if preferred to raisins.

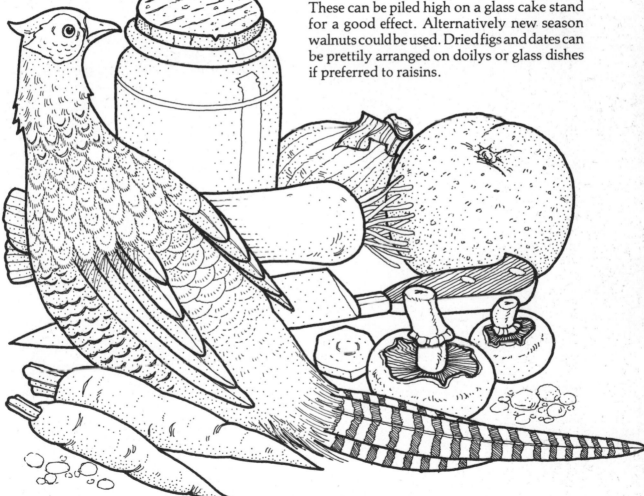

14.

Impromptu Parties

There is always the occasion when a brief gathering of friends, or an outing somewhere, turns into so much fun that you say 'Let's continue the party back at my place!' and then realize you have a houseful of hungry guests and no food to give them. And, depending on your lifestyle, it's more or less likely that you will be taken by surprise by unexpected guests. Since the urge for celebration always seems to strike when the shops are shut, a small but judicious stock cupboard of items will provide quick, simple and tasty dishes to satisfy hungry revellers.

Having standby meals in the house is also useful for those occasions when you are not able to get out from work during the lunch hour to do some shopping, or perhaps when the opportunity to do something more exciting comes up you can say yes to it knowing there is a meal at home either for yourself or others you might have to cater for.

Even the best regulated households can be taken by surprise. After saying goodbye to weekend guests (having been eaten out of house and home) we have seen them return a little while later when their car has broken down. Although it's nice to see them again it's surprising how soon visitors can become peckish once more.

If you have children in the house, the recipes in this section will be useful for those occasions when they forgot to tell you they had invited their friends home to tea.

Living in the country it is not always possible to pop out for something when people do drop in. In some cases shopping trips may be limited to once a week, or even less frequent, so store cupboard standbys are a must.

The following list of foods is probably in most cook's fridges or cupboards, but it is a good idea to make them regular buys:

- tinned tomatoes
- wholemeal pasta
- brown rice
- tinned tuna
- tinned sweetcorn kernels
- tinned, cooked beans (kidney, butter, borlotti, chick peas)
- tomato purée
- shoyu/soya sauce
- Parmesan cheese
- dried beans (haricot, butter, kidney)
- onions
- nuts
- free-range eggs
- garlic
- lemons
- oranges
- wholemeal bread

If you are not in a hurry for the meal then dried beans and other pulses may be used instead of canned, ready-cooked products. Cartons of juice may be used if fresh fruit is not available. Fresh is always best, but for store cupboard meals products such as fruit tinned in its own juice or apple juice is useful.

Unexpected guests may bring an appeasing bottle of wine with them, but it's worth having a bottle or two in your 'cellar' for the impromptu party.

Bean and Pasta Salad

Serves 4; 340 calories per portion

6 oz (175g) wholemeal macaroni or pasta shapes

14 oz (400g) tin cooked chick peas

7 oz (200g) tin broad beans

3 tablespoonsful olive oil

Juice of 1 orange

Freshly ground black pepper

Freshly chopped parsley or chives

1.   Boil the pasta in plenty of water for about 12 minutes until *al dente* (that is, cooked but still offering some resistance to the teeth). Drain and run under cold water.

2.   Drain the beans and mix together in serving bowl with the pasta.

3.   Place the oil, orange juice, pepper and herbs in a clean screwtop jar and shake vigorously. Pour over the salad and toss.

Note: If you are not in a hurry for the meal there is no reason why dried beans cannot be used in place of tinned beans. If you have fresh broad beans available they are even better, but these

meals are constructed from your store cupboard standbys. Cartonned orange juice may be used if you have no fresh oranges.

Tuna Salad

Serves 4; 270 calories per portion

4 oz (100g) brown rice

7 oz (200g) tinned tuna

5 oz (150g) tinned sweetcorn kernels

2 free-range hard-boiled eggs

Freshly chopped parsley, if available

1.   Wash the rice in a sieve and then cook in plenty of boiling water for about 25-30 minutes. Top up from time to time with more boiling water, if necessary. Drain, if all the water has not been absorbed.

2.   Drain the oil or brine from the tuna and flake into a bowl with the rice, which can be used either hot or cold.

3.   Drain the sweetcorn kernels and add to the fish. Mix thoroughly.

4.   Stir in the parsley, if using, and mix thoroughly. Place in serving dish.

5.   Shell the eggs and slice thinly. Arrange around the top of the dish.

Tomato Pasta

Serves 4; 160 calories per portion

6 oz (175g) wholemeal spaghetti or other pasta

2 onions, diced

1 clove garlic, crushed

1 red pepper, diced (if you have no fresh pepper use 2 dried chillies for flavour)

1 tablespoonful tomato purée

14 oz (400g) tin tomatoes

½ pint (300ml) water

1 teaspoonful marjoram, dried

1 teaspoonful dried basil

1.   Boil the spaghetti in plenty of water for about 12 minutes until *al dente* (that is, cooked but still offering some resistance to the teeth when bitten). Drain.

2.   Meanwhile place the onions in a saucepan with a teaspoonful of oil and add garlic and pepper or chillies. Cover and sweat for 5 minutes.

3.   Add tomato purée and tinned tomatoes, water and herbs. Cover and cook for further 10 minutes.

4.   Put the spaghetti onto plates and top with sauce.

5.   Offer Parmesan cheese separately.

Instant Casserole

Serves 4; 190 calories per portion

1 onion, diced

2 cloves garlic, crushed

14 oz (400g) tinned tomatoes

14 oz (400g) tinned butter beans

1 dessertspoonful tomato purée

1 tablespoonful mixed dried parsley, basil and marjoram

Freshly ground black pepper

4 thick slices wholemeal bread, 1½-inches (4cm) thick

1.   Place the onion and garlic in a saucepan with a smear of vegetable oil and cover. Sweat for 5 minutes.

2.   Stir in the tomatoes, beans, purée, herbs and pepper and cover. Continue to cook over a low heat for 15 minutes.

3.   Toast both sides of the bread and place each slice on a serving plate. Pour over the tomatoes and beans, serve at once while hot.

Cashew Risotto

Serves 4; 500 calories per portion

8 oz (225g) brown rice
1 onion, diced
1 red or green pepper, diced
12 oz (325g) sweet corn kernels
6 oz (175g) toasted cashew nuts
3 oz (75g) raisins or sultanas

1.   Wash the rice in a sieve and boil in plenty of water for about 25 minutes or until cooked. Top up with boiling water as necessary. Drain if all the water has not been absorbed.

2.   Stir the rest of the ingredients into the rice and serve, either warm or when the rice is cold.

Sweet and Sour Stir-Fry

Serves 4; 85 calories per portion

If your guests are lucky enough to find you have a fridge (or better still a garden) full of fresh vegetables, a stir-fry meal can be easily cooked and quickly produced. It is also, of course, full of vitamins and preferable to the store cupboard canned foods. Add some nuts for protein.

Sweet and sour sauce (page 180)
5 oz (150g) tinned bamboo shoots
2 leeks, washed and sliced
2 onions, diced
1 green pepper
1 clove garlic, crushed (optional)
8 oz (225g) beansprouts

1.   Make a quantity of sweet and sour sauce and place in a wok or large frying pan. Heat.

2.   Add the vegetables to the hot sauce in order of hardness, i.e. the bamboo shoots first and the beansprouts last. Stir-fry in the sauce over a high heat until the vegetables are just-cooked but still crunchy. Add a little more boiling water to the sauce during cooking, if necessary.

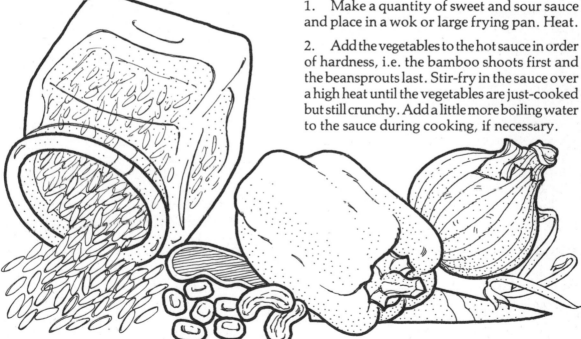

15.

Lunch Parties

Sunday is usually the day when family and friends are invited to lunch. Usually the meal centres around a roast joint or some other form of roast meat with vegetables and a sticky, sweet pud. Here are five menus that suggest more adventurous meals you might like to use for a Sunday lunch. Some are vegetarian and some include fish.

For the guests who would like something nearer to the traditional lunch the Pâté en Croûte menu is most suitable. The menu based on stuffed vegetables makes an excellent buffet lunch and can be served either hot, cold or warm without spoiling. It also uses salmon as a starter which is something most guests will appreciate as a treat. This traditional Scandinavian way of serving fish is easy to prepare in larger quantities, so it is ideal for a buffet and its cost is offset by the relative cheapness of the stuffed vegetables.

Each of the lunches has a course that features a slightly unusual food and this makes it more exciting for guests. Mixing the relatively unfamiliar (e.g. globe artichokes) with the familiar (e.g. baked apples) is a good way of introducing new foods to people. As is the Pâté en Croûte in a menu with the fruit flan.

The menus include only one roast lunch because a wholefood diet uses meat as an accompaniment to vegetables, and this variation on the Sunday roast theme emphasizes a large selection of vegetables and uses a dried fruit stuffing to give the meat some fibre; it's also delicious. If you are using meat for everyday or entertaining purposes then choose lamb, free-range poultry or game.

Lamb is slightly fattier than other meats but because it is killed young it is less likely to contain drug or growth-promoting hormone residues. White meat like poultry is less fatty, and a free-range bird should be tastier and free from drug residues. Similarly, game is a healthier meat and it is also lower in fat than other meats.

There is no need to add fat during the cooking of meat. It can be seared in a hot pan, without fat in the case of beef, and then roasted, covered for $2/3$ of the time and uncovered for the remainder at a high temperature. Lamb can be stuck with herbs like rosemary, or with garlic cloves, and roasted without added fat. Stand meats to be roasted on a rack inside a roasting pan and the fat will drain away. If it is drying out baste a little with its own fat, or better still cover it. Allow the meat to 'rest' for a few minutes before carving and serve with its own juices. A roasting brick can also be used. This is soaked in water for about 20 minutes before use and is especially good for poultry and game. The bird sits in the brick and cooks in its own juices, especially delicious if the body cavity is filled with your favourite herbs and with lemon, or even orange, quarters.

Chicken can be boned and skinned and cooked in light sauces made from puréed fresh vegetables, or baked wrapped in spinach leaves, or sautéed in a vegetable stock.

There is one traditional-style Sunday lunch in the following menu suggestions. Two menus are vegetarian and a third has a vegetarian main course with a fish starter which may be swapped to make a completely vegetarian lunch. The fifth lunch is a buffet which uses salmon in an unusual way with stuffed vegetables.

All the menus are suited to light white wines or, in the case of the lamb, perhaps a rosé wine from Provence. For other wine suggestions see the Cheese and Wine chapter (pages 58-75). Whatever you choose make it light, so that your guests do not feel like sleeping all afternoon.

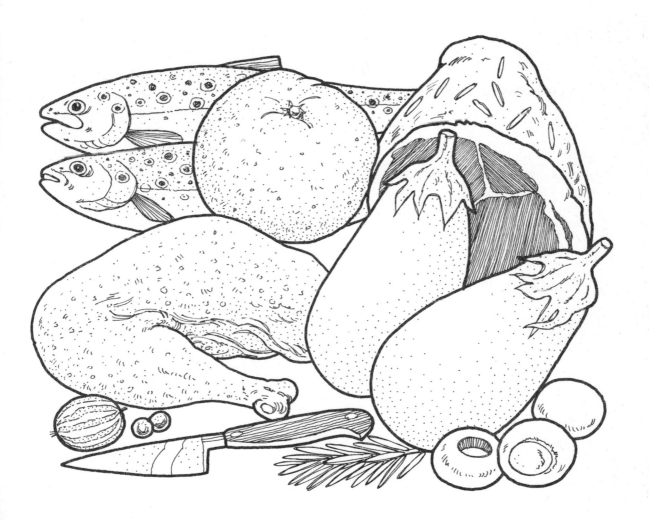

Lunch Menus

MENU I

*Fresh Mackerel and
Gooseberry Mousse*

Mushroom Moussaka and Green Salad

Fresh Fruit

Fresh Mackerel and Gooseberry Mousse

Serves 6; 275 calories per portion

8 oz (225g) fresh gooseberries

4 tablespoonful boiling water

½ oz (12g) gelatine or agar agar

1 dessertspoonful clear honey

2 lb (900g) fresh mackerel, to weigh 1½ lb (675g) when gutted and filleted

Freshly ground black pepper

Blade of mace, freshly ground

Juice of 1 lemon and rind of ½

2 free-range egg whites

1. Top and tail the gooseberries and wash. Place in a saucepan with 6 tablespoonsful of water. Cover and cook over a low heat for 15 minutes or until soft enough to purée. Drain, reserving liquid.

2. Dissolve the gelatine in the boiling water and leave to cool.

3. Purée the cooked gooseberries in a food processor and add the honey.

4. Stir the gelatine into the gooseberry mixture and place in the bottom of a wetted fish mould or small soufflé dish with a 1½ pint (900ml) capacity. Place in the fridge to set.

5. Wash the mackerel and arrange in the bottom of a grill pan.

6. Season mackerel with freshly ground black pepper and sprinkle with 1 teaspoonful of freshly ground mace.

7. Pour the juice of half the lemon over the fish and grill under a high heat for 10 minutes.

8. Remove the fish from the skin and bones and place in a liquidizer. Blend until smooth with the juice from the rest of the lemon, the grated rind from half the lemon and more black pepper to taste. If mixture is too dry add the reserved gooseberry liquid.

9. Whisk the egg whites until stiff. Fold a couple of tablespoonsful into the mackerel mixture to lighten, then quickly fold in the rest using a metal spoon.

10. Spoon on top of the set gooseberry mixture and smooth surface. Leave in the fridge for a couple of hours before unmoulding and serving.

Mushroom Moussaka
Serves 6; 145 calories per portion

3 aubergines, sliced ½-inch (1.5cm) thick
1½ lb (675g) mushrooms, sliced
½ oz (12g) unsalted butter or soft vegetable margarine
1 onion, diced
1 clove garlic, crushed
14 oz (400g) tin tomatoes
1 tablespoonful tomato purée
Pinch basil
Pinch oregano
1 oz (25g) unsalted butter or soft vegetable margarine
1 oz (25g) wholemeal flour
½ pint (300ml) skimmed milk
1 teaspoonful ready-made stoneground mustard
Freshly ground black pepper
3 oz (75g) Parmesan cheese
2 free-range eggs, separated

1.   Heat the oven to 350°F/180°C (Gas Mark 4) and bake the aubergine slices for 30 minutes.

2.   Sauté the mushrooms, onion and garlic in the butter in a large saucepan for about 10 minutes, stirring to ensure even cooking.

3.   Add the tomatoes, purée and herbs and continue cooking over a low heat, uncovered.

4.   Put the butter and flour in a saucepan and make a roux. Cook, stirring, for 2 minutes.

5.   Gradually stir in the milk to make a thick sauce. Season with mustard and pepper.

6.   Remove from heat and stir in the cheese and egg yolks.

7.   Remove the aubergines from the oven and spread a layer in base of a lightly-oiled ovenproof dish. Pour on the mushroom sauce. Top with the rest of the aubergines.

8.   Whisk the egg whites until stiff. Using a metal spoon fold 2 tablespoonsful into the cheese sauce to lighten, then fold in the rest.

9.   Pour over the aubergines and return to the oven for 35-40 minutes.

Fresh Fruit

Offer a selection of fresh fruits that are different from the perennial apples, pears, bananas and pineapples. As the menu contains gooseberries it will be seasonal from late May to August. During that time there are soft fruits such as strawberries, raspberries and cherries available, as well as other summer fruits like peaches, nectarines, apricots and plums. If the weather is cold try halving some of the stone fruits and poaching lightly in a little white wine mixed half and half with water. Otherwise offer fruit whole or slice the fruit and place some on each dessert plate so everyone has a taste of each of the fruits. Arrange them attractively and this can be one of the most enjoyable desserts.

MENU II

*Gravad Lax and Mustard
Sauce or Dill Mayonnaise*

*Stuffed Potatoes, Peppers,
and Aubergines*

Apricot Profiteroles

Gravad Lax
(Dill-cured Salmon)

*Serves 10; 185 calories per portion
(Illustrated opposite page 160)*

2 lb (900g) middle cut or tail piece of salmon
2 oz (50g) sea salt
2 oz (50g) Demerara sugar
About 40 black peppercorns
Bunch of fresh dill or 2 level tablespoonsful dried dill, chopped

1.   Either ask the fishmonger to prepare the salmon in two triangular fillets or do it yourself by slicing along the backbone, removing the backbone and smaller bones.

2.   Mix together the other ingredients to form a pickling marinade.

3.   Lay one piece of fish on a dish, skin side down and cover with the pickling mixture. Place the second piece of fish on top with the thick part lying on top of the thin part of the bottom half.

4.   Place a weighted plate or chopping board on top and place in the fridge for a minimum of 24 hours and a maximum of 5 days, turning once a day.

5.   To serve, discard the peppercorns and dill and slice thinly. Serve with dill mayonnaise or mustard sauce or simply with lemon wedges and wholemeal or rye bread.

Note: Salmon is expensive but this way of serving makes it go a long way. It is also refreshingly different from the more usual party dish of smoked salmon. To give a Scandinavian authenticity try to buy one of the attractively wrapped large 'wheels' of rye crispbread. They are about the size of a small tray with a hole in the middle so that they can be hung up in old-fashioned Scandinavian kitchens on a piece of string near the kitchen range. There it is easy to break off a piece to eat with a thin slice of cheese as a snack, or to give visitors or neighbours as a token of hospitality.

Mustard Sauce

About 800 calories
(Illustrated opposite page 160)

2 tablespoonsful ready-made wholegrain mustard

½ tablespoonful light Muscovado sugar

1 free-range egg yolk

6 tablespoonsful olive oil

1½ tablespoonsful white wine or cider vinegar

1 tablespoonful freshly chopped dill

Freshly ground black pepper (optional)

1.   Beat the mustard, sugar and egg yolk together until smooth.

2.   Gradually add the oil and vinegar, mixing thoroughly between additions. Season with dill and freshly ground black pepper if desired.

Dill Mayonnaise

About 750 calories

1 tablespoonful ready-made wholegrain mustard

1 tablespoonful ready-made smooth mustard

½ tablespoonful light Muscovado sugar

6 tablespoonsful olive oil

1½ tablespoonsful white wine or cider vinegar

Freshly ground black pepper

4 tablespoonsful chopped dill

1.   Mix together the mustards and sugar to form a paste.

2.   Gradually stir in the oil and vinegar, mixing well after each addition.

3.   Season to taste.

4.   Stir in the dill.

Stuffed Potatoes

Serves 6; 60 calories per portion
(Illustrated opposite page 160)

6 even-sized flattish potatoes

4 shallots, diced

1 dessertspoonful olive oil

8 oz (225g) mushrooms, finely chopped

½ stock cube

½ pint (300ml) water

1 teaspoonful ready-made stoneground mustard

Freshly ground black pepper

1 tablespoonful freshly chopped parsley

1.   Scrub the potatoes and cut out the central flesh very carefully using a sharp knife and leaving a ½-inch (1cm) thick shell.

2.   Cube the flesh taken from the centre of the potatoes.

3.   Place the shells in a lightly-oiled ovenproof dish and pre-heat the oven to 375°F/190°C (Gas Mark 5).

4.   Place the shallots in the oil and cook gently for 5 minutes.

5.   Add the mushrooms, potato cubes, stock cube, water and seasoning and cook for 5 minutes, not allowing the potato to disintegrate. Add mustard and pepper.

6.   Stir in the parsley and spoon into the prepared shells. Pour any excess liquid, making it up to about 1 pint (600ml), around the potatoes before covering and cooking for 30 minutes. Baste from time to time.

Stuffed Green Peppers

Serves 6; 250 calories per portion
(Illustrated opposite)

6 green peppers, small and even-sized
4 oz (100g) brown rice
2 oz (50g) pine kernels
2 oz (50g) flaked almonds
2 oz (50g) raisins or sultanas
½ 'no-added-salt' stock cube
½ pint (300ml) water
1 teaspoonful ground allspice
Freshly ground black pepper
Grated rind ½ lemon
¼ pint (150ml) boiling water

1.   Slice the tops off the peppers, about ½-inch (1cm) from top, reserve. De-seed and place in a lightly-oiled ovenproof dish. Pre-heat oven to 375°F/190°C (Gas Mark 5).

2.   Wash the rice and put it in a saucepan with three times its volume of boiling water and cook for 20 minutes.

3.   Drain the rice and rinse to remove any starchiness. Return to the saucepan and add the pine kernels, almonds, raisins, stock cube, water, allspice, pepper and lemon rind. Stir well over a moderate heat.

4.   Allow to cook for a further 10 minutes until the raisins have become plump and the liquid reduced.

5.   Spoon the rice mixture into the prepared peppers; replace their lids.

6.   Pour the water around the base of the peppers. Cover the dish with a lid, greaseproof paper or foil and cook in the oven for 40 minutes.

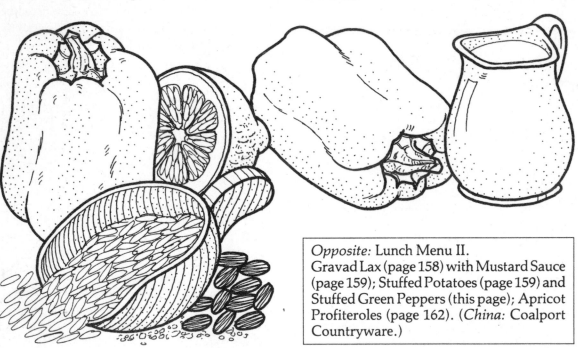

Opposite: Lunch Menu II.
Gravad Lax (page 158) with Mustard Sauce (page 159); Stuffed Potatoes (page 159) and Stuffed Green Peppers (this page); Apricot Profiteroles (page 162). (*China:* Coalport Countryware.)

Stuffed Aubergines

Serves 6; 240 calories per portion

3 large aubergines
2 large onions, diced
2 cloves garlic, crushed
1 dessertspoonful olive oil
14 oz (400g) tin tomatoes
8 oz (225g) cashew pieces
Freshly ground black pepper
¼ pint (150ml) water
1 tablespoonful tomato purée

1.   Halve the aubergines and, using a grape-fruit knife, carefully cut out the central flesh leaving a ½-inch (1cm) rim around the edge.

2.   Plunge the shells into boiling water and cook for 1 minute. Plunge into iced water to stop them cooking. When cold, drain and reserve.

3.   Lightly oil an ovenproof dish and place the shells in the dish. Pre-heat the oven to 375°F/190°C (Gas Mark 5).

4.   Chop the flesh from the centre of the aubergines into small cubes.

5.   Put the aubergine cubes, onions and garlic in a pan with the oil and cook over a low heat until the onion is transparent. Do not brown the onion or garlic.

6.   Add the tomatoes, cashews and pepper and continue to cook for 5 minutes. Transfer mixture to the aubergine shells.

7.   Mix together the water and tomato purée and spoon around the shells. Cover the dish and bake for 40 minutes.

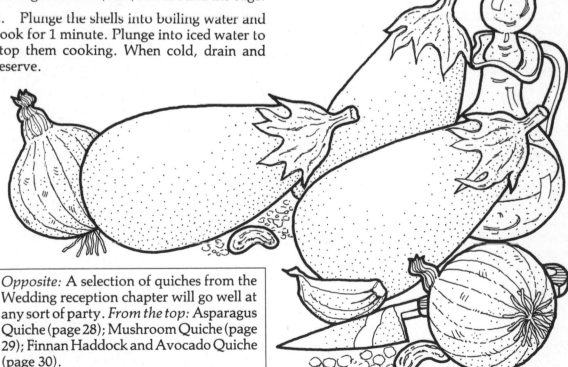

Opposite: A selection of quiches from the Wedding reception chapter will go well at any sort of party. *From the top:* Asparagus Quiche (page 28); Mushroom Quiche (page 29); Finnan Haddock and Avocado Quiche (page 30).

Apricot Profiteroles

Serves 6; 200 calories per portion
(Illustrated opposite page 160)

¼ pint (150ml) water
2 oz (50g) unsalted butter
2 free-range eggs, beaten*
2½ oz (65g) 85 per cent wholemeal flour
6 oz (175g) dried apricots
12 oz (300g) Quark or similar low-fat soft white cheese

1.   Place the water and butter in a saucepan and heat until the fat has melted and the water is boiling.

2.   Add the sieved flour all at once and beat (off the heat) until the mixture is smooth and shiny and leaves the sides of the pan cleanly.

3.   Allow to cool a little before beating in one egg at a time ensuring each is completely integrated before adding the next. The paste should be stiff enough to pipe so do not add all the egg if the mixture is getting too wet.

4.   Place mixture in a piping bag with a ½-inch (1cm) plain nozzle and pipe onto a lightly-oiled baking sheet. Use a sharp knife dipped in hot water to cut the paste after piping each ball onto the tray.

5.   Brush with a little beaten egg or milk and bake at 425°F/220°C (Gas Mark 7) for 20 minutes then lower the heat to 375°F/190°C (Gas Mark 5) for a further 5 minutes to dry out the balls.

6.   Remove from tray and leave to cool on a wire baking rack before filling with apricot mixture.

Apricot Filling:

1.   Wash the apricots and cook in plenty of boiling water for about 25 minutes. Drain reserving some cooking liquid.

2.   Purée the apricots, using a little cooking liquid if necessary to make a soft purée.

3.   Allow to cool before mixing thoroughly with the cheese.

*About 4 oz (100g) weight in shells is required. Free-range eggs are larger than standard eggs, so weigh before use; only 1½ eggs may be required. Adding too much egg will make paste too wet and it will not rise.

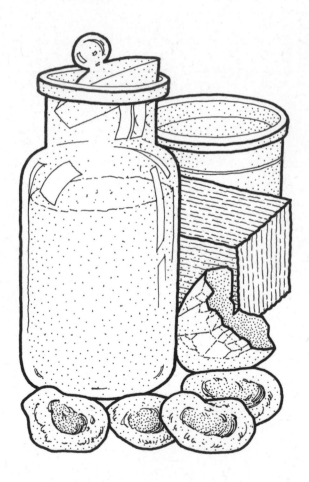

MENU III

Ricotta Salad

Pâté en Croûte

Raspberry and Blackcurrant Sponge Flan

Ricotta Salad

Serves 8; 145 calories per portion

1 large Webb's or other crispy lettuce

2 juicy oranges

12 oz (325g) Ricotta cheese

4 oz (100g) pistachio nuts, shelled

1.   Cut the Webb's lettuce into shreds and wash well. Shake off all excess water and place a bed of lettuce in each serving dish.

2.   Peel and remove pith from the oranges. Slice into thin rounds, removing pips as you go. Place the rounds of orange in a circle on top of the lettuce.

3.   Spoon a mound of cheese on top of the orange circle and sprinkle with pistachio nuts.

Pâté en Croûte

Serves 8; 290 calories per portion

Flaky Pastry:

7 oz (200g) wholemeal flour

4 oz (100g) unsalted butter

1 teaspoonful lemon juice

2½ fl oz (75ml) cold water

1.   Sieve the flour twice.

2.   Rub a quarter of the fat into the flour and mix to a soft dough with lemon juice and water.

3.   Flour the work surface and roll the dough to a long rectangle about 18 inches (45cm) by 10 inches (25cm), keeping it as square as possible at the corners.

4.   Using another quarter of the butter place small knobs at even intervals across the top two-thirds of the dough.

5.   Fold the bottom third up and the top third down over it. Press the edges together with a rolling pin to prevent air escaping.

6.   Turn the dough one turn to the left (this is the position the dough should be in at the start of the rolling). Cover dough and leave in fridge to rest for 15 minutes.

7.   Repeat the rolling and folding adding the third quarter of butter. Cover and rest for 15 minutes.

8.   Repeat the rolling and folding adding the fourth quarter of butter. Cover and rest for 15 minutes.

9.   Repeat the rolling and folding without the addition of fat. Cover and leave to rest before using.

10. To make the plait, roll out the pastry into a rectangle. Place the filling in a strip down the centre, leaving a space at top and bottom.

11. Snip the dough with kitchen scissors at about 1-inch (2.5cm) intervals, from the edge to the filling. Fold the ends up over the filling then alternately bring up the strips of dough to make a plait.

12. Egg wash and carefully lift onto a non-stick or lightly-oiled baking tray and bake in a pre-heated oven at 400°F/200°C (Gas Mark 6) for 35 minutes.

Filling:

6 oz (175g) aduki beans, soaked overnight
1 large onion, diced
2 cloves garlic, crushed
8 oz (225g) mushrooms, diced
1 teaspoonful corn/soya oil
1 teaspoonful cayenne pepper
4 oz (100g) walnuts, ground
2-5 fl oz (60-150ml) vegetable stock

1. Place the beans in a saucepan with plenty of boiling water and cook for about 40 minutes until soft. Drain.

2. Place the onion and garlic in a saucepan with the oil and sauté for 10 minutes.

3. Add the mushrooms, cover and continue cooking for 10 minutes.

4. Place the onion mixture in a food processor or liquidizer and blend. Season with cayenne pepper.

5. Add the cooked beans and blend again. Mix in the walnuts and gradually add the vegetable stock to moisten the mixture, but do not make it sloppy. Adjust the seasoning and the filling is ready for use.

Raspberry and Blackcurrant Sponge Flan
Serves 8; 130 calories per portion

2 oz (50g) soft vegetable margarine
2 oz (50g) clear honey
2 free-range eggs
3 oz (75g) wholemeal flour, sieved
8 oz (225g) raspberries
8 oz (225g) blackcurrants
½ oz (12g) gelatine or agar agar

1. Cream the margarine and honey together.

2. Gradually add the beaten eggs, adding some flour if the mixture starts to curdle.

3. Fold in the flour and pour the mixture into a lightly-oiled sponge flan ring.

4. Bake at 350°F/180°C (Gas Mark 4) for 25 minutes until firm to the touch. Allow to cool before removing from the tin.

5. Meanwhile, wash the raspberries. Wash the blackcurrants and remove from the stalks.

6. Place fruit in a stainless steel or glass saucepan and heat gently until the juices begin to run. Drain, reserving juice.

7. Place the drained fruit in the cooled flan case and return juice to the saucepan. Add water to the juice to bring the quantity to ¼ pint (150ml). Heat until just boiling.

8. Remove from heat and sprinkle over the setting agent, stirring all the time until dissolved. Leave to cool and when on point of setting spoon over the fruit as a glaze.

MENU IV

Globe Artichokes

Courgette and Pepper Quiche

Baked Apples

Globe Artichokes

Serves 6; 45 calories per portion

6 globe artichokes
4 tablespoonsful freshly chopped parsley
3 cloves garlic, finely chopped
1 tablespoonful salt

1. Soak the artichokes in a large bowl, or the sink, full of cold water to which the salt has been added. Try to wedge them in upside down to get all the grit or dirt out from between the leaves.

2. Drain and place the artichokes in a large saucepan or a couple of smaller ones with the parsley, garlic and plenty of boiling water.

3. Boil for 30-40 minutes until the outside leaves come away easily.

4. Either drain and allow to cool and serve cold with vinaigrette or serve hot with mustard sauce (page 159).

Courgette and Pepper Quiche

Serves 6; 100 calories per person

1 large onion, diced
1 tablespoonful vegetable oil
8 oz (225g) courgettes, thinly sliced
1 red pepper, de-seeded and cut into rings
2 oz (50g) mature English Cheddar cheese, grated
2 free-range eggs
½ pint (300ml) natural yogurt
1 teaspoonful wholegrain ready-made mustard
Freshly ground black pepper

1. Line a lightly-oiled 8-inch (20cm) flan dish or ring with half fat to flour pastry using 5 oz (150g) wholemeal flour and bake blind for 5 minutes in a pre-heated oven at 400°F/200°C (Gas Mark 6). Remove paper and baking beans and bake for another 5 minutes before filling.

2. Sauté the onion in the oil for 5 minutes.

3. Add the courgettes and pepper and cook for another 5 minutes.

4. Place the vegetables in the base of the prepared pastry case. Sprinkle the cheese on top.

5. Beat together the eggs, yogurt and seasoning and pour over.

6. Return to the oven and bake for 35 minutes until firmly set and golden brown.

7. Serve this quiche with a large mixed salad and, if your guests are very hungry, add a baked jacket potato as well!

Baked Apples

Serves 6; 160 calories per marzipan apple,
120 calories per average sultana apple

As the oven has been on for quiche and the baked potatoes it makes sense to use it for a dessert. Baked apples when stuffed with unusual fillings make nice, light lunch desserts. Choose a slightly tart cooking apple for baking. Unfortunately choice is becoming more restricted with fewer varieties in the shops. Bramley apples are over-used; they have a good flavour but there are better varieties. Personally I prefer Newton Wonder and the earlier Grenadier variety. Many gardens and orchards contain unknown varieties that are good to experiment with if you can obtain some.

To bake, slit the skin of the apple with the point of a knife around the circumference and bake at 350°F/180°C (Gas Mark 4) for about 40 minutes.

Stuffings:
a)   One favourite with guests is marzipan-stuffed apples. Marzipan is, of course, sugary but not much is needed to stuff an apple. After the apples have been cored use the corer to cut a piece the same size as the core from a bar of raw cane sugar marzipan. I chose this marzipan from health food shops not because I believe that brown sugar is 'healthier' than white (all sugar is equally harmful) but because these products are free from the colouring, flavourings and preservatives found in other marzipans, and because they have a better flavour.

b)   Sultanas can be used, as can any soaked and chopped dried fruit tossed in cinnamon or mixed spice. Drizzle a teaspoonful of clear honey over the stuffed core cavity.

MENU V

Stuffed Shoulder of Lamb

Selection of Steamed Vegetables

Blackcurrant Brulée

Stuffed Shoulder of Lamb

Serves 8; 780 calories per portion

4 lb (1.8 kilos) boned shoulder lamb
6 oz (175g) dried apricots
1 large onion, diced
½ oz (12g) unsalted butter
4 oz (100g) wholemeal breadcrumbs
1 tablespoonful freshly chopped parsley
Freshly ground black pepper

1.   Poach the apricots in a little water for 20 minutes. Drain.

2.   Sauté the onion in the butter until transparent.

3.   Finely chop the apricots and put in a mixing bowl.

4.   Add the onions, breadcrumbs and parsley and mix thoroughly. Season.

5.   Stuff the main shoulder cavity and close the cavity using string and a trussing needle.

6. Place the stuffed joint on a rack in a roasting pan and place in a pre-heated oven at 425°F/ 220°C (Gas Mark 7). Roast for 2¼ hours. Baste from time to time with fat which will run from the meat. Cover with foil after first hour to prevent over browning or drying out.

Gravy:
Ask the butcher to give you the bones from the shoulder and put these in a saucepan with water to cover, a bay leaf, parsley stalks, peppercorns and a diced carrot and simmer for 30 minutes. Strain and place in saucepan when ready to make the gravy. Add the juices from the meat pan after skimming off the fat, or skim off the fat and make the gravy in the roasting pan. Add water from the cooking vegetables if more liquid is required and thicken with arrowroot or cornflour slaked in water.

Vegetables:
Serve a selection of three or four steamed vegetables such as courgettes, peas, broccoli or cauliflower, runner beans, carrots, baby turnips etc.

Blackcurrant Brulée
Serves 8; 130 calories per portion

2 lb (900g) fresh blackcurrants
6 sprigs of mint
¼ pint (150ml) water
2 teaspoonsful arrowroot or cornflour slaked in 2 tablespoonsful water
4 tablespoonsful cassis liqueur or syrup
½ pint (300ml) soured cream
2 oz (50g) light Muscovado sugar

1. Wash and pick over the blackcurrants, and place in a saucepan with the mint and water.

2. Cook over a gentle heat for about 10 minutes until juices run from the fruit, but they remain whole.

3. Remove from heat and stir in the thickening agent and the cassis. Leave to cool.

4. Pour into a shallow ovenproof serving dish and top with the cream, spread thinly over the top. Sprinkle over the sugar.

5. Flash the dish under the grill until the sugar caramelizes.

Note: Blackcurrants are one of my favourite fruits. They have a superbly distinctive flavour and a wonderful mixture of tartness and natural sweetness when they are plump and ripe. They are very high in fibre and a beautifully dramatic colour. *Brulées* do use cream and sugar which are often part of traditional Sunday lunches, but this recipe uses a lot less and it makes minimal use of the sugar which is necessary for the characteristic crunchy topping.

16.

The Office Party

This office party caters for 10-12 people. It can be used for any occasion, such as an office lunch to celebrate a birthday or when a colleague is leaving. It can also serve for an evening party near Christmas or for any special occasion when everyone has to work late on a particular project. At the *Here's Health* office we don't need much prompting to have a party and we much prefer to bring in exciting dishes cooked at home rather than rely on disappointing and expensive pub meals in smoky atmospheres when celebrating birthdays. If you have like-minded colleagues who enjoy good food then try a self-catering party. In good weather you can take the celebration lunch to a nearby park, or if you are lucky enough to be working near the sea, jump in a car and take the picnic to the beach! Share the preparation between those who enjoy cooking, and the others can help pay for ingredients, or bring along the wine or mineral water and fruit juices, plus paper plates and cutlery and cups.

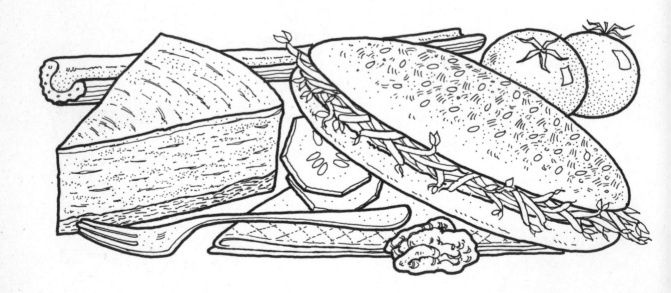

**An Any Occasion
Office Party Menu**

*Curd Cheese and Tomato Flan
Wholemeal Egg Rolls
Piquant Salad
Falafel
Hummus*

*Coffee and Walnut Swiss Roll
Ginger Cheesecake*

Curd Cheese and Tomato Flan

*Makes 2 × 8-inch (20cm) flans. Serves 12
slices; 310 calories per portion*

12 oz (325g) wholemeal flour
6 oz (175g) soft vegetable margarine
Water to mix

1. Sieve the flour into a mixing bowl and add the fat.

2. Rub the fat into the flour until the mixture resembles breadcrumbs in consistency.

3. Make a well in the centre and add enough water to make a soft paste.

4. Turn onto a lightly-floured work surface and roll out to line two lightly-oiled 8-inch (20cm) flan rings.

5. Cover with greaseproof paper and fill with baking beans. Bake in a pre-heated oven at 400°F/200°C (Gas Mark 6) for 10 minutes. Remove from heat and remove beans and paper before filling with curd cheese mixture.

Filling:

6 ripe but firm tomatoes
1 large bunch spring onions
12 oz (325g) low-fat curd cheese
½ pint (300ml) natural yogurt
3 free-range eggs
¼ pint (150ml) skimmed milk
2 tablespoonsful freshly chopped chives

1. Wash the tomatoes and cut in half. Place 6 halves in each baked pastry case. Arrange evenly around the circumference of the flan base.

2. Wash the spring onions and cut into small pieces with kitchen scissors.

3. Place the onions, cheese, and yogurt in a large mixing bowl and stir well until thoroughly mixed.

4. Lightly beat the eggs in another bowl with the milk and add to the cheese mixture. Stir well.

5. Pour half the cheese mixture into each flan and sprinkle the chives into the centre of the flans.

6. Bake for 25-30 minutes until golden-brown and firmly set.

7. Allow to cool completely before slicing and packing to take to the office.

Egg Rolls

Makes 20; 125 calories per portion

1½ lb (675g) wholemeal flour
¾ oz (18g) fresh yeast
¾ pint (450ml) lukewarm water
1 teaspoonful corn or soya oil
25g vitamin C, crushed

Filling:
1 punnet sprouted alfalfa seeds
4 free-range hard-boiled eggs
2 tablespoonsful cold-pressed safflower mayonnaise

1.   To make the rolls sieve the flour into a mixing bowl.

2.   Crumble the yeast into the water. Add the oil and vitamin C tablet. To achieve the right temperature of water use ⅓ boiling to ⅔ cold.

3.   Leave the yeast mixture to stand for 10 minutes, then pour into the flour and work in to form a soft dough.

4.   Turn the dough onto a lightly-floured surface and knead for 10 minutes.

5.   Shape into bridge rolls and place on a lightly-oiled baking tray. Cover and leave in a warm place until doubled in size.

6.   Meanwhile set the oven to 425°F/220°C (Gas Mark 7).

7.   Glaze the rolls with beaten egg or milk and bake for about 20 minutes until golden-brown and hollow-sounding when tapped. Allow to cool on a wire tray before filling.

8.   To make the filling mash the boiled eggs together with the mayonnaise and freshly ground black pepper to taste.

9.   Spread the egg mixture on the base of the rolls and place a generous amount of washed alfalfa sprouts on top before replacing the lid. Alternatively only slice the rolls partly through so the top does not become detached. Take along any unfilled rolls for those extra-hungry office workers.

Piquant Salad

Serves 12; 80 calories per portion

2 bunches watercress
8 oz (225g) beansprouts
12 oz (325g) tin sweetcorn kernels
2 large beetroot
6 ripe tomatoes
6 oz (175g) carrot
4 tablespoonsful olive oil
2 tablespoonsful raspberry vinegar
Freshly ground black pepper

1.   Wash all the salad ingredients and pack into a large polythene container and leave overnight in the fridge for a quick getaway to the office the following morning.

2.   Place the olive oil, vinegar and pepper in a screwtop jar with a non-corrosive lid (such as an empty mayonnaise jar) and shake vigorously. Store in the fridge.

3.   Just before serving the lunch mix the watercress and beansprouts together. Drain the sweetcorn and stir that in.

4.   Dice the beetroot and tomatoes and add to the other salad ingredients.

5.   Grate the carrots and stir those in. Toss in the dressing just before serving.

Falafel

Serves 20; 70 calories per portion

10 oz (275g) chick peas *or* 1½ lb (675g) cooked chick peas
1 free-range egg
2 medium onions, minced to a pulp
2 cloves garlic, crushed
½ teaspoonful each of cayenne pepper, ground cumin, turmeric and freshly ground black pepper
3 tablespoonsful tahini
Sesame oil for frying
4 oz (100g) wholemeal breadcrumbs (optional)

1. If using uncooked chick peas soak for 12 hours before use, then cook in plenty of boiling water for about 1½ hours until soft enough to mash to a pulp. A pressure cooker will speed up the job considerably.

2. Place the mashed chick peas in a liquidizer and blend until smooth.

3. Add the eggs, onion, spices and tahini to the liquidizer and blend again until thoroughly mixed.

4. Remove from the liquidizer and mould into small balls which are to be fried in the lightest possible smear of oil until golden brown, about 10-15 minutes on a low to moderate heat. The breadcrumbs are for use if the mixture is too soft to form into balls that will not disintegrate in the pan. The ability to form a binding pulp is different with each batch depending on how long the chick peas have been cooked, etc.

Note: Falafel are usually served hot after being deep fried, but this method of cooking them in a frying pan in a little fat results in fewer calories. They are just as good eaten cold as part of a buffet.

Whoever makes the Falafel might also like to make the Hummus because they both involve cooking chick peas and these can take a long time to cook. So, rather than have two people spending a long time in the kitchen one person can cook twice the quantity! Having said that, there are ready-cooked chick peas available in tins and this would save a lot of time for party preparations.

Hummus

Serves 20; 55 calories per portion

6 oz (175g) chick peas *or*
14 oz (400g) cooked chick peas
5 oz (150g) tahini
2 cloves garlic, crushed
Juice of ½ lemon
1 tablespoonful of olive oil
Freshly ground black pepper

1. If using dried chick peas soak for 12 hours before cooking. Then cook in plenty of boiling water for about 1½ hours, until soft enough to mash to a pulp. A pressure cooker will greatly speed up the job.

2. Put the mashed chick peas into a liquidizer and blend until smooth.

3. Add the tahini, garlic and lemon juice and blend again until thoroughly mixed.

4. Spoon into serving dishes and drizzle the oil over the surface of the hummus to prevent it from drying out. Cover and place in the fridge until ready to take to the office the next day.

5. Garnish with the parsley before serving.

Coffee and Walnut Swiss-Roll

Serves 10; 90 calories per portion

3 oz (75g) wholemeal flour

3 free-range eggs

3 tablespoonsful clear honey

2 tablespoonsful boiling water mixed with
3 teaspoonsful instant decaffeinated coffee

2 oz (50g) finely chopped walnuts

Filling:

4 oz (100g) low-fat soft white cheese, such
as Quark

4 tablespoonsful of 'no-added-sugar' jam
(optional)

1.   Line a Swiss-roll tin with greaseproof paper oiled on both sides. Pre-heat the oven to 425°F/220°C (Gas Mark 7).

2.   Sieve the flour and place most of the bran from the sieve into the prepared tin. Shake to cover the paper evenly.

3.   Place the eggs and honey in an electric beater and whisk for several minutes until thick and ropey. Alternatively, place in a basin over a double boiler and whisk until thick and ropey.

4.   Carefully fold in half the flour using a metal tablespoon.

5.   Add the coffee and then the second half of the flour and the nuts and fold in as quickly as possible making sure all the flour is thoroughly mixed in.

6.   Pour at once into the prepared tin and smooth the mixture to cover the whole tin. Bake for about 10 minutes until well risen and springy to the touch.

7.   Remove from oven and turn out onto a sheet of greaseproof paper. Peel off the paper. If it will not come off easily then cover for a minute or two with a cold, wet teatowel.

8.   When the paper is removed, trim the edges of the cake then roll up, starting from the shortest side and incorporating the greaseproof paper on which the cake is lying into the roll. This enables it to be unrolled when it has become quite cold. It can then be filled with a layer of cheese then a layer of jam (optional) before being rolled up again.

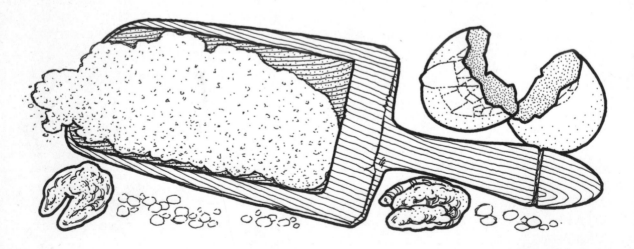

Ginger Cheesecake
Serves 10; 135 calories per portion

Base:
Make a pastry case for two 8-inch (20cm) flans as described in the Curd Cheese and Tomato Flan recipe (page 169). Choose a loose-bottomed flan tin for the cheesecakes because this is a more attractive way to present them. Bake blind as before.

Filling:

6 tablespoonsful *Just Ginger**
1 lb (450g) cottage cheese
Grated rind of 2 lemons
½ pint (300ml) natural yogurt
¼ pint (150ml) double cream
4 free-range egg whites
2 free-range egg yolks

1. Spread the *Just Ginger* equally over the base of both flan cases.

2. Sieve the cottage cheese into a mixing bowl and stir in the lemon rind and yogurt.

3. Whip the double cream until just stiff and stir into the mixture with the lightly beaten egg yolks.

4. Whisk the egg whites until stiff and quickly fold into the mixture using a metal spoon.

5. Pour at once into the two prepared flan cases and bake at 350°F/180°C (Gas Mark 4) for 25-30 minutes until set and just turning golden-brown.

* Just Ginger is a purée of fresh ginger and sugar made by Parrish & Fenn and available from health food shops and delicatessens.

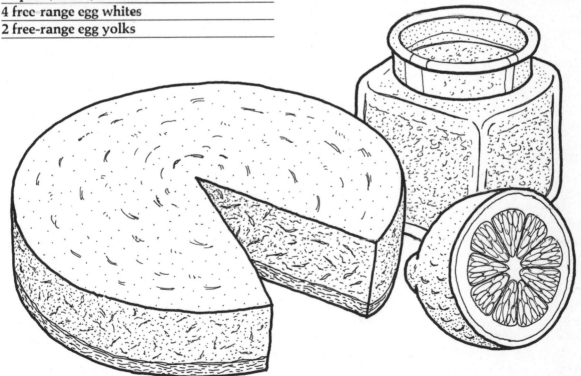

17.

Outdoor Parties

Some of the nicest meals I have had have been the evening barbecues on holiday in Spain, France and Portugal. The smell of barbecuing food mixed with the heavy evening scents gives a new appetite to any jaded palate.

After a day's swimming or walking there's a feeling of real hunger, unlike the hunger after a day in the office or at home. It's so nice, too to make the most of being outside in the fresh air and when the weather is fine it's a crime to spend any time inside.

If you are abroad, try locally caught fish or a couple of free-range chickens barbecued with fresh herbs and served with a salad and the local wine. The simplest food is often the nicest and when it can be bought so fresh each day it makes it a real effort to come home to the supermarkets.

Small barbecues are excellent for trips to the beach. The food can be taken ready prepared in a coolbox with plenty of icepacks and kept in a shady place until it's needed. A beach barbecue is best held during the evening when other people are leaving and the smell or smoke (there should not be much from a properly controlled barbecue) will not disturb others. It's often too hot to eat much during the day at the beach and if you are in and out of the water you will not want to eat until later.

Pack the barbecue sauces and any salad dressings in screwtop jars. Choose jars that have a plastic coated top, so that any acidic matter will not come directly into contact with a metal lid — old mayonnaise or 'no-added-sugar' preserve jars are better than honey jars for this.

It is better to pack the kebab ingredients in the cool box, cut and wrapped in the case of fish or meat, but uncut in the case of vegetables. These are easy and not messy to cut on site: Remember to pack some kitchen roll or a damp flannel for wiping hands, and a bottle of fresh water for washing/rinsing hands. Do not dress the green salad until ready to serve or it will go soggy.

Choosing a barbecue

When buying a barbecue there are several points to consider. Make sure the barbecue is right for the job you want it to do. If it is for large parties, choose one with a large grill area; there are some available which are about 4 feet (120cm) long and 1½ feet (45cm) wide, built in sturdy steel with nickel chrome grills and griddles. Two grills and a griddle are useful, especially when they are on runners so that the positions can be altered.

By varying the density of charcoal under

each grill, different heats can be obtained and the food can be transferred between grills to bring it on together. When cooked it can be kept hot on the griddle. Alternatively, the griddle can be used to cook Teppan Yaki (Japanese) style.

If buying a smaller barbecue, buy one with a pan in the base on which the coals are placed. This prevents them being in touch with the metal framework of the barbecue and therefore heating it or causing it to go rusty. If you buy a cheaper barbecue without a grill pan special under-charcoal material is available on which to place the coals to protect the sides of the barbecue.

Other things to look for are rungs which allow the cooking grills to be lowered or raised away from the heat. The grills on most barbecues have handles so the food can be whipped away from flare ups. The cause of flare-ups is usually too much charcoal in the pan.

Portable barbecues are also available. Some fold up like a sandwich maker with the coals inside and form a chimney to get the fire going quickly. They then unfold to provide two grills for cooking. Generally, the fire should be lit 30-40 minutes before it is wanted, to allow the coals to become glowingly hot.

Other barbecues have lids, hinged or loose, and this facility allows food to be smoked at the same time as it is cooked. Most lids should have a vent to control air and smoke. Special hickory chips (pieces of hickory wood) are available to flavour the smoked food, or barbecued food. The wood chips are soaked in water before being thrown onto the hot coals.

Battery and clockwork operated rotisseries are also available. These are best used on barbecues with lids which will keep in the necessary heat to cook something like a chicken. Larger barbecues can, of course, cook a whole lamb or boar, but these are specialist jobs that take about four and nine hours respectively. Barbecues and barbecuers can be hired for this!

Fish is probably more the requirement of the wholefood cook but this can give problems by sticking to the rungs of the grill. The answer is *not* to place the fish or other food on a piece of foil because this will prevent the heat getting to it. Fish broilers are useful. These are wire grill 'sandwiches' into which the fish is placed. It can then be easily cooked on both sides without sticking or breaking when being turned. Fish broilers come in individual, or up to three fish, sizes.

A good pair of tongs is also essential. These come as either regular tongs or tongs shaped like a fish slice with a fork on top. They are very useful for burgers and other foods. Toasting forks and skewers are also useful. And a good pair of gloves will prevent burns to the hands and protect from splashes of hot fat. Kitchen paper is useful to have around to absorb excess fat on food before serving.

Specialist equipment is available from barbecue shops like The Barbecue Shop, Portsmouth Road, Cobham, which also offers personalized designs for barbecues to be built as permanent structures in gardens or on special trolleys which may be wheeled to the edge of the swimming pool, or wherever else they are required. They have even built barbecues into balconies of top floor flats!

Even if you do not have a swimming pool it is attractive to barbecue or picnic near water, but make sure it's moving. Stagnant ponds and lakes attract a lot of nasty insects and flies that will find you and your food fascinating. Similarly, there are always flies where there are cattle and often where there is shade beneath any trees that are in bloom.

A shady spot is important for comfort when eating, so stay out of the sun for the picnic; you can always sit in it afterwards. Take a book or last week's Sundays newspapers to read and perhaps a ball or a Frisbee to work off the meal. Serious picnickers will prefer a cricket bat and stumps! A nice walk before the picnic is often a good idea. Choose a circular route so you come back to the parked car and do not have to carry the picnic things around with you for a long distance.

Picnic preparations

A picnic basket not only looks nice but is practical too, because it is so light and a lot can be packed into it. Make a checklist before you leave, if necessary, to remember to pack:

- Plates.
- Cups.
- Cutlery.
- Cruets (if necessary).
- Bread knife.
- Vegetable knife.
- Corkscrew.
- Small gas burner or a vacuum flask of hot water.
- Coffee/teabags.
- Milk.
- Butter/polyunsaturated margarine.
- Paper napkins.
- Serviettes.
- Table cloth.
- Picnic table and chairs/rugs, beachmats and a teacloth.
- And don't forget the food!

For the 'posh picnic' pack the iced soup in a vacuum flask that has been standing in the fridge or freezer to chill.

Butter can also be softened and packed into a Thermos, then chilled. This is also useful for camping holidays and it will last well if kept in this way.

Pack the tomato sauce for the terrine in a screwtop jar and do not cut the terrine until it is to be served, so that it does not dry out.

It is always nicer to drink out of a glass than a plastic or paper cup, especially wine, so pack some wine glasses, carefully wrapped in a thin teatowel or packed with kitchen roll. Nice cutlery is also a bonus. If you enjoy picnics it might be worth buying a special set which can stay in the picnic basket ready for use. There are some good Italian picnic cutlery sets that have holes in the handles for hanging on racks or tieing together with string so you do not lose your spoon and fork! They are now being used for general household use because they are so attractive.

Vegetable tartlets, and any quiches or flans and tarts will probably travel better with the protection of the flan ring around them, but loosen them and remove the ring before packing the picnic so you do not have to wrestle with it on site. The quiche or tart can even be ready cut, but left as a whole to keep fresh and held together with the flan ring.

Choosing a site for a picnic is important. Obviously it should be away from a main road and the quieter the better. Do not picnic in a field that is full of crops, and if you are afraid of animals do not set up in a field of bullocks. Even if they are at the opposite end of the field they are curious and friendly and it will not be long before they join you, bringing lots of flies with them!

Opposite: A Barbecue Party.
Barbecued Trout (page 181); Fish Kebabs (page 179); Barbecued Fresh Fruit (page 183).

Barbecue Menu

Beefburgers with Barbecue Sauce
or Chilli Sauce

Fish Kebabs and
Sweet and Sour Chicken Kebabs
with Savoury Rice

Barbecued Fish Steaks
with Avocado Sauce
Barbecued Stuffed Fish

Vegetable Kebabs

Barbecued Fruit

Beefburgers
Makes 8; 250 calories per burger

2 lb (900g) steak
1 free-range egg
2 onions, finely diced
4 oz (100g) wholemeal breadcrumbs
2 tablespoonful tomato purée
2 teaspoonful ready-made mustard
Freshly ground black pepper

1. Trim any fat from the meat and mince it.

2. Stir in the rest of the ingredients and form into burger shapes.

3. Cook over a hot barbecue for 10 minutes each side. Brush with Barbecue Sauce to prevent drying out.

Note: Vegetable Burgers (page 82) are just as good barbecued.

Opposite: A 'Posh' Picnic.
Chicken Terrine on Tomato and Chive Sauce (pages 184-85). (*China:* Royal Worcester Viceroy Gold.)

Barbecue Sauce
366 calories in total

1 teaspoonful corn or soy oil
2 large onions, finely diced
1 tablespoonful molasses sugar
1 tablespoonful cider vinegar
1 tablespoonful Worcestershire sauce
¼ pint (150ml) natural tomato ketchup *or*
3 tablespoonsful of tomato purée
2½ fl oz (75ml) water if using ketchup *or*
¼ pint (150ml) water with tomato purée
Juice of 1 lemon

1. Place the oil in a saucepan and add the onion. Cover and cook over a low heat for 10 minutes.

2. Add the rest of the ingredients, stir well and continue to cook for a further 10 minutes.

3. Allow to cool slightly and, if preferred, liquidize until smooth.

Chilli Sauce
Sufficient to top 8 burgers;
20 calories per topping

1 fresh green chilli
½ red pepper
2 shallots
½ tablespoonful sunflower oil
2 fresh ripe tomatoes
1 dessertspoonful tomato purée
½ teaspoonful oregano

1. Wash and de-seed the chilli and chop very finely. (NB: When working with chillies, do not rub your eyes or lips because the chilli will sting any tender flesh.)

2. Finely chop the flesh of the pepper and peel and dice the shallots.

3. Place the prepared vegetables in small, heavy-based saucepan with the oil. Cover and sweat for 5 minutes.

4. Wash and finely chop the tomatoes. Place flesh and all juice and seeds from chopping in the pan.

5. Stir in the purée and oregano. Cover and leave to cook over a low heat for 10 minutes.

6. Remove from heat and liquidize. Serve at once or return to pan to heat through.

Fish Kebabs

Serves 8; 330 calories per kebab
(Illustrated opposite page 176)

2 lb (900g) monkfish, fresh tuna or other fish of choice
2 tablespoonsful olive oil
6 tablespoonsful lemon juice
Chervil or chives, finely chopped
Freshly ground black pepper
1 large red or green pepper
½ pineapple
2 oz (50g) button mushrooms
1 large onion
8 very small tomatoes washed and left whole

1. Cut the fish into bite-size chunks large enough to stay on the kebab skewer.

2. Mix together, in a clean screwtop jar, the oil, lemon juice, herbs of choice and pepper.

Shake vigorously and pour over the prepared fish. Leave to marinate while preparing the other vegetables.

3. Wipe the mushrooms if necessary and add to the marinade.

4. Wash and de-seed the pepper and cut into 'squares' suitable for skewering.

5. Peel the pineapple, remove the central core and cut into largish cubes.

6. Cut the onion into quarters and divide the 'layers' ready for placing on skewer.

7. Assemble the kebabs by alternating pieces of fish with the vegetables. They look nicer on the barbecue if they are all the same arrangement.

8. Barbecue or grill for about 5-7 minutes, basting with the marinade and turning to prevent burning.

Note: A closely textured fish such as monkfish or fresh tuna is best used for kebabs so that the fish does not disintegrate on the kebab skewer.

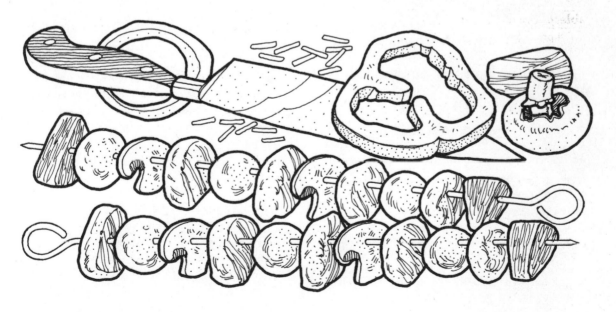

Sweet and Sour Chicken Kebabs
Serves 8; 160 calories per kebab

Choose free-range poultry because, theoretically, it should not have been treated with any drugs and therefore there should be no risk of drug residues in the fat or flesh. It is also often preferred for animal welfare reasons. Very often buying a free-range chicken is easier abroad than in England. So on holiday you might take a trip to a local market where the poultry is often far fresher than at home. However it might upset some people if they see live chickens in the market. Choose members of this shopping trip carefully!

Sweet and Sour Sauce:

4 tablespoonsful cider or wine vinegar
4 tablespoonsful water
Juice of 1 orange
1 dessertspoonful clear honey or Demerara sugar
1 dessertspoonful tomato purée
2 tablespoonsful shoyu/soya sauce
1 tablespoonful dry sherry (optional)

1. Place all the ingredients in a heavy-based saucepan. Cover and cook gently over a low heat until the sugar has dissolved.

2. Remove from heat and allow to cool.

Kebabs:

1 free-range chicken, or chicken portions, 4 oz (100g) per person
2 green peppers, de-seeded
4 oz (100g) button mushrooms
16 small tomatoes

Using a sharp knife remove the flesh from the chicken and cut it into cubes. Place in the sweet and sour sauce to marinate for at least two hours.

2. Cut the pepper into 'squares' to fit on the skewers.

3. Wipe any dirt from the mushrooms and leave whole.

4. Wash the tomatoes and leave whole.

5. Add the whole mushrooms to the marinade for the last 30 minutes.

6. Arrange the ingredients uniformly on kebab skewers and barbecue or grill for 15 minutes. Turn during cooking and baste with the remainder of the sweet and sour sauce.

7. Serve with a freshly tossed green salad, and wholemeal bread, if liked.

Savoury Rice
Serves 8; 70 calories per portion

The kebabs are usually served at the table and then each guest can push the contents off their kebab onto a bed of rice. Also offer a simple salad. To give the rice more flavour try cooking it as below. If at home, the rice may be cooked indoors. If camping, it is probably easier to cook the rice over a gas burner, in a small saucepan.

1 lb (450g) brown rice
1 tablespoonful olive oil
2 cloves garlic, crushed
2 dried red chillies, chopped
1 red pepper, de-seeded and diced
Plenty of boiling water

1.   Wash the rice in a sieve.

2.   Place the oil, garlic, chillies and peppers in a saucepan. Cover and sweat for 5 minutes.

3.   Stir in the rice and continue to cook for about 5 minutes. Stir from time to time to prevent rice sticking to bottom of saucepan.

4.   Add plenty of boiling water and simmer for 25 minutes, or until cooked. Top up from time to time with more boiling water if necessary.

Barbecued Fish Steaks

Choose a fish suitable for cutting into steaks or buy steaks freshly cut from the fishmonger. If abroad on holiday find the local fish market. In many Mediterranean ports or small inland towns these are quite exciting places with their fabulous displays of colourful fish rarely seen in Britain. I remember one in particular where I was gazing so intently at one fisherman cutting up octopus that I failed to get out of the way of someone dragging a whole, small shark across the floor and I had a very smelly, sticky foot until we could get to the beach!

Fresh tuna steaks are popular in Mediterranean markets and these are ideal for barbecuing or grilling. If you have not tried fresh tuna you will not be disappointed. You will probably also see swordfish steaks and halibut. Whatever the locals cut up for fish steaks (within reason!) will probably be your best bet. It's also easier for most people to buy steaks rather than wrestle with metric weights and a foreign language.

At home we are more limited in our choice of fish because the fishmonger's customers are so conservative he will not risk buying many unusual types of fish. There are the usual cod

and haddock and coley steaks, and if you are feeling extravagant salmon or turbot. Why not try a piece of monkfish? This closely textured fish is very good grilled or barbecued, but it will not be cut into steaks, it will appear as a fish 'tail'. It is simply cut off the bone by slipping a knife along the bone and removing the fish whole. Luckily it has no small bones in, so it's suitable for children, too, at barbecues.

Juice of 2 lemons
Chervil leaves or basil, finely chopped
Freshly ground pepper
1 dessertspoonful olive oil
8 fish steaks of choice, 4 oz (100g) to 6 oz (175g) per person

1.   Mix together the lemon juice, herbs, pepper and oil and brush over the fish.

2.   Place over moderate heat barbecue and cook, without turning, for 10-15 minutes until fish flakes easily. Baste from time to time with lemon mixture.

Avocado Sauce
950 calories in total

2 ripe avocado pears
½ pint (300ml) natural yogurt
Juice of ½ lemon
Freshly ground black pepper

1.   Peel avocado and remove stone. Mash together or liquidize with rest of ingredients until smooth and runny.

Note: This is delicious served with freshly barbecued or grilled fish steaks.

Barbecued Stuffed Fish

Serves 8; average 300 calories per portion
using oily fish
(Illustrated opposite page 176)

8 fish of choice (see note)
1 oz (25g) vegetable oil
2 onions, diced
3 sticks celery
2 tablespoonsful finely chopped parsley
8 oz (225g) cooked rice
2 oz (50g) almond flakes
Juice of 3 lemons
Freshly ground black pepper

1.   If the fish have not already been prepared remove heads and guts. Wash under running cold water.

2.   Place the oil in a pan and sauté the onion and celery for 5 minutes. This can be done over the barbecue if necessary.

3.   Stir the parsley and rice into the sautéed vegetables and add the almonds to the stuffing.

4.   Stuff the gut cavity and arrange the fish on the barbecue.

5.   Baste with lemon juice and sprinkle with pepper. Barbecue or grill for about 15 minutes, basting frequently.

6.   Alternatively, the fish may be basted then wrapped in greaseproof paper inside cooking foil, and left to cook over medium heat coals for about 1 hour. Turn once or twice during cooking.

Note: Choose slightly oily fish for barbecuing because these need no extra oil adding during cooking. They do not flake like white fish and they come in conveniently small sizes for grilling whole with stuffing! Red mullet or red snapper are good choices if abroad. At home, mackerel make good barbecued fish, as do larger herrings and, of course, the over-used trout.

These fish are just as good barbecued without stuffing, when they can be served with barbecued vegetables or a simple salad. Putting some slices of lemon or sprigs of fresh herbs inside the gut cavity makes all the difference to the flavour. Try fresh fennel with trout, tarragon with herring and fresh rosemary with mackerel. Fennel seeds can be used if fresh fennel is not available. Look out for fennel on holiday because it grows wild all over Mediterranean countries.

Vegetable Kebabs

Grilled or barbecued vegetables are delicious just on their own. Spear a selection onto a kebab skewer. Choose from baby tomatoes, small par-boiled onions, whole mushrooms, par-boiled potato slices or new potatoes, tiny par-boiled corn on the cob, slices of red and green peppers, slices of courgettes. Barbecue over medium hot coals and baste with a mixture of lemon juice and olive oil with freshly chopped herbs of choice added. Turn the skewer from time to time.

Serve barbecued vegetables with barbecued sardines, cooked whole, or prawns or crayfish, or Barbecued Fish Steaks (page 181), or barbecued Beefburgers (page 177).

Barbecued Fruit

(Illustrated opposite page 176)

Hot summer fruits are absolutely delicious straight from the barbecue. They make a lovely finish to an outdoor meal, especially if the English evening is turning a little chilly. Somehow the flavour of the fruit is also enhanced when it is warmed.

Try barbecuing a selection of the following fresh summer fruit:

- Halved peaches.
- Halved or whole apricots.
- Slices of pineapple.
- Horizontally halved small bananas.
- Slices of orange.

1.   Baste the fruit with 2 tablespoonsful or raw cane sugar or honey mixed together with the juice of 1 orange and the juice of 1 lemon.

2.   Alternatively, you can put the fruit onto the cleaned barbecue kebab skewers (when the first course has been removed) and cook the warm fruit over the dying embers. Remember to baste so it does not dry up.

3.   For better flavour the fruit can be marinated in the juice beforehand. Add a tablespoonful of liqueur or brandy to the marinade for special occasions.

'Posh' Picnic Menu

Cold Watercress Soup

Chicken Terrine
Vegetable Tartlets

Nectarine Franzipane

and simmer for 20 minutes. Remove from the heat.

5.   Remove the bay leaf and, when the soup is cool enough, press through a sieve or liquidize.

6.   Season to taste with nutmeg and allow to cool. Stir in the yogurt then chill in fridge.

7.   Place several ice cubes in a vacuum flask and place the lid on to cool the flask. Alternatively place the flask in the freezer for 30 minutes before adding the soup to transport it to the picnic.

8.   Serve with thin slices of wholemeal bread, offer unsalted butter or soft vegetable margarine separately.

Cold Watercress Soup
Serves 6; 45 calories per portion

2 bunches watercress

8 oz (225g) new potatoes

1 onion, diced

2 pints (1.2 litres) vegetable stock

1 bay leaf

Sea salt

Freshly ground black pepper

Freshly grated nutmeg

6 tablespoonsful thin natural yogurt

1.   Wash and trim the watercress and discard any yellowing leaves.

2.   Scrub the potatoes and chop roughly; slice if large.

3.   Place watercress, potatoes onion and stock in a large saucepan together with the bay leaf and seasoning (except the nutmeg).

4.   Cover and bring to the boil. Lower heat

Chicken Terrine
Serves 6; 160 calories per portion,
or 240 with Tomato and Chive Sauce
(Illustrated opposite page 177)

4 chicken breasts, boned

3 oz (75g) green beans

3 oz (75g) new carrots

2 free-range egg whites

7 oz (200g) Quark or similar low-fat soft white cheese

1.   Line a 6×4×3-inch (15×10×7.5cm) terrine or bread tin with greaseproof paper.

2.   Mince the chicken and place in a mixing bowl.

3.   Wash the vegetables. Top and tail beans. Cut carrots into julienne strips and boil or steam for 5 minutes. Remove from heat and place under cold running water. Drain.

4.   Whisk the egg whites until stiff.

5.   Stir the cheese into the chicken.

6.   Fold 2 tablespoonsful of egg white into the mixture to lighten it then quickly fold in the rest.

7.   Place a layer of chicken mousse in the terrine followed by three rows of beans running the length of the terrine with a space between each row. Top with mousse and follow with a layer of carrots. Finish with a layer of mousse.

8.   Place terrine in a baking tray or roasting tin of boiling water and bake for 40 minutes in a pre-heated oven at 425°F/220°C (Gas Mark 7).

9.   Remove from oven and allow to become cold before removing from tin. Place in fridge to chill before serving. To serve place a slice of terrine on top of the Tomato and Chive Sauce.

Tomato and Chive Sauce

6 ripe tomatoes
2 tablespoonsful freshly chopped chives
4 tablespoonsful olive oil
1½ tablespoonsful wine or cider vinegar
Freshly ground black pepper

1.   Liquidize the tomatoes and stir in the chives.

2.   Place oil, vinegar and pepper in a screwtop jar and shake vigorously.

3.   Thoroughly mix the two lots of ingredients and chill before serving.

Vegetable Tartlets
Serves 6; 115 calories per tartlet

8 oz (225g) shelled fresh broad beans
8 oz (225g) baby carrots
8 oz (225g) fresh garden peas
6 × 3½-4-inch (9-10cm) tartlet shells, baked blind for 20 minutes (page 98)

Dressing:
1 clove garlic, crushed
4 tablespoonsful olive oil
1½ tablespoonsful white wine vinegar
1 tablespoonful freshly chopped chives

1.   Place all the prepared vegetables in a divided steaming basket, keeping them separate, and cook over a small amount of water for 10 minutes until cooked.

2.   Shake all the dressing ingredients together in a clean screwtop jar.

3.   Toss in dressing while hot, still keeping the vegetables separate.

4.   Allow to cool and transport to the picnic in sealed containers.

5.   Assemble the tartlets at the site of the picnic, filling a third of each tartlet with a portion of a different vegetable.

6.   Decorate with a sprig of fresh mint.

Nectarine Franzipane

Serves 6; 320 calories per portion

Base:

5 oz (150g) wholemeal flour
3 oz (75g) unsalted butter or soft vegetable margarine
1 tablespoonful light Muscovado sugar
1 free-range egg yolk
Water to mix
1 tablespoonful 'no-added-sugar' apricot jam

1.   Sieve the flour into a mixing bowl and add the fat.

2.   Rub the fat in until the mixture resembles breadcrumbs in consistency.

3.   Stir in the sugar.

4.   Beat the egg yolk with a little water and mix into the flour, adding more water if necessary, to make a soft dough.

5.   Roll the pastry out on a lightly-floured surface and line a lightly oiled 8-inch (20cm) loose-bottomed flan tin.

6.   Prick the bottom of the pastry with a fork and smooth the jam over the base.

7.   Bake in a pre-heated oven at 400°F/200°C (Gas Mark 6) for 10 minutes.

Filling:

2 oz (50g) unsalted butter or soft vegetable margarine
1 oz (25g) light Muscovado sugar
1 free-range egg
1 dessertspoonful skimmed milk
2 oz (50g) ground almonds
2 nectarines
1 tablespoonful 'no-added-sugar' apricot jam

1.   Cream the fat and sugar together until pale in colour and fluffy in consistency.

2.   Beat in the egg and milk.

3.   Stir in the ground almonds. Spoon mixture into the part-baked base.

4.   Wash and stone the nectarines. Cut into thin slices, but do not peel. Arrange the nectarine slices on top of the flan case filling, lightly pressing into the mixture.

5.   With the remaining pastry, make a lattice work top to the tart. Glaze with egg and bake in a pre-heated oven at 350°F/190°C (Gas Mark 4) for 35 minutes.

6.   Remove from the oven and brush with the apricot jam while still hot. Transport to the picnic in its tin.

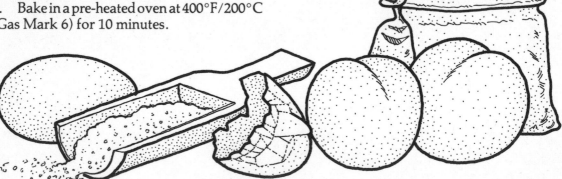

Party Notes

Date   Guests   Menu

Date	Guests	Menu

Index